GHANAIAN
LITERATURES

GHANAIAN LITERATURES

Edited by
RICHARD K. PRIEBE

Contributions in Afro-American and African Studies, Number 120

GREENWOOD PRESS
New York • Westport, Connecticut • London

Library of Congress Cataloging-in-Publication Data

Ghanaian literatures / edited by Richard K. Priebe.
     p.   cm. — (Contributions in Afro-American and African
studies, ISSN 0069-9624 ; no. 120)
   Bibliography: p.
   Includes index.
   ISBN 0-313-26438-4 (lib. bdg. : alk. paper)
   1. Ghanaian literature—History and criticism. 2. Ghanaian
literature (English)—History and criticism. 3. Oral tradition—
Ghana. I. Priebe, Richard. II. Series.
PL8021.G5G43 1988
809'.889'9667—dc19   88-16110

British Library Cataloguing in Publication Data is available.

Library of Congress Catalog Card Number: 88-16110
ISBN: 0-313-26438-4
ISSN: 0069-9624

First published in 1988

Greenwood Press, Inc.
88 Post Road West, Westport, Connecticut 06881

Printed in the United States of America

The paper used in this book complies with the
Permanent Paper Standard issued by the National
Information Standards Organization (Z39.48-1984).

10 9 8 7 6 5 4 3 2 1

Dedicated to Ghana,
the people and the land

ACKNOWLEDGMENTS

I wish to thank the following individuals and publications for permission to reprint the essays which appear in this book. Every effort has been made to trace copyright holders. I would be interested in hearing from any copyright holders not acknowledged here.

"Comic Opera in Ghana," by E. J. Collins from *African Arts* vol. 9, no. 2; reprinted by permission of the Regents of the University of California and the author. "Ayi Kwei Armah and the 'I' of the Beholder," by D. S. Izevbaye from *A Celebration of Black and African Writing,* ed. Bruce King and Kolawole Ogungbesan; reprinted by permission of Ahmadu Bello University Press. "Armah's *Fragments* and the Vision of the Whole," by Edward Lobb from *Ariel* vol. 10, no. 3; and "Kofi Awoonor's Poetry," by L. R. Early from *Ariel* vol. 6, no. 1; reprinted by permission of *Ariel.* "Kofi Awoonor and the Ewe Tradition of Songs of Abuse *(Halo),"* by Kofi Anyidoho; printed by permission of the author. "Three Young Ghanaian Poets: Vincent Okpoti Odamtten, Kofi Anyidoho and Eugene Opok Agyemang," by Kofi Awoonor; printed by permission of the author. "The Language of the Proverb in Akan," by Lawrence Boadi from *African Folklore,* ed. Richard M. Dorson; reprinted by permission of Doubleday and Company. "Atukwei Okai and His Poetic Territory," by Kofi Anyidoho from *New West African Literature,* ed. Kolawole Ogungbesan; reprinted by permission of Heinemann Educational Books. "The Character of Popular Fiction in Ghana," by Ime Ikiddeh from *Perspectives on African Literature,* ed. Christopher Heywood; "Kwesi Brew: The Poetry of Statement and Situation," by Edwin Thumboo from *African Literature Today* vol. 4; and "Language and Drama: Ama Ata Aidoo," by Dapo Adelugba from *African Literature Today* vol. 8; reprinted by permission of Africana Publishing Company, a division of Holmes and Meier Publishers. "Drama in Ghana," by Charles Angmor from *Theatre in Africa,* ed. Oyin Ogunba and Abiola Irele; reprinted by permission of the author and Ibadan Uni-

ACKNOWLEDGMENTS

versity Press. "Three Ghanaian Novels: *The Catechist, The Narrow Path,* and *A Woman in Her Prime,*" by Robert E. McDowell from *New African Literature and the Arts* vol. 2, ed. Joseph Okpaku; reprinted by permission of the author. "Structure and Image in Kwei Armah's *The Beautyful Ones Are Not Yet Born,*" by Gareth Griffiths from *Studies in Black Literature* vol. 2, no. 2; reprinted by permission of *Studies in Black Literature.* "Ama Ata Aidoo: The Art of the Short Story," by Lloyd W. Brown from *World Literature Written in English* vol. 13, no. 2; reprinted by permission of *World Literature Written in English.* "The Making and Breaking of Kwame Nkrumah: The Role of Oral Poetry," by Kwesi Yankah; printed by permission of the author. "Storytelling of the Akan and Guan in Ghana," by James Yeboa-Dankwa; printed by permission of the author.

I would never have finished this project without the patient help and hard work of three individuals to whom I owe special thanks: Diane Marshall, who put the text on a word processor, and Barbara Hobson and Greg Jenkins, who proofread copy. Finally, I would like to thank the Office of the Dean of the College of Humanities and Sciences at Virginia Commonwealth University for extensive support in the preparation of the manuscript for publication.

Richard K. Priebe
Richmond, Virginia

CONTENTS

CONTENTS

INTRODUCTION

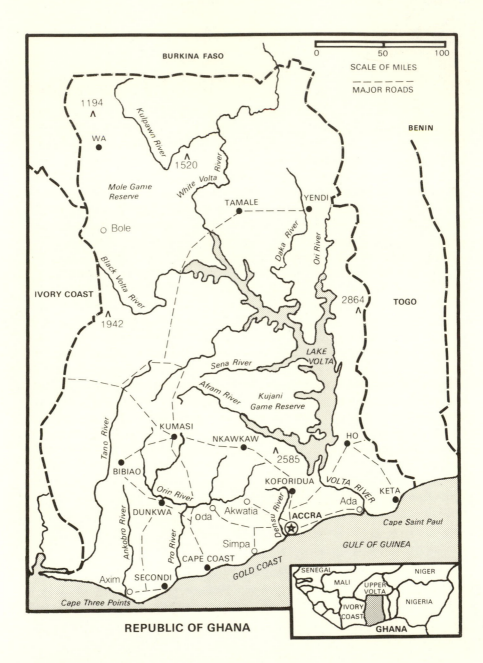

REPUBLIC OF GHANA

Map by Max K. Winkler

INTRODUCTION

Ghana is one of the smaller countries in Africa. Though larger than its West African neighbor, Togo, it is roughly one fourth the size of Nigeria. Its population of ten million people is roughly one tenth that of Nigeria. Still, the land and the people historically have had a disproportionally large impact, economically, politically and culturally, on the rest of Africa and the larger world. Over the past ten years the country has been going through the shattering experience of an economic collapse, and such an experience affects negatively the arts no less than every other aspect of life. Very little has been published by Ghanaian writers in this period, but we should keep that rather bare fact in perspective. However poor Ghana may now appear, it is a country endowed with substantial natural resources, and this is no less true of its cultural resources. Though the primary purpose of this book is to serve as an introduction to, and survey of, the literatures of Ghana, I would hope that in some small way it also shows there are reasons to be optimistic about the future of this beautiful land.

In writing of literature in Africa one is almost invariably drawn into the necessity of having to use the plural, "literatures," even when dealing with the literature within the geographical boundaries of one country. Good arguments can be advanced for the study of national literatures in Africa, but literary boundaries can never be as neatly drawn as the political ones. What, for example, really distinguishes Ghanaian and Nigerian literature? I might hazard some tenuous distinctions. Clearly Kwame Nkrumah's leadership in gaining independence earlier than it was gained in other African countries and the charismatic way he promulgated a Pan-African vision, affected writing in Ghana. The novels of Ayi Kwei Armah and Kofi Awoonor often argue with what Nkrumah did, but in the works of these writers we find a far more pervasive Pan-African outlook than in Nigerian writers. Still, I am not sure we can go very far drawing distinctions of this kind. The question of national literatures, at any rate, is a moot one; the countries exist politically, and thus it has become convenient for scholars to classify and discuss African literatures in terms of national divisions.

Yet within a country the size of Ghana there are at least two basic reasons we must think of literatures. Ghana is, of course, a pluralistic society, linguistically as well as culturally. First of all, English is the official language, and most writers have opted to use it, but there are also literatures in the vernacular languages, especially Ga, Ewe, and the Akan languages, though pieces have been written in several other languages as well. And even when writers write in English, some of the most distinctive elements of their style might be traceable to their traditional linguistic and cultural heritage. We hear and see Ama Ata Aidoo's Fante background in her drama and fiction just as we find Awoonor's Ewe background in his poetry and fiction. Secondly, and completely aside from differences based on languages and ethnic groups, there are differences based on audience and modes of transmission. Like the differences between national literatures in Africa, the difference between ethnic literatures within Ghana are not always clear enough to warrant making fine distinctions (though obviously, the more we are dealing directly with traditional oral literature, the less valid this observation is). When, however, we consider transmission and audience, we have three literatures in Ghana that are very different even to the most untrained and casual observer: folk, popular, and elite. Since these are also the divisions scholars have mainly followed, they are the ones I have used in organizing the articles in this collection.

It is my hope that this book primarily will serve as an introduction to the scholarship on the literatures of Ghana. My central guideline in selecting pieces for inclusion have been essentially two: the quality of the individual piece and the extent to which it is representative of a significant area of the literary scholarship that exists on Ghana. A few of the essays are appearing for the first time in this collection, but for the most part, the collection is more a reflection of the range of work scholars have published in journals than it is a judgement on which areas are most important. Most of the criticism of Ghanaian literature, for example, has focused on a small handful of writers. There is, in contrast a vast body of oral art, and also of popular literature, that has been surprisingly understudied. Moreover, there are some excellent writers, such as Ama Ata Aidoo and Joseph Abruquah, who have been given very little attention. Obviously, there are important gaps that should be filled and inbalances that should be redressed, but I hope this collection will serve to call attention to those needs, just as it points to the solid work that has been done. Regarding the selection of essays, I should add that there was some excellent material I had to exclude due simply to the high cost of reprint rights and there were other essays I could not use simply because there was such an abundance of material on the subject (as in the case of Ayi Kwei Armah).

ORAL ART

While all three literatures now exist simultaneously in Ghana, the folk tradition is the oldest one. As some folklorists are quick to argue, the terms "folk literature," or even "oral literature," are unfortunate collocations. As "literature" means something written, we have a contradiction in terms. It also invites comparison with written literature and the use of the literary critic's analytical methods, but an apple will never have the taste of an orange. Perhaps the term "oral art" would be a more felicitous choice. At any rate, if we stop to consider the extent to which oratory skill is prized in Ghana, and also the range and richness of oral art that exists there, it's surprising how fully this material has been overlooked. If an individual knows of only one African folktale, it is likely to be a Ghanaian Anancy tale. R. S. Rattray's early collection of these tales and others are widely known, but following his seminal work, there is a clear dearth of material.

Fortunately, this situation has begun to change. With J. H. Nketia's work on Akan funeral dirges published in the fifties *(The Funeral Dirges of the Akan)* and Kofi Awoonor's work in the early seventies on Ewe poetry *(Guardians of the Sacred Word)**, and the work of several other Ghanaian scholars, we have the start of a new interest and focus on traditional material where the field work and analysis is done by Ghanaians. The importance of this recent work cannot be overstated. These pioneers have already inspired a new generation of Ghanaian scholars (See in this collection the work of Jonas Yeboa-Dankwa, Kwesi Yankah and Kofi Anyidoho). Our attention has been drawn beyond the Anancy tale to a variety of poetic genre (the dirge, praise poetry, abuse poetry) and gnomic forms (the riddle, the proverb). The prose forms are important, and though they may be the easiest forms for an outsider to collect and analyze, they represent only a part of the broad spectrum of traditional forms. Moreover, even with prose narratives, the outsider has not always given context the close attention that Yeboa-Dankwa gives it in his essay on the folktale in Ghana. The intimate knowledge of language and culture these scholars have has also served to break down several misconceptions about oral art. From the outside, oral art has often appeared simple and merely functional. The insider, however, has shown us that there is often a complex aesthetic that operates with even a "simple" form such as the proverb. In addition, he can establish for us

---

*These and other references in the Introduction are to be found in the Bibliography at the end of the book.

what some of the rules are in Ghanaian poetics. Lawrence Boadi, for example, does an excellent job of this in his article on the Akan proverb. These new scholars are also impressing on us a clear sense of how very dynamic traditional oral art is. Indeed, the fact that it is "traditional" means that it is conservative vis-à-vis change, but not immune to it. As Kwesi Yankah and Kofi Anyidoho show, politicians, or even writers, may effectively appropriate traditional forms and style for their own ends, but as Yankah also shows, they can never "own" those forms. They go on, sometimes with modification, with a life of their own. Thus Nkrumah used praise songs to help bolster his image, but there were also abuse songs that criticized him when he went astray in the eyes of the folk.

POPULAR LITERATURE

Popular literature is the most recent literature in Ghana, and given the present economic situation, it is in the most precarious position. Essentially, it is literature, either written or oral that has a mass appeal in Ghana. This mass audience contrasts with the folk audience of traditional oral art in that it is, for the most part, multi-ethnic. The manner of transmission, furthermore, is not always the face-to-face interaction of the traditional performance; instead, mass media such as television, newspapers, pamphlets, and even loudspeakers are employed. As we can see here in the articles by E. J. Collins on comic opera and Ime Ikiddeh on popular fiction, popular literature in Ghana has developed along three lines. First, we have the lyrics of highlife music, syncretic western and African music that developed all along the West Coast of Africa in the thirties and forties with particular styles developing in Ghana. The lyrics may be either in English or vernacular languages (often Ga, Ewe or Fante-Twi) and may be on anything from love to economic problems or some topical or political issue. The form has continued on its own to the present day in Ghana, but it was also joined from the thirties on in the development of a second stream of popular literature, the concert party (or comic opera), a multi-generic dramatic event involving comic sketches as well as highlife. Professional groups involved in the performance of these events would drive in vans from village to village putting on their acts in bars, or even setting up loud-speaker systems in a large open public area. In addition to Collins' articles on the subject, Charles Angmor discusses the concert party in the larger context of the development of drama in Ghana.

The third stream of popular literature in Ghana, popular writing, needed two factors to get off the ground: mass literacy and indigenous printing presses. Local papers aimed at a small educated elite can be found even at the turn of the century in Ghana (then the Gold Coast), but not until after World War Two, and not really until after independence in 1957, was there any extensive indigenous popular writing in Ghana. The colonial government in the Gold Coast had by the late forties started to develop a broad program of education, and the universal primary education and adult literacy campaigns of the fifties and sixties were among the most significant achievements of Nkrumah. From the early part of this century on, there were some private printing presses and some missionary presses in Ghana. During the Nkrumah era a very sophisticated government press was established at Tema followed by a number of small privately owned presses in the late sixties after the Nkrumah government was overthrown. As I have shown more fully in an article on popular writing, "Popular Writing in Ghana: A Sociology and Rhetoric," the nexus of literacy and technology in the late sixties gave rise to a flowering of popular writing that was only cut short by the economic problems of the seventies.

A wide range of material is to be found in this third stream of popular literature. In addition to the chapbook novelettes that Ime Ikiddeh discusses in his article, there is material in popular magazines (short stories, serialized novelettes and poetry), and in literary sections of newspapers (material similar to what we find in the magazines, but also including serialized comic strips). Unlike the highlife lyrics and concert party, this material is much more commonly found in English than in any of the indigenous languages. In some cases it is very similar to material found elsewhere in West Africa. The romances, for example, are very similar to those found in the Onitsha chapbooks. Still, when we go over this material closely, we find much of it has a distinctly Ghanaian flavor. In one of the most popular comic strips of the early seventies, for example, the central figure was the folk trickster, Kwaku Anancy.

Though most popular writing has been in English, there is a body of literature in vernacular languages to which little attention has been paid. In his book *African Language Literature*, Albert Gérard has given an excellent historical and descriptive overview of this material, and in his critical study, *The Breast of the Earth*, Kofi Awoonor provides some summary and analysis of several pieces of Ewe writing, but that is the extent of the scholarship. If we adopt a strictly geographical criterion for Ghanaian writing, we might argue that the first major Ghanaian writer was Umar ibn Abu Bakr ibn Uthman al-Kabbawi al-Kanawi (1858–1934) who may have composed as many as 1,200 poems in Arabic and Hausa. Several other Islamic writers lived near him in the same area of northern Ghana, and also wrote in Hausa and Arabic, but it is not clear to what

7

extent they can be considered Ghanaian writers beyond geographical circumstance.

In the southern part of Ghana, the situation is somewhat different. As in the north, where vernacular writing was related to the religious presence of Islam, the roots of vernacular language writing can be traced to the presence of Christian missionaries who were, of course, concerned with the translation of the Bible, hymns, and *The Pilgrim's Progress* into vernacular languages. By the time the Vernacular Literature Bureau was established in 1951 (now the Bureau of Ghana Languages), a few pieces of short fiction had been published in the south. After independence the Bureau pushed for more creative writing in vernacular languages, and though they had some success, they were fighting a battle against the prestige English had as the official national language. A few collections of poetry came out, but most of the publications were novelettes of the popular sort that appeared in English, or reworkings of traditional folktales. One of the most successful writers in a vernacular language was Ferdinand Kwasi Fiawoo, an Ewe from eastern Ghana. He wrote three plays that were well received by readers and audiences in his region. Perhaps his most successful was *Toko atolia (The Fifth Landing-Stage)* which he wrote in 1932. This play, and the other two which he wrote in the 1940s and 1950s, focuses on traditional customs of the Ewe and looks critically at these practices from a Christian perspective.

ELITE LITERATURE

Regardless of the extent to which a country is literate, the audience for elite literature is bound to be relatively small. The average American, if he chooses to read any literature at all, is more likely to pick up a Mickey Spillane novel about the detective Mike Hammer, than any of Faulkner's novels (despite the interesting fact that Faulkner wrote a few novels aimed at a popular audience). For the most part, the consumption, and often even the production of elite literature today is tied to universities. If we look at the popular writers in Ghana, we find that many were, and still are, journalists. Elite writers such as Kofi Awoonor, Kofi Anyidoho, Ama Ata Aidoo, Ayi Kwei Armah, and Atukwei Okai have all taught in the university. Some of these writers were educated abroad, just as most of their works were published outside Ghana, mainly in the United States or England. The development of an elite literature is not so directly tied to the development of an indigenous technology as is the case with popular literature, since the audience that consumes the literature need not be an indigenous audience. Yet even though the individual writer might be educated abroad, it would look as if a strong university system is vital for the nourishing and development of an elite literature. Not surprisingly, Ghana despite its size has had one of the finest university systems in Africa.

Elite literature started to develop only slightly earlier than popular literature in Ghana. In fact, the concert party, as E. J. Collins shows us, started out as an art form by and for the educated elite. One writer stands out very clearly as an individual who raised issues and developed themes that were to be central in Ghanaian writing almost a half century later. In his time, Kobina Sekyi (1892–1956) was better known as a journalist and lawyer, deeply involved in nationalist politics and well-educated in the areas of philosophy and sociology. He was truly one of Ghana's great intellectuals, and he did well in the small amount of poetry and short fiction he wrote. It is, however, for one play, *The Blinkards,* that Sekyi is an important figure in the history of Ghanaian literature. Though written and produced in Cape Coast in 1915, the play was, surprisingly, never published until 1974. A light, satirical comedy, it voices concern for the increasing Anglicization of Ghanaian (Gold Coast) society and the rejection of traditional culture. Sekyi goes after the Anglo-Africans who foolishly ape mannerisms and distort language. For the first time in West African literature, the African who has spent time in Europe, the "been-to" appears as a comic figure.

Christian missionaries were very important in setting up the foundations, not merely for vernacular literatures, but for literature written in European languages. They established the first schools where these languages were taught, but no less important a foundation can be seen in the early sermons and religious tracts that were a result of the missionary education. Most of these foundations were laid in the nineteenth century, but to get a clearer historical perspective we need to go back to the early part of the seventeenth century. Anton Wilhelm Amo was born in 1703 near Axim. At an early age he was brought to Amsterdam where he was educated. He earned his Doctor of Philosophy at Wittenberg in 1730 and a few years later became a professor there. Most of his writings were on law and philosophy and were written in Latin, though one poem that he wrote in German is still extant (Jahn, 38–39).

By the nineteenth century there was a very important group of German-Swiss missionaries among the Ewe in Eastern Ghana, but it was the English speaking missionaries who were to have the most significant impact. Very little work has appeared on the sermons and tracts of the late nineteenth century (See studies by Gérard), but clearly this is an area where a lot of significant research might be done. At the turn of the century the work of lawyers educationists and journalists was gaining ascendency, and Gold Coast writing was becoming more nationalistic. The work of three Fante intellectuals might be studied very fruitfully from this perspective: James Aggrey (1875–1930) was the most religiously oriented of the three, while John Mensah Sarbah (1864–1918) and J. E. Casely-Hayford (1866–1930) were the most nationalistic in their writings.

Casely-Hayford was, in fact, the most important leader of African nationalism in the early twentieth century, and both his wife and daughter made important contributions to the development of Ghanaian literature. His wife, Adelaide (1868–1959) is important as an autobiographer and short story writer, while his daughter, Gladys May (1904–1950), gained some recognition for her stories, sketches, and poetry. The most important literary contribution, however, came from her father. The first Ghanaian novel (actually, the first West African novel), was J. E. Casely-Hayford's *Ethiopia Unbound*, published in London in 1911. In these early years of colonial Ghana, educated elite were more involved in journalism than the development of a literature. *Ethiopia Unbound* is heavy moralistic reading, but this loosely structured narrative set the stage for other works about the African torn between two cultures, yet fighting for his cultural and political independence. Not for another thirty years did a second Ghanaian novel appear. Then, in 1943 in England, R. E. Obeng published *Eighteenpence,* a very moralistic study of a man trying to live a good life in a traditional society.

Despite numerous artistic flaws, both works are informed by a deep sense of *gravitas:* a serious concern with the political well-being of the state in *Ethiopia Unbound* and the moral well-being of the individual in *Eighteenpence*. Most Ghanaian writers, and virtually every Ghanaian novelist, popular and elite, since Casely-Hayford and Obeng, have shown a concern with political or personal morality and in some cases both. Interestingly, the professions of these two pioneer writers point, not only to the professions of the more recent post-independence writers, popular and elite, but also to the most important subjects and characters of this newer generation of writers. Casely-Hayford was a journalist and a lawyer; Obeng a teacher and a catechist. Most post-independence writers are journalists or teachers who write about students and lawyers or about schools, religion, the legal process (or the failure of the legal process) and traditional culture.

It was a long time, however, before another important work followed. As independence approached, and then arrived in March 1957, no writer stepped forward to assert cultural independence with a voice as strong as Chinua Achebe's in Nigeria. In 1958 the Ghanaian Ministry of Information brought out an independence anthology, *Voices of Ghana,* a very quiet assertion by over thirty writers, but no major works appeared until after Kwame Nkrumah was overthrown in February, 1966.

Rarely can we find easy answers for why a literary silence existed, but speculation may at least prove profitable. Prior to independence a great amount of excellent writing was being produced in Ghana, though it was mainly in the area of journalism. There is a long and significant history of serious journalism in the Gold Coast, and many journalists of the thirties went on to become major political figures in West Africa. In the forties through the fifties, journalistic writing became an increasingly important tool in the independence movement, but when independence was achieved, the situation very suddenly changed. Nkrumah did not allow for political dissension, and the consequences, namely detention, were made quite clear. Ironically, the most important "Ghanaian" work of this period was written by a non-Ghanaian, a South African. On the eve of independence Peter Abrahams published a novel that was a thinly disguised attack on Nkrumah. *A Wreath for Udomo* (1956) was an important work, but it would be another ten years before a Ghanaian would dare to make such a written statement.

In 1960 Nkrumah shut down the Ghanaian edition of *Drum* magazine after voicing objections to some of the material Henry Ofori, the editor, was publishing. A few years later a private publishing house withheld the release of a collection of Ofori's short stories. Printed in 1965, it was not released until after the coup, since the company was afraid of political repercussions, even though the stories had nothing sharper than light satire in them (personal communication with Ofori, 1974).

Censorship and fear of censorship were not, however, the most important factors in contributing to the literary silence of the Nkrumah years. It would, in fact, be a distortion of history to dwell on it. Many writers and potential writers were engaged in the task of nation building in a very practical and immediate manner. They were involved in the massive literacy and adult education programs I referred to earlier. One poet, G. Adali-Mortty, played a key role in this campaign. As he saw it, teaching was at the time a much higher priority than writing (personal communication, 1974). In addition, private investment was very strictly controlled and limited by the state, so little money was available for private presses such as the ones that were developing in Nigeria.

This is, of course, something of an oversimplification of the Nkrumah period. Those were very heady years, and a sense of cultural nationalism was stirring the very rapid development of Ghanaian poetry. A number of young poets were translating traditional poetry, and Albert Kayper-Mensah published much of his poetry in the 1950s and 1960s. Moreover, Michael Dei-Anang published three volumes of very patriotic poetry, *Africa Speaks* (1959), *Ghana Semi-Tones* (1962) and *Ghana Glory* with Yaw Warren (1965), and Frank Kobina Parkes published *Songs from the Wilderness* (1965). A good deal of this verse is apprenticeship poetry

11

marred by too much uncontrolled exuberance, but a lot of young writers were also being inspired to develop their talents.

If we turn to the Ghanaian universities, specifically the University of Ghana at Legon, we can get a good sense of how this talent was developing. There was an excellent journal at Legon, *Okyeame,* and if we look at the issues of the early sixties we have a who's who in Ghanaian literature: Efua Sutherland, Kwesi Brew, Kofi Awoonor (George Awoonor-Williams), Frank Parkes, Albert Kayper-Mensah, Ama Ata Aidoo, S. Adali-Mortty, and J.C. de Graft all wrote for the journal. Later in the sixties, the works of Ayi Kwei Armah, Atukwei Okai (John Okai), Kofi Sey and Kojo Kyei also appeared in it. These writers were also publishing a considerable amount of their work in *Présence Africaine* and *Black Orpheus.*

While collectively these pieces are very important in the development of Ghanaian writing, there are only two book-length works of the early sixties that stand out as landmarks. One is Kofi Awoonor's *Rediscovery and Other Poems* (1964). Some of the work in the collection was clearly the work of a young poet, but no other poet in Africa prior to this work (and I would include the very remarkable Nigerian poets of this period) had done such fine work of melding the themes and forms of traditional verse with the rhythms of the English language. The other work is Joseph Abruquah's *The Catechist* (1965). Despite the lack of political engagement, the novel rather neatly fits the patterns set by *Ethiopia Unbound* and *Eighteenpence,* but is much more successful aesthetically than those earlier works. The story is essentially a fictionalized biography of Abruquah's father whom we follow from his early years in a small village through his death as an old catechist. We see a bright and ambitious individual who is often abrasively vain, arrogant and stubborn, but also recognizes the value and significance of a Western education as his culture begins to undergo changes he cannot entirely comprehend. Abruquah, himself a teacher for many years, very effectively avoids making any direct authorial assertions, letting the narrative carry the impact of the conflicts that develop.

For roughly ten years following the Nkrumah period there was simply an amazing amount of literature, in quantity and quality coming from Ghanaians. The writers who were being nurtured in *Okyeame* clearly came of age, and several were soon established with major international reputations.

In a double sense, Kwesi Brew is the elder statesman for the writers of this remarkable phase of Ghanaian writing. His major career has been in Ghana's diplomatic service where he served as ambassador to several different countries. As a poet he had also been publishing a number of individual poems in journals and anthologies before his first volume, *Shadows of Laughter* came out in 1969. Though his poetry is rarely stunning, it marks a clear break with the earlier poetry in English that was marred by excessive sentimentality. There is a firm, mature sense of *gravitas* in this poetry that examines the past and raises questions about the future. However personal he becomes, his poetry is anchored in a concern for the community. As Edwin Thumbo shows us, Brew is important for what he does with "statement and situation."

Kofi Awoonor is also a poet of and for the community. As a result of his numerous articles and several book-length critical studies, especially *The Breast of the Earth,* he has become one of the most important critics of African literature. More recently, he has also started on a diplomatic career as Ghana's ambassador to Brazil. Despite these other careers, there is no sense of either distance or subjective romanticization when he draws from traditional Ghana in his poetry. His voice is bardic, at times vatic, and even if you know nothing about Ghana or Africa, you cannot fail to be impressed by his dexterity and virtuousity in blending sounds, developing cadences, and shaping images. As all three articles here on his work show, however, any sense of his writing is enriched by knowing the very specific ways he has bridged traditional oral art and elite literature, traditional Ghana and contemporary Ghana. In even the best of the earlier poets we find a quest after the voice of the traditional poet-cantor that is often self-conscious. The anguish of this quest is surely something we can relate to, and while in Awoonor's poetry we also see and hear an anguished questing, the questing is never after the poet-cantor's voice. Whether drawing on the plaintive and elegaic dirge tradition or the sharp-tongued, caustic abuse tradition, Awoonor always has that voice. The voice may often be pained, but it is always self-confident in its exploration of ways it can speak of the joys and sorrows of the community.

With the arrival of Atukwei Okai on the poetry scene in the late sixties we can begin to sense a definite trend in Ghanaian poetry toward the adoption of the poet-cantor's voice. Just as Awoonor went beyond Brew and some of the earlier poets in adopting the voice, Okai goes beyond Awoonor. Okai certainly is the most controversial Ghanaian poet; you may find his work brilliant or bothersome, but it is hard to be indifferent to it. He is a more intensely personal poet than Awoonor, but he also sees himself speaking for the community in much the same way Whitman saw himself speaking for America. And like Whitman, he announces his bardic voice in a loud insistent, even brash manner.

Kofi Anyidoho, who has so effectively written on Okai, is, in turn, one of the subjects in Kofi Awoonor's essay on the newest generation of Ghanaian poets. Awoonor is intrigued by the ways these writers have avoided the trap of servile imitation of older African writers, a trap into which a number of younger West African writers have fallen. Kofi Anyidoho might well be the most promising poet of the three, yet Vincent Odamtten and Opoku Agyemang are developing their own styles, with Odamtten being more overtly political than Anyidoho and Agyemang being more personal. Still, all three are also well within the Ghanaian tradition of *gravitas,* of adopting the poet-cantor's voice, and of freely adopting style and content of traditional oral art. Indeed, there may be more imitation here than Awoonor had granted, but imitation in the finest sense that these poets are looking not just at the specific work of the older poets, but at the process through which a style was developed within a tradition.

Despite the fact that there was a lot of attention given in post-independence Ghana to the development of elite drama and theater, they never quite got off the ground the way the popular concert party did. Three names stand out, Ama Ata Aidoo, Efua Sutherland and Joe de Graft, but collectively they have only written a half dozen plays. Charles Angmor gives an interesting historical overview of the development of theater and dramatic writing in Ghana, tracing the origins back to the early concert party and analyzing the strengths and weaknesses of the best plays of the above three writers. Dapo Adelugba then takes us into a more detailed study of two plays by Ama Ata Aidoo and demonstrates how the dramatic force of her plays resides in her very apt and felicitous use of several kinds of English.

We should not think too narrowly, however, when considering drama in Ghana. A quality of much of the poetry since Awoonor's first poems, is the dramatic intensity of the writing; it is poetry to be performed. Public readings were frequent and well-attended in Accra in the sixties and seventies and clearly those who are most likely to be enthusiastic about the poetry of Okai are those who have seen and heard his exuberant performances. More attention should also be given to the radio play. The B.B.C. did a lot throughout West Africa to promote the writing and production of such plays, and Awoonor is one of the more important writers to try his hand at this genre. Finally, we see that where Ama Ata Aidoo is a good playwright, she is an outstanding writer of short fiction and this is due to her fine eye for dramatic scene and her ear that is so well tuned to the subtleties of dialogue. As Lloyd W. Brown shows in his essay on her stories, we tend always to feel in her best writing that she is allowing us to overhear the rich and often poignant discourse of ordinary Ghanaian women and their lives of "quiet desperation."

The final four essays, by Gareth Griffiths, D. S. Izevbaye, Edward Lobb and myself, all focus on the fiction of the two most important contemporary Ghanaian writers, Kofi Awoonor and Ayi Kwei Armah. For the most part, it has been their work that has drawn the attention of the world to the literary scene in Ghana. Consider that the articles and reviews on the work of these two writers is almost equal to all the articles written on the other writers. The attention has been warranted, but it might easily blind us to the fact that these men were not writing out of a literary vacuum in Ghana. Most of this introduction clearly argues with that notion, but we might also think about the recent development of the novel.

As I indicated above, the years following the fall of Nkrumah were very rich in terms of the production of Ghanaian literature. They were especially fertile years for the growth of the novel, and roughly three times the number of novels, popular and elite, came out in this period as in all the other periods combined. In his brief but insightful essay, Robert McDowell gives us a look at three of these novels: Joseph Abruquah's *The Catechist* (1965), Asare Konadu's *A Woman in Her Prime* (1967), and Francis Selormey's *The Narrow Path* (1966). These novels are in several ways more representative of the period than the works of either Armah or Awoonor, and if we look closely, we might find some interesting areas of contrast and comparison.

Once again we see the deep sense of *gravitas* that pervades Ghanaian literature, but all three novels are virtually devoid of any political commentary. Rather, they are, like the earlier *Eighteenpence,* serious explorations of the moral implications of being and growing in a community. The novels by Abruquah and Selormey are, in fact, *Bildungsromanen,* where the focus is on the development and education of an individual. (We could also consider Amu Djoleto's *The Strange Man* (1967), Cameron Duodu's *The Gab Boys* (1967), or Joseph Abruquah's *The Torrent* (1968) in this light.) Like many of the novels of this period there are fairly simple characters and plot, a lack of moral ambiguity, a central focus on personal relationships and the keys to success, and, perhaps most importantly, an emphasis on naturalistic detail.

In 1968 Armah's *The Beautyful Ones Are Not Yet Born* came out, and then in 1971 Awoonor's *This Earth, My Brother* appeared. How very different from their predecessors these novels seemed to be. Their experimental narrative styles seemed more in line with post-modernist fiction in Europe than developments in Ghana. Where earlier Ghanaian novels followed an objective and realistic mode of representation with a strictly linear chronological structure, these novels followed a more subjective and impressionistic mode of representation with a very fragmented chronological structure. In fact, the movement away from temporal time takes us in the direction of myth, and both writers seem to shape their work around the symbolic structures of myth and ritual. Yet these two works are also more overtly political than most Ghanaian novels of the period, and they offer some scathing commentary on post-independence problems.

The areas of divergence from the other novels of the time is quite clear. It is no less important to see that there are areas of convergence, common Ghanaian ground that they do share. From the external education of the individual in the *Bildungsroman* we have a shift to the internal searching and anguish of good men in a corrupt world, but in both cases we have a serious concern with the well being of the community. The other novels offer a rather straight didactic argument that the answer is in hard work, education, and moral direction on the part of the individual. These two works are more troubling in that they provide no easy answers, but simply argue for a broad (I would even say "mythic") vision that encompasses past and present, as well as the shared needs of all in the community. There is sufficient naturalistic detail that we can see that "community" here, no less than in the other novels, can be read as Ghana. But their breadth of vision is such that we can see that Awoonor and Armah are effectively speaking of Africa. If we look back, we can see a connection with Casely-Hayford's *Ethiopia Unbound*. If we look forward, we see this vision broadening into the epic structures of Armah's most recent work, *Two Thousand Seasons* (1973) and *The Healers* (1978).

Very little creative writing has come from Ghanaian writers since *The Healers*. What can we really say about the future of Ghanaian letters? The social milieu of the post-Nkrumah period was, at first, clearly conducive to the rapid growth of written literature. Other coups, however, have followed the one that toppled the Nkrumah government, and the quality of life has gotten worse for the average Ghanaian. The general malaise that has resulted from the political and economic instability has affected Ghanaian writers no less than other citizens. A number of critics have seen *This Earth* and *The Beautyful Ones,* their abundance of scatological images, as constituting depressing nay-saying commentary on all that is in Africa. Extending this literalist interpretation into the present silence we might "read" that silence as an even more profound negation. Only a Pollyana or a Pangloss could be blind to the severity of the situation in Ghana, but I will risk sounding like one and return to the optimism of my opening statement in relation to the one consistent characteristic I see in Ghanaian writing, the concern with the *polis,* the community.

In *This Earth,* Awoonor writes of his protagonist "dashing through traffic across a senseless roundabout which used to be [named] for the man they threw out, now for the abstraction for which they threw him out." For the protagonists of Armah and Awoonor, history is, in the

Joycean sense, a nightmare from which they are trying to escape. The best of the past, in myth and ritual, is put forth by both writers as the source of positive vision that will enable their society to transcend the nightmare. In the early post-independence period such a vision led poets like Adali-Mortty, to put his concern with a literacy campaign before his personal interests as a writer. From such a perspective we might view the present period for many Ghanaian writers more as a period of hibernation in terms of their art than as an abnegation of responsibility to their craft. It might be argued that writing is ultimately an individual act, yet the Ghanaian writer has effectively argued through his art that the art must be grounded in a serious committment to society. There is, then, a profound eloquence in the present literary silence. In 1976 Awoonor spent a year in prison as a result of his opposition to the military regime. More recently, Ama Ata Aidoo served as Ghana's Minister of Education. And just a year ago, Kofi Anyidoho returned to Ghana to teach, having completed his doctoral studies in the United States. I see in these moves a positive interconnection, a statement in effect that the writer in Ghana today can do more by going to jail or serving the state or teaching than he can through seeing a piece of literature through to publication. In one sense this is a sad comment on the present state of affairs, but such commitment to society will surely make possible a renaissance of Ghanaian literature.

ORAL ART

THE LANGUAGE OF THE PROVERB IN AKAN

Lawrence A. Boadi

The view is often expressed that the most important distinguishing feature of the proverb and other related spoken art forms is didacticism. Scholars say that, especially in preliterate societies, the main role of the proverb is to provide a storehouse of native wisdom and philosophy and a code of behavior for children and youth. This view seems to me too pragmatic and limiting and excludes much about certain aspects of the proverb as an art form. It ignores the importance that some societies attach to linguistic and literary features associated with the proverb, especially the sharp wit, the sarcasm, the humor, the rhetoric, and, indeed, all the aesthetic and poetic values of language use. Unless further elaborated, the didactic view would also lead one to believe that in Akan, for instance, any short utterance that expresses a moral truth is a proverb. The Akan language is spoken by between three and four million people in the West African country of Ghana and by a few thousands more in neighboring Ivory Coast.

A careful observation of language in context will reveal that in Akan society the primary function of proverbs is aesthetic or poetic and not didactic. Naturally, in most discussions and dialogues each participant is involved in putting across a point, exhorting, admonishing, or concealing a fact, and these ends could, in the majority of cases, be achieved without resort to proverbs. Yet a speaker often selects a particular proverb or striking metaphor because he wishes to embellish or elevate his message with a poetic dimension, or demonstrate to his opponent his superior sophistication, education, eloquence, or sensitivity in the use of his language. These goals need not be moral or didactic. My own experience with situations in which brilliant speakers use proverbs supports the view that they are motivated in the main by a desire to heighten their message poetically.

What I have said implies that native speakers are linguistically sensitive enough to be able to tell what constitutes a proverb in Akan and to distinguish proverbs from mere sayings intended to put across a moral point. The truth of this implication is borne out by the fact that Akan speakers do not react to translations of foreign proverbs into Akan as they do to native proverbs. For example, although most Akan Christian converts accept as incontrovertible the moral truth embodied in the sayings of the Old Testament Book of Proverbs, they intuitively exclude them from the class of native proverbs. Apparently, Old Testament verses do not capture features associated with Akan proverbs that the adult native speaker has grown to recognize. Mature native speakers of Akan deny the status of proverbs to the following biblical quotations:

> ". . . tie woagya nte so, na mpo wo na mmara."
> (Hear the instruction of thy father, and forsake not the law of thy mother.) *Proverbs* 1,8.

> Iehawa suro ne nyansa-hu mfiasie; agyimifo bu nyansa ne net so animtia.
> (The fear of the Lord is the beginning of wisdom: but the foolish despise wisdom and instruction.) *Proverbs* 1,7.

They also deny that translations of the following English sayings are proverbs in the Akan sense of the term.

> A stitch in time saves nine.
> Honesty is the best policy.
> A friend in need is a friend indeed.

One could give a variety of explanations for native attitudes to these proverbs. The thesis I would like to develop is that native speakers are sensitive to the poetic value of proverbs whether or not these contain a moral truth. Further, the varied emotional and intellectual reactions shown by native speakers to proverbs are conditioned more evidently by the aesthetic value of these proverbs—the quality of the imagery and of the wit—than by their moral content or truth value. Native speakers do not evaluate all proverbs equally but seem to arrange them on a hierarchical scale, with some having more rhetorical or poetic value than others. The structure of the hierarchy needs detailed study, but for my present purpose I will recognize two levels: highly valued proverbs used in serious discussions and debates, generally by adults; and little-valued ones mostly used by non-adults or by adults with children, especially during classroom instruction. (It is common for an adult to use a proverb when talking to a child, but the reverse is unusual.) Proverbs are assigned to places in the hierarchy not on the basis of their factual content and validity but on the quality of their imagery. The more concrete and unusual the image, the higher the proverb rates. Consider the following proverbs:

1. s woamma wo y nko antwa nkron a, wontwa du.
   (If you do not allow our neighbor to cut nine, you will not cut ten.)

2. Dabi y bio.
   (Some day [the future] is another, i.e., first fool is not a fool.)

The explanation for (2) is that the future will offer another, similar opportunity and a chance to retaliate. This proverb is used as a threat on occasions when a person discovers he has been cheated and regrets having helped a friend. All adult native speakers would recognize these as Akan proverbs by their sentence structure, rhythm, and context. At a certain level of discourse and in certain social contexts, however, both these proverbs would be considered trite and uninteresting although they both convey a moral truth and may have been appropriately used. Any serious adult public speaker who hoped to drive a point home to his audience and used these proverbs to illustrate his argument would be judged an incompetent speaker. Very likely, he would receive evaluative comments such as *n' ano ntee* ("His lips have not dried up yet"). I am not saying that these are not proverbs or that they are never used, by that neither would occur in a serious debate because the imagery is too ordinary, uninteresting, and lacking in concreteness. As a step toward a taxonomy of proverbs I would rate (1) and (2) low on the scale.

In Akan society, rhetoric is a far more important part of an adult's linguistic equipment than in most other societies. A mature participant in a dialogue or public discussion always strives to use vivid language because his audience is continually making folk-literary analyses of his speech. The importance attached to brilliance and imaginativeness in public speech leads those who aspire to enter traditional public life and hope to exert influence, especially in the courts and in politics, to cultivate the use of striking images. It is not unusual for courtiers in the course of their training and education to be attached to foreign courts in order to practice the technique of public speech, in which the witty use of striking metaphor and imagery is an important ingredient.

Let us now turn to a few of the proverbs that are highly valued in the culture.

3. aserewa su agyenkuku su a ne to pae.
   (If the aserewa attempts to sing like the agyenkuku, his posterior explodes.)

4. aserewa mo danta k se a, etu no hwe h.
   (If the aserewa puts on a large loincloth, it is thrown off balance.)

23

The *aserewa* is the smallest bird recognized in the culture, and the *agyenkuku* is one of the larger ones. In order to produce the deep notes of the *agyenkuku,* the *aserewa* has to overstrain it vocal muscles and he may explode his lungs or belly thereby. The proverb is used in situations in which a person attempts to do what is far beyond his natural ability.

The *danta* is a large piece of cloth folded several times and used as a loincloth by men working in the fields or fighting on the battlefield. It can also refer to the bandages worn by women to cover their private parts. The weight of the huge *danta* throws the little bird off balance and swings him down.

What distinguishes (3) and (4) from (1) and (2) are not features such as rhythm and alliteration, but unique and concrete images. Each of these latter two proverbs in a comment on overambition, a highly abstract notion. As with most proverbs, the implied comment is very general and can apply to a wide range of situations. But the vocabulary is not general or abstract. The comment is given a poetic dimension through a series of concrete images whose semantic features are interrelated, as in (3), excepting one or two purely grammatical words which act as structural links. *Aserewa* and *agyenkuku* are exotic but also concrete. The verbs *su* and *pae* both imply activity, the latter denoting, in addition, physical violence. But the wit and humor of this proverb derive from a subtle interplay of the semantic features of the images. The two nouns are matched in semantic features but they offer a contrast in content between a small and a large bird. Both verbs denote activity, but are opposed to each other in semantic features: *su* carries with it suggestions of spontaneity and volition, whereas *pae* implies rigidity and inertia; *su* connotes joy, vitality, life; *pae* connotes pain, annihilation, and final destruction. The selection of starkly concrete images and the irony that often results from the complex relations between the semantic features of these images characterize highly valued proverbs.

The second proverb expresses basically the same idea and shares an image with the first. Here we are given a series of physical images that conjure up a picture of an insignificant, diminutive bird dressed in a huge loincloth made of bales of cloth. The irony results from the vivid contrast between two opposites, the small size of the bird and the huge *danta*. The picture is one of grotesqueness. There is, of course, an additional concealed suggestion of sexuality in the image of this insignificant bird aping humans by covering its private parts. The verb in the second part of the proverb expresses physical and highly muscular action. Clearly, the interest raised by the imagery, wit, humor, and suppressed irony is outside the practical meaning or the moral philosophy of the proverb.

Proverbs at the low end of the hierarchy lack a complexity of relationships. Compare (3) and (4) on the one hand with (5), which purports to express basically the same idea.

5. abofra te fufuo a, te nea bek n' ano.
   (The child should take a morsel small enough to fit his mouth.)

Although (5) seems to have the same meaning as (3) and (4) and lends itself to use in the same situation, an Akan adult would avoid (5) in a serious discussion or even in conversation with other adults. He might use it when talking to children and non-adults. The imagery of (5) appears too ordinary to interest mature adults. The proverb does contain concrete nouns, but their semantic features are not related to each other in any interesting or significant way. Indeed, the impression Akan people probably get on hearing this proverb is that it is not concrete at all. Proverbs such as the following share similar properties and certainly belong to a lower level of intensity.

6. wunni yaanom a, yemfr yaanom.
   (If you have no friends you do not call friends.)

7. nda nyinaa ns.
   (All days are not equal.)

8. obi nkyer abofra nyame.
   (Nobody shows the child where God is.) [The Akan believe that the heavens are inhabited by God, who reveals himself as the gray clouds, one of the first things seen by the child when it is born.]

9. ade nyansa w nto.
   (Wisdom is not bought.)

Each of these sayings has at least one linguistic feature associated with Akan proverbs. Example (6) is distinguished by the rhythmic balance and the recurrence of certain phonological segments, (7) by its conciseness and generality, and (9) possibly by the stylistic use of inversion. But there is nothing strikingly concrete or stark about the imagery. Although (6) or (8) may occur in an adult conversation or a serious debate, a mature speaker would, if he had other alternatives, select those with more striking images. The fact that (6) and (8) have a greater chance of entering a serious debate by adults than, say (7) and (9) suggests that the division should not be restricted to the dichotomy of highly-valued and low-valued proverbs.

It might strike people of European descent as odd that Akan adults should prefer the concrete to the abstract proverb, because in European culture the adult mind is expected to express itself abstractly. The door is open for speculation as to whether the adult Akan speaker indulges in abstract thinking at all. But the adult Akan speaker prefers concreteness of expression in proverbs over abstractions.

In discussing the language of the proverb one should not forget the social context with which it is closely associated. The proverb is an important aspect in the training of courtiers, who are required to show brilliance, wit, and sophistication in debates. Concrete imagery is in keeping with the dramatic setting and color of the court. An image must be startling or dramatic (e.g. *etu no hwe h*, "It swings him, it uproots him").

With the vivid concreteness of the higher-level proverbs go directness and frankness. Imagery is drawn not only from exotic animal but also sex, body parts, and body functions. The free selection of sexual imagery to reinforce an argument in a public debate or discussion sometimes strikes foreigners as an unnecessary indulgence in obscenity. Indeed, in the past, foreign collectors of proverbs have completely ignored these proverbs, judging them to be embarrassingly crude and primitive.

Akan adults do not consider these proverbs obscene. In spite of repeated condemnations from missionaries, proverbs that allude to sex and body parts persist. Here are a few examples:

10. ayamtubin, y mb no boa mu.
    (Loose excrement, one does not pack it in a basket.) [A basketlike container made from palm branches is used to carry solid loads from the farm to the house. The idea being expressed here is that some situations are so delicate and complex that they can only be saved by extreme care and tact.]

11. woho b n a, yeta fra wo mu.
    (If your body stinks, people in your company take the advantage to fart.) [If you are universally known to be a thief, for example, other people will steal when you are about, hoping that you will be blamed for their thefts.]

12. wonta nsuro k tep n.
    (The twin-bearer is not frightened by the supreme penis.) [Twins in Akan culture are regarded as mystical, and the woman who bears twins is considered unusual.]

13. s wo k te awu a, no ara na wo dwons fa mu.
    (Although your penis may be dead, it still is your only
    means for passing water.) [You do not reject your parents
    or spurn your birthplace however poor or humble these
    may be.]

There are, of course, situations in which the use of these texts might be
considered obscene, for example if a person went about saying them out
of context or outside the appropriate occasions. In serious and heated
debates, however, it is accepted that a speaker can freely use proverbs
alluding to bodily parts and functions. The value of these proverbs lies in
the starkness of the imagery, which here is much franker than what is
heard in ordinary discourse.

It should be clear from the preceding paragraphs that there exist in the
language multiple proverbs which, while expressing a common central
idea or philosophy, differ in the intensity and quality of their language and
imagery. In attempting to characterize the imagery, I have proposed a
tentative two-level hierarchy. Very likely, an extensive study would
reveal that the scale is not dichotomous at all but that there are intermedi-
ate levels. Take this saying:

14. wo se akyi apor a h ara na wotafe.
    (The back of your teeth may be rotten, nevertheless it is
    the only spot that you suck.)

This proverb occurs in serious dialogues, as we would expect from the
concrete imagery derived from a body part and body function, and from
its direct and frank character. Nevertheless, in a debate between adults,
this proverb is likely to be less valued than its near-synonym (13). Thus,
the existence of proverbs such as (14) argues strongly against a purely
dichotomous scale. Furthermore, the place of a proverb on the hierarchy
is not fixed. Conceivably, the value of a proverb may change if a new one
expressing the same central idea is created or an old one lost through
time.

These uncertainties aside, the available evidence shows that native
speakers recognize a hierarchy. The question that we ask is: are reactions
to conceptually related proverbs uniform, and if not, what is the motiva-
tion for the different reactions? I contend that the different reactions from
a mature native speaker are determined not by the truth-value of proverbs, but by the quality of the imagination or poetry that has gone into
them.

STORYTELLING OF THE AKAN AND GUAN IN GHANA

Jonas Yeboa-Dankwa

Many authorities have written about storytelling in some parts of the world. There have been very few such works on storytelling in Ghana. An example is R.S. Rattray's *Akan-Ashanti Folktales*. But even this work is not devoted solely to storytelling; neither does it mention the Guan whose customs are similar to those of the Akan. The aim of this work, therefore, is to write about storytelling of the Akan and Guan in Ghana. A brief account is given about these two ethnic groups in order to put the work in a better perspective.

There are three language groups in Ghana.[1] These are Gur, Mande, and Kwa. According to Joseph H. Greenberg these three languages are part of the Niger-Congo branch of the Congo-Kordofanian language family.[2] Akan, which is the language of the ethnic group called Akan, is made up of Fante and Twi. The Fante live along the coast in the Central Region while the Twi live in the interior. The Akan alone occupy more than one third of the area of Ghana and according to Abu-Hassan more than forty per cent of the people speak Akan.[3] There are other ethnic groups which have cultural similarities with them; some of these are the Guan, the Nzema and the Aowin. The 1970 Population Census of Ghana also put the Akan together with the other related ethnic groups as making up well over sixty per cent of the population in five out of the nine regions in the country.[4] All this shows that the Akan and the other related ethnic groups form the single dominat group in the country.

The indigenous Akan and Guan peasant farmers always long for the good storytelling sessions. At these occasions they enjoy the company of other people in the community in order to keep their physical strength and restore their moral and spiritual powers after the day's hard work on their farms. The experience I got from my father is this. The night seems very long for these farmers. As a result they usually sit for long hours by the fire under the stall in the yard or on the veranda when they have sleepless nights. Therefore, the stories which last long into the night are a good repose for them.

The Akan and Guan tell stories for other reasons. They indirectly use them in training their children in good morals. They are taught to be honest, truthful, dutiful, serviceable, skillful, brave and thrifty. Good parentage and good administration are also taught with these stories. Some of these stories are used to comment on the behavior of a child, a wife, a husband, and even those in authority such as the chief. R. S. Rattray points out that it was a recognized custom, especially in the olden days, "for anyone with a grievance against a fellow villager, a chief or even the King of Ashanti to hold him to . . . disgrace in ridicule, by exposing some undesirable in his character—greed, jealousy, deceit . . ."[5]

The point being made is that in normal life the chief of an Akan or Guan town, or the King of Ashanti, in particular, is neither insulted, ridiculed nor disgraced by any citizen. Anyone who violates this tradition is severely punished. The belief is that the chief or the King who is the religio-political head of the community is the representative of the ancestors. To disrespect him implies that the ancestors are not honored. The ultimate result might be a calamity in the community. But in storytelling the tradition of respecting those in authority, however bad they might be, is ignored. Moreover, anonymity is the rule in storytelling. As the storyteller mentions no one's name, even though such people can be inferred, nobody becomes outwardly offended. Furthermore, if the narrator does not want to mention the name "Onyankopon" (God) the creator and owner of all the folktales, he says, "Ananse Kokuroko" (Great Spider).

The Spider is the trickster in Ghanaian folktales. Originally, all folktales were called "Nyankonsem" (God's words). When God wanted to name them after anyone who would be able to buy them with a live lion, a live python, a live dwarf and the live insect called "mmoboro," it was only Ananse who could achieve this feat. Thus folktales among the Akan and Guan are called "Anansesem" (Spider's words).

The folktales, which are differentiated by their characters, deal with almost everything in the world. These stories include wild and domestic animals, people such as bad wives and bad and unfaithful husbands, disobedient beautiful young women who refuse all suitors from their hometowns, supernatural beings such as "sasabonsan" (the half-man-half-beast with over-grown hair who lives in tall trees in the forest), spirits, "mboatia" (the short men in the forest or dwarfs), trees, rivers, the sea, and even stones. The characters are also determined by the locality of the ethnic group. For example, the Fante who are along the coast may use the whale as a character in a story about death while the Asante may use the elephant or the python. But all of them will use "Ananse" (the spider), the trickster in Ghanaian folktales. Other common characters in both the Akan and the Guan include the hare, the tortoise, the deer, the antelope, the parrot, the sunbird, the crow, the vulture, the ant, the rat, and the squirrel.

The characters can be put into binary groups such as the big and the small, the strong and the weak, the tall and the short, the dead and the living, the wise and the foolish, the rich and the poor and the quick and the slow. The purpose of matching these opposing characters shows that life does not always favour the strong, or the wise and the rich, but the weak, the foolish and the poor at times succeed in life. They also play a useful role in the world and are at times more successful than their seemingly superior counterparts.

Stories can be told by any person irrespective of age or sex. But storytelling goes with knowledge and wisdom, so the good narrators are old men and old women. It is the grandfather or grandmother, the father or the mother or an adult member of the family who tells stories in an Akan or Guan community.

There is no formal training for storytelling. Children listen to the stories told by their grandparents, parents, brothers, and sisters or other members of their families or storytellers in the community. So individual children from their childhood develop an interest in stories and storytelling. This is evident in the fact that every Akan or Guan child can tell some folktales and has his own repertoire.Furthermore, as will be shown later in this work when actual storytelling is discussed, individuals, as a result of their traditional relationships, are given the opportunity to tell stories at storytelling sessions. Children also organize themselves to tell stories. Parents at times ask their children to tell them stories; so also do grandparents ask their grand children. As a result of the introduction of Western education,storytelling in Akan is included in the curriculum of Akan and Guan primary schools, especially, in the lower classes. This is mostly done on Friday afternoons. So at present the Ghanaian educational system provides for direct training in storytelling at the primary level. There are other facilities for indirect training in storytelling in Ghana. An example is the Ghana Broadcasting Corporation which has a program for Akan storytelling once every week. Guan is not a written language, so both Akan and Guan children benefit from this informal training in storytelling. All this points to the fact that even though there is no conscious or direct effort made to train storytellers among the Akan and the Guan, the facilities available, both indigenous and literary, make individual good storytellers come out by the time they reach adulthood. A good example of a good narrator without formal education is Nana Osei Wusu from Chechewere in the Offinso district who is about eighty-eight years old. But it must be pointed out that very few become good narrators. For example, even though Nana Osei Wusu is illiterate, he is recognized as the best storyteller in his traditional area and the whole of Offinso district. Again, as a result of storytelling in the primary schools, the school children tend to develop their own versions of traditional stories. One main characteristic of these "school" stories is that they are short because some of the incidents are left out.

There are usually two places where stories are told. They are in the home either by the fire under a stall or in the open in the yard, on the verandah or in the kitchen, or in the bedroom, and on the "prama" (the open space in the town or village).[6] When parents or grandparents tell stories to their children or grand children, it is mostly by the fire. The verandah is used when they are not sitting around the fire in the yard especially during the rainy season. The kitchen is mostly used by the mothers to whom their children and other children in the house go. The bedroom is either used by the parents and their children, or the grand-mothers in particular and their grand children when the latter sleep with them in the same room. On many occasions it is the children who ask their parents, grandparents, or other adults in their family to tell them stories. The children are never denied this unless circumstances do not allow it. Not all stories are told to the children, especially the young ones. Stories about ghosts, supernatural beings, death and other frightful ones are not told them, especially in the bedroom, for there is the obvious concern that the tales might make them have nightmares. Children might even express their fear and not go to sleep until their parents or grandparents are ready to go to bed.

The appropriate time for storytelling is in the evening after the last meal of the day. Moonlit nights are the most suitable, especially for storytelling on the prama. But when there is no moon, lanterns are used. The stories are not told during the day because the people believe that it is not good. There are sanctions for this prohibition. Anyone who tells a story in the day is supposed to grow a hump at the back. Being peasant farmers, the Akan and Guan are almost always in their farms working; there is not time for storytellng during the day. The prohibitions are thus used as a check against the lazy children who do not want to go to the farm or work, but would always like to play or loiter about. They also put fear in them in order that they might conform to the social practices. However, moderni-zaiton is eroding these indigenous social sanctions of the Akan and Guan. As a result of the introduction of Western educaiton and the establish-ment of the Ghana Broadcasting Corporation, folktales are told in the afternoon. Moreover, researchers from the Language Centre and the Institute of African Studies, both of which are in the University of Ghana, Legon, and the School of Ghanaian Languages at Ajumako, together with the Department of Ghanaian Languages, University of Cape Coast, go round collecting and recording folktales from storytellers during the day.

There is no official or formal costume for storytelling. The men put on their "mmarimatam" (men's cloth) which is a long broad piece of cloth. Some of these cloths are sewn with one piece of material of twelve yards long. The women put on "ntama" (ordinary cloth) which is made up of two pieces and a blouse to cover the shoulder. The boys dress as their fathers, but their cloths are smaller, and the girls as their mothers, but they have one piece of cloth and a shoulder cover. When it is cold the girls put on another piece of cloth over the shoulder cover. The women can use the second piece of cloth to cover themselves, while the men and boys can always wrap themselves in their mmarimatam.

It is the children in the village or town who always gather together first before a storytelling session starts. While they are waiting, and in order to entertain themselves, they can play riddles or sing the songs callled "mmoguo"[7] (sing for nothing songs). The Fante even use drum accompaniment in these inital interludes. When the storytelling is by a group, such as the "Abetifi Anansesem Kuo" who I heard in 1980 when I did my fieldwork, the members who gather together early also sing these mmoguo. These mmoguo before the actual storytelling are longer than those which are used during the stories themselves.

The storyteller, or any member of the audience, can sing a mmoguo which is made up of short repetitive sentences, phrases or words. If it is the storyteller who is to sing or lead, there is no signal to inform the audience that he is going to interrupt his story with a song. All that he has to do is to stop at a convenient point and pick up his tune. The storyteller can sing a few lines, according to the structure of the song, before the audience joins in a chorus, or he can sing through the whole song first before they repeat or sing their part.[8] On other occasions there is an alternation of the lines sung by the leader and the chorus.[9] If it is a member of the audience who is to sing the song, there are conventional expressions that he must use to ask the storyteller to stop the narration. But these expressions are never used when the storyteller has not come to the end of a sentence or has not completed an action. Therefore, the mmoguo is always sung at a convenient point in the story.

The mmoguo may be known by the storyteller and all the audience. It does not matter if it is a new one, because the response is always given in a chorus. Again, you can hum if you do not know the words. One interesting thing about Akan and Guan songs is that the words are repeated, and thus it is very easy to pick up a tune and sing in harmony with the group.

The conventional expressions used to interrupt the narration for the mmoguo to be sung depend upon the ethnic groups. For example, while the Akuapem Twi and Guan (Okere) will use this common one:

> Da no na mewo ho.
> (On that day I was there),

Gomua, an ethnic group of the Fante, will use:

> Opanyin, so wo fien.
> (Elder, hold your story, or Storyteller, stop your narration and
> let me sing a mmoguo.)

The Akuapem expression presupposes that the leader of the interlude, or any other member of the group, was at the scene of the incidents about which the story is told. The mmoguo is repeated a few times before the storyteller continues his narration.

The mmoguo is very important in Akan and Guan storytelling. It keeps up the morale of the audience. It also helps them to participate fully in the narration, and this is a good sing of the interaction between the storyteller and his audience. There are other uses of the mmoguo, especially to the storyteller. It helps him to have a rest because storytelling among the Akan and Guan is really dramatic. He may be tired, out of breath or he might have lost his voice. During the rest period he may either join the audience, recollect the incidents that come next or even those which seem to elude him. It also helps those who might be feeling sleepy to wake up. So after every mmoguo there is renewed interest by the audience. This can be found from the comments they make, their laughter and their facial expressions. Those who are tired will be seen stretching up in their seats.

The audience sit in a semi-circle facing the storyteller. But during a good performance, before the session ends, the narrator would be encircled by a large number of people. Each person brings his or her stool. The children bring their parents' or those of any adult members in their families. The stool for the storyteller is brought by a child in his house.

The Akan and Guan folktale has three parts: the introduction or opening, the story itself and the ending. The introduction or opening formulas which set the stage and are a prelude to the "Once upon a time" formula, which takes the audience into the world of fantasy, depend upon the ethnic groups. For example, the Twi and Okere (Guan) of Akuapem will say: "Abraa! Abraa!" (Listen! Listen!) and the audience will respond "Yon! Yon!" (We're listening! We're listening!). After this opening the storyteller will ask a question such as, "Do you know the reason why if you marry from your own hometown, you do not regret?" And the audience will answer "No!" When anyone says "Yes!" it is somewhat an insult. He does not want the performance to come on. But this is very, very rare. The Agona of the Central Region will say, "Da bi ara ne nne!" (Today is like any other day!) Most of the Fante will also say, "Kodzi wondze ndzi oo!" (Folktales, they don't believe them!)

The narrator can also start the story with a statement which is either a summary or the moral of the story. An example for such a summary is, "why the cat is called Okra (the soul)." An example of a moral also will either be a question or an ordinary statement such as, "Why everyone should do good."

Another common opening expression is, "Yesise, sise oo!" (We say, we say!) The audience's response is "Yesise no sen?" (What do we say?) In other words, the storyteller with this expression is informing the audience that he is going to tell them a story and they in turn are asking him what kind of story he is going to tell them. When this particular formula is used the narrator goes on to the "Once upon a time" formula which is inversely put in a negative form thus, "Was it not one day . . ." Or, he can use the positive form, "One day," or "Once upon a time." Two other opening formulas are, "In the days of . . ." and "Long, long ago . . ." The particular version or a combination of these versions of the introductory or opening formulas depends upon the storyteller and how good he is, the audience and the particular occasion.

When the story has started the success of a storyteller depends upon how skillfully and creatively he can use his language, how he can perform and not simply narrate the story, how he can lead the audience in singing the mmoguo if he is the reader and how he can sustain their interest throughout the period.

Even though the language a storyteller uses is the everyday conversational one, he uses it in such a way that it is full of descriptive expressions, imagery such as metaphors and similes. It is the effective use of some of the above devices singly or in combination that helps him to describe the incidents in a story. Direct speech for the dialogue between or among characters is another useful technique freely and effectively employed by good storytellers such as Nana Osei Wusu of Chechewere. For example, in one folktale Ananse collected all wisdom into a pot and tried to hang the pot on top of a big tall tree in the forest. His son Ntikuma followed him from afar. With the wisdom pot in front of Ananse he could not climb the tree. Ntikuma told him to change the position of the pot and hang it at his back. This incident Nana Osei Wusu put in an effective dialogue with Ntikuma speaking slowly with fright and Ananse turning round, though afraid, shouting at the person speaking to him.

Dramatization of the actions of the characters is one effective technique also. The storyteller uses changes in his facial expression, his hands and bodily movements or actual mimicry for these actions. For example, the fright of Ntikuma when he was speaking to Ananse was depicted with a flushed face by Nana Osei Wusu; he also showed how Ananse quickly turned with a pulled face and a hoarse voice because he was taken by surprise. Changes in voice are also used by the good Akan and Guan storytellers to show pitch, loudness, softness, surprise, anger, joy, happiness, hatred, love, and even death. These exaggerations in the use of the voice help the narrator to create the correct atmosphere so that the audience can picture the incidents being described in the fairyland of the story. Onomatopoeia is never left out, and the good storytellers are effective in using this technique. For example, when Ananse did wrong against God he was punished. When he was almost caught by his assailants when he was running away, he jumped to the ceiling "Kado!" "Kado" is the sound made when something is thrown at the ceiling. When the hunter shot the old large male baboon from the top of the tall tree it fell "Tuu!" "Tuu" is also the sound made when something from a great height falls to the ground. What is interesting about these sounds is that apart from making the narration real, dramatic and interesting, they all create laughter as a result of how they are made by the narrators. Repetition in the use of reduplication is one of the devices for exaggeration. It is used to show size, height, length, and shape. Verbs and adjectives are the parts of speech that are mostly reduplicated. For example, Ananse walked very, very fast to the forest with the wisdom pot would be "Ananse nantew *ntemntemntem . . .*" When Ananse went to the "food dish" he hid on the ceiling, he ate very, very, very quickly would be, "Ananse didii *hareharehare,*" or *"ntemntemntem."* The needle-like legs of "Nankorohwea," one of Ananse's sons, would be described as *"nketenketenkete."* They very beautiful young woman who despised all men in her hometown and finally married a tiger would be described as *"fefefefefefe"* or *"fefeefe."* Another way of storytellers using reduplication to show exaggeration to achieve their aim is the prolongation of either medial vowel or the final vowel sound. The palatable food Ananse ate would be described as *"dedeede."* The beautiful young woman referred to would be described as *"fefeefe."* Ntikuma also walking very slowly following Ananse in the forest would be described as *"breoo."* The tall big tree in which Ananse wanted to hang the wisdom pot would be described as "dua *tenteenten, kakraa . . ."* The hands are used to show size, length, and shapes of objects. Weight can be shown by the hands, facial expressions together with other actions. Length too can be shown by the paces the narrator takes in front of the audience. Different facial expressions and parts of the head for example, the nose, eye, and mouth can be used to show a bad smell, a stern gaze and a sweet or bitter thing respectively.

There are certain rules in Akan and Guan storytelling. One of them is complete silence; therefore there is this expression, "Anansesem kyi kasa" (Folktales hate speaking). But this does not mean that occasional comments which do not disturb are not made. Neither is laughter forbidden because it is natural and spontaneous; you cannot suppress it. It is when individuals speak undertone or even loudly and when they try to do anything to disturb the performance that the rules are applied. The people near them ask them quietly to stop what they are doing. They may wink at them or they may lightly push them with their elbows. If all these measures fail, you will her individuals or the whole audience shout at the particular person or persons disturbing to stop misbehaving. But there might be one or two reasons why there could be genuine cases of disturbance. When the story tends to be too long and uninteresting or, when the storyteller tends to tell too many lies, there is nothing that can be done. These individuals are by their actions asking the storyteller to cut his story short.

When the stories are very long, when there is too much exaggeration or when lies are being told, because most of these stories are known by the audience, you will hear a listener immediately say, "Wosisi me!" (You're cheating me! And the storyteller will respond, "Mesisi mo makoda!" (I'm cheating you all in order to go to sleep!) The narrator himself, as Nana Osei Wusu does, can also say, "Anansesem ye nsisie!" (Folktales are cheating!) or "Anansesem nkye myin!" (Folktales don't take a long time to grow!) There is always laughter after these impromptu interpolations. They bring life to the atmosphere again.

There are conventional expressions or ending formulas for ending the stories. The narrator can use any of the following:

> Manansesem a metoe yi, se eye de o, se enye de o, momfa bi
> nko na momfa bi mmra!
> (The folktale I've just narrated, if it is good, or if it's not good,
> you should take some away and bring some.)

The response from the audience is:

> Ehee!
> (Alright!)

Or,

37

Manansesem a metoe yi, se eye de o, se enye de o, mede
soa . . .
(The folktale I've just narrated, if it's good, or if it's not good, I
pass it on to . . .)

In the first example after the response by the audience one of them
starts his story. In the second one it is the person named who starts the
new story. The narrator can also end the story by repeating the moral or
lesson he used at the beginning. The moral or the lesson can be a proverb
which is used throughout the narration where appropriate. A suitable
proverb for Ananse being unable to gather all the wisdom in the world into
the wisdom pot can be, "All wisdom is not in one man's head." Two
proverbs for the gluttony of Ananse would be "Glutony results in death,"
and "Gluttony is illness." The storyteller can ask the audience to congratulate him by saying, "Mompene no e!" (Congratulate him!) The usual
response is "Ehee!" (Well done!) If the story is really a good one, you can
tell from the loudness of the response, or the number of times it is
repeated. A listener can also ask the audience to congratulate the narrator; he uses the same formula used by the storyteller. There is also
another formula for ending the story and beginning the new one. As soon
as the narrator ends, a member from the audience will say,

W'anansesem a wotoe yi, woboa!
(This story you have narrated is a lie!)

The storyteller asks that listener,

Meboa no sen?
(How do I lie?)

The expression used by the listener is a way of informing the audience
that he is the next person to tell a story. The response of the storyteller
gives him permission to do so.

As a result of the various ways in which the narrator ends his story, no
one knows who is to tell the next story until the final formula. As the end
of the story can be determined by the ending formulas, there is great
anxiety or keen expectation at this point. The anxiety or expectation can
be determined by the facial expressions of the listeners or their restlessness. As a good narrator knows the others who are fairly good, he makes
sure that one of them has his or her turn first. But individual listeners can
be quick to sense this, so they use the ending formula which allows them
to tell the next story. A casual look at the ending formulas used might

indicate some confusion when the narration is completed. But here is never any confusion. The story always ends on a peaceful note despite the anxiety of the listeners. This peaceful ending brings the audience from fairyland and gives them inner joy and satisfaction.

There is no specific time or a formal way of closing a storytelling session. The stories usually last for a long time, especially the community ones. Whenever any listener feels tired or sleepy, he takes his stool and quietly moves away. After some time when there is only a handful of listeners left, the performance ends.

Storytelling among the Akan and Guan of Ghana is one of the greatest pastimes, particularly in the rural areas. Individual good storytellers are found only in large areas. The good storyteller is usually an old man or an old woman who has amassed a large repertoire and developed a unique style from an early period by being a member of the family or community storytelling sessions. The introduction and the spread of literacy from the second half of the nineteenth century, and the impact of the mass media, such as the newspaper, the radio and the television, have to some extent affected the role and status of both the folktale and the storyteller. However, a critical examination of the function of these institutions reveals that the folktale is only being adapted to the social changes in the country.

APPENDIX

"MMOGUO": SONGS[10]

The part for the chorus is indented.

1. Let us go to look at "by the tree."
   The squirrel, the squirrel "by the tree."
     Let us go to look at "by the tree."

2. Ntonko o![11]
     I shall grow to get horns.

3. Spider, spider, spider,
   The food you left us with
   Some animals, some animals have eaten it all.
   He says, "Stop!
   I have eaten it myself.
   Stop! Lazy woman."

    Stop! I have eaten it myself.
A woman who hates the farm.
    Stop! I have eaten it myself.
A harlot (woman).
    Stop! I have eaten it myself.

4. Adenne!
    Where is mother gone?
      Adenne!
    Mother is gone to the farm.
      Adenne!
    With whom did she leave you?
      Adenne!
    With Okuafo Yeboawa.
      Adenne!
    Roast a piece of yam for me (to eat).
      Adenne!
    Fetch some water for me (to drink).
      Adenne!
    She refused to fetch the water.
      Adenne!
    Where am I going?
      Adenne!
    I am going to the water pot.
      Adenne?
    There is no water in the pot.
      Adenne!
    I went towards the river.
      Adenne!
    The road is flooded.
      Adenne!
    I went just a little further.
      Adenne!
    A tall palm-tree is possessed.
      Adenne!
    Small palm-trees are singing for it.
      Adenne!

5. Who is standing there very, very black?
    Who is standing there very, very red?
      Amerenyawa!
    Standing there for what?

Amerenyawa!
Making threads from raffia leaves.
Amrenyawa!
Making threads for whom?
Amrenyawa!
Making theads for my girl-friend.
Amrenyawa!
Your girl-friend called what?
Amrenyawa!
Yaa Afoakwa.
Amrenyawa!
Is it Kwakye's child, Takari?
Amrenyawa!
Kwaw who lives at Oda?
Amrenyawa!
She did not turn up.
Amrenyawa!

NOTES

1. *Map of Ghanaian Languages,* 1980.
2. Joseph H. Greenberg, *The Languages of Africa,* p.8.
3. Abu-Hassan, *Developing Human Resources of the Book Industry in West Africa: Report on a UNESCO Mission to Ghana.*
4. *1970 Population Census of Ghana,* Vol. II, pp. XXVI-XXVIII.
5. R. S. Rattray, *Akan-Ashanti Folktales,* p. xi.
6. C. A. Akrofi, *Twi Nsem Nkorenkore Kyerewbea (Twi Spelling Book),* p. 105 refers to "prama" as the lane between two rows of houses.
7. The Appendix shows a few collections of the "mmoguo."
8. Refer to "mmoguo" Number 8 in the Appendix.
9. Refer to "mmoguo" Numbers 4 and 5 in the Appendix.
10. Each of the "mmoguo" has a story to go with it.
11. "Ntonko" is the largest type of pepper the Akan and Guan farmers have. There are many kinds.

BIBLIOGRAPHY

Abu-Hassan, *Developing Human Resources of the Book Industry in West Africa: Report on a UNESCO Mission to Ghana,* (15 March–17 May, 1981.)

Akrofi, C. A., *Twi Nsem Nkorenkore Kyerewbea (Twi Spelling Book),* (Accra, Waterville Publishing House).

Ben-Amos, Dan, "The Elusive Audience of Benin Narrators," *Journal of Folklore Institute,* 9 (1972–73), 177–184.

Finnegan, Ruth, "Story-Telling," *Limba Stories and Storytelling,* (Oxford, The Clarendon Press, 1967).

Georges, Robert A., "Towards an Understanding of Storytelling Events," *Journal of American Folklore,* 82 (1969), 318–328.

Greenberg, Joseph H., *The Languages of Africa,* (Bloomington, Indiana University Press, 1963).

Herskovits, Melville J., "The Study of African Oral Art," *Journal of American Folklore,* 74 (1961), 451–456.

Jordon, A. C., "Tale Teller and Audience in African Spoken Literature," *Proceedings of Conference of African Languages and Literature,* (1966), 33–43.

Musson, Margaret, *Mr. Spider and His Friends,* (London, Oxford University Press, 1953).

Pelton, Robert D., *The Trickster in West Africa* (New York, Garland Publishing, 1981).

Rattray, Robert Sutherland, *Akan-Ashanti Folktales,* (Oxford, The Clarendon Press, 1969).

1970 Population Census of Ghana, Vol. II (Accra, 1972), xxvi-xxviii.

Map of Ghanaian Laguages, (Language Centre, University of Ghana, and Ghana Institute of Linguistics, 1980).

THE MAKING AND BREAKING OF KWAME NKRUMAH: THE ROLE OF ORAL POETRY

Kwesi Yankah

The use of folklore for political purposes is a world-wide phenomenon. Its roots in the Western world may be traced as far as 18th century Germany, where Gottfried Herder, championing the cause of nationalism drew attention to German folklore as the repository of the soul of the people. In Finland, USSR, Turkey, and the U.S. different forms of folklore have been exploited during wars, political crises or nation build-ing, as effective channels for disseminating, political ideology (See Oinas 1972). In Africa the close link between folk poetics and modern politics is exemplified in places like Zambia, Kenya, Guinea, and several parts of Southern Africa, where the song has been used as a medium for state or political propaganda (Finnegan 1970).

In exploiting forms of folklore to serve the ends of modern politics, the rationale is evidently that of appealing to the romantic disposition of the broad masses of people through channels that have been influential in the past. While the politicization of folklore forms continues to receive scholarly attention, there seems to be missing an attempt to critically examine and monitor the efficacy of the traditional modes of communica-tion in serving modern roles. Such a task is an enormous one, owing to the wide diversity of cultures that exploit the medium, and the different epochs in which the phenomenon transpires. The task, on the other hand, becomes easier, and the effort more realistic, if we attempt to monitor the modern exploitation of folk wisdom in the political career of a single personality. For here, we are enabled by the specificity of the endeavor to be more circumspective.

It is with this in mind that I intend, in this paper, to examine the various ways in which the wisdom of the folk was exploited to shape the destiny of Kwame Nkrumah, the first President of Ghana.

The circumstances surrounding the rise of Nkrumah to the forefront of Ghana's struggle for independence; his political leadership in Ghana from 1957, when Ghana attained independence, to 1966 when he was over-thrown from power; Nkrumah's commitment to African unity, and the pioneering role he played in the attempt to free the entire African continent from colonial rule—all these are indeed cliches in the lexicon of political historians.

But politics being what it is, Nkrumah will continue to receive both favorable and unfavorable reviews from political activists, Ghanaians, and scholars as a whole. Viewed positively or negatively, however, there is one attribute on which supporters and opponents of Kwame Nkrumah are in essential agreement. I refer to Nkrumah's well-publicized charisma. In the eyes of the Ghanaian who lived through Nkrumah's role, however, this charisma carried with it an aura of enigma, mysticism and invincibility, that blew the image of Kwame Nkrumah out of proportion with that of his local peers and opponents—a fact which led to such utterances and publications after his overthrow as "The myth surrounding Kwame Nkrumah is broken." (See, for example, Ocran 1968.)

In seeking to identify the source of Nkrumah's enigma, one could not discount Nkrumah's personal life style, and the possibility of innate mystique. References have been made by such scholars as Marais (1972) and Timothy (1981) to, for example, Nkrumah's meditative tendencies, his withdrawal into silent meditation when faced with critical issues. One recalls also Nkrumah's characteristic use of the white handkerchief and walking stick, which many believed embodied mystical power. Then of course was the well-established rumor that Nkrumah had a personal fetish, called Kankan Nyame, who administered to his spiritual needs. But whether these accounts were based on fact or fantasy, they fitted squarely into the plot of Kwame Nkrumah's factual biography. In his autobiography, he states,

> I had heard many stories about ghosts, for such things are real in tribal society. Instead of being afraid of these tales, however, I remember sitting for long enough on my own wishing that I could die simply because I should often rank among those privileged souls who could pass through walls and closed doors, sit among groups of people unobserved and make a genuine nuisance of themselves!
>
> I don't know whether this longing for things supernatural indicated psychic power, but my mother has many times related the following incident which occurred one day. When, strapped to her back in the normal manner of a young African child, I was travelling with her on one of our frequent journeys together. It happened that she had to wade through a stream on the way, and as we neared the center, I suddenly cried out in excitement that I was standing on a fish. Although startled by

44

my sudden and noisy outburst, my mother was even more surprised when she discovered to her amazement that she had actually trapped a fish with one of her feet. It ended happily, for she managed to catch it and we had it for dinner that evening (Nkrumah 1957:9).

The aura of mysticism surrounding Kwame Nkrumah was indeed thickened by the proliferation of Nkrumah's effigy on stamps, currency, in cloth design, and in the form of statues in several parts of the country. Then, of course, was the Ghana Young Pioneer Movement—a club of youthful Ghanaian primary and secondary school kids who were not only inculcated with the ideals of Nkrumaism and pan-Africanism, but were also taught to recite pledges and chants that idealized Nkrumah's virtues and enigma.

But Nkrumah's credo and enigma were, perhaps given the greatest booster through the institution of traditional appellation poetry. A fact not yet broached in any of his reviews, Kwame Nkrumah had a salaried traditional poet whose duty it was to preface all Nkrumah's speeches with an unlimited outpouring of awe-inspiring appellations. Thus, whether Nkrumah spoke in public, in parliament, or on the radio, there was always a prelude of a well-articulated appellation performance often ending with the words,

> Kwame kasa kasa kasa
> Kwame speak, speak, speak.

It is indeed from the lexicon of this poetic institution that Kwame Nkrumah acquired the title Osagyefo (Savior-at-war) which eventually replaced the presidential title. Other appellations by which Nkrumah came to be known are Kantamanto (One-who-never breaks-his-oath) Oseadeeyo (He-who keeps his word), Oyeadieyie (One who repairs damage) and the like.

The performance of Nkrumah's title before he spoke had a special significance. Beside boosting Nkrumah's ego and credo, the appellation recital, with its foregrounding of Ghanaian verbal wit also harmonized with Nkrumah's own rhetorical talent. To many who ever heard Nkrumah speak, the power and flow of his words were captivating. To Genoveva Marais who knew Nkrumah well, "When he spoke, his words not only inspired others but seemed to act as a spur to his own further inspiration. His audience listened to him spell bound" (Marais 1972:128). In the words of Bankole Timothy

> Nkrumah was at his best when addressing a political meeting.
> He was an effective spellbinder and rabblerouser. He could
> make his audience become incensed or sorrowful according to
> the effect he wished to produce.
>
> As an orator, Nkrumah brought all his theatrical skill into play:
> he was a born actor who played on the emotions of his
> audience. For effect, he used his hands while speaking: he
> shook his head, paced along the dais, and gave a captivating
> smile. His eloquence was fiery. . . . Even his political oppo-
> nents recognized his forceful oratory (Timothy 1981:112).

Nkrumah's eloquence while at the forefront of Ghana's politics was infact
not a newly found talent. It was a follow-up of his debating capabilities
during his college career (Nkrumah 1957:19–30). Nkrumah's own talent in
oratory then made the traditional appellation poetry eloquently recited
before his speeches all the more significant; for being evocative and
dignifying the traditional poetry performance was an appropriate signal
for the brilliant display of rhetoric that followed. Part of the words of the
traditional poet even highlighted Nkrumah's speech-making talent; to him
Nkrumah was, The Ever-present-master-at-war, who assembles a crowd.

But how traditional was Nkrumah's appellation performance? In essence, it seemed to be a novelty. Beside the novelty of utilizing appellation in modern Ghanaian politics, the Nkrumah inspired phenomonon
was not of the nature of informal, spasmodic *abodin* (appellation) recitals
uttered among friends and relatives among the Akan, and other ethnic
groups in Ghana. Neither was it of the character of the rigidly-sequenced
formal Akan appellation genre, *apae,* specifically performed by professional bards, *abrafo,* for Akan chiefs as they sit in state on public
occasions. It was a half-way house between these two. It was spontaneous, improvised, and unmarked by stanzas. The novelty of the phenomenon is made even more evident by the background of Nkrumah's poet.

Okyeame Boafo Akuffo was before his assignment to Nkrumah attached to the chief's court in Akuropon. But he was not an *obrafo,* royal
appellation reciter. He was the royal spokesman, *Okyeame,* a position
which required competence in oratory, proverbial lore, and oral traditions. As a royal spokesman, his duty was to embellish words meant for
the chief's audience, and in poetic terms reformulate messages directed
at the chief. He had learnt appellations while at the chief's palace,
through the oral channel, and through his knowledge of the drum language. As a royal spokesman, the performance of libation poetry on
formal occasions was part of his duties. This involved the use of appella-

tion; for the libation ritual is an act of communication with significant entities, such as the Almighty God, gods, titular and ancestral spirits, etc., each of whom had appellations worthy of highlighting on public occasions. The poetic manipulation of words as well as the use of appellations were thus the poet's stock-in-trade before he met Kwame Nkrumah. Indeed, he attracted the attention of President Nkrumah in December 1960 during one of his libation poetry performances on a public occasion in Koforidna, Eastern Ghana. The fluent articulation of high-sounding appellations by Okyeame Akuffo during this performance drew a thunderous applause from the audience, including President Nkrumah. Less than a week after this episode, Nkrumah appointed Okyeame Boafo Akuffo as his poet, a novelty in modern Ghanaian politics. In this role, the poet was called upon to use appellations not as part of a larger discourse unit as he used to, but as an end in itself. He was indeed performing a role similar in a sense to that of the traditional royal bard in *apae* performance who stood in front of the chief and performed his appellations (see Yaukeh 1983). Nkrumah's inspired performance, however, did not conform to the traditional one in which the performer half-covers his upper lip with his left hand while reciting, and where ends of stanza were marked by drumming and blowing of horns. Neither were Nkrumah's appellations fixed. The performances were often a poetic capsule of Nkrumah's speech that was going to follow. If Nkrumah was going to make a policy statement on agriculture, this was foreshadowed in the appellation performance; if it was on the subject of African Unity or Africa's total liberation, the recital was fashioned to suit the topic. Beside this, the appellation performances often made allusion to on-going and past political events within and outside Ghana that the poet considered consequential in boosting Nkrumah's ego.

But whether Nkrumah's inspired appellation performance were dynamic in theme or not, the significant point is that they had their main source in the traditional repertoire of the royal appellations of the people of Ghana.

Indeed the building blocks of Nkrumah's appellations were basically a crystallization of the appellations of all the paramount chiefs in Ghana. He had authorized his personal poet, Okyeame Boafo Akuffo, to go to all the royal paramountcies in Ghana, collect awe-inspiring royal eulogies and plant the Nkrumah image on these. Thus, though Nkrumah was an Nzema, born in Nkroful in the Western Region of Ghana, he was, according to his eulogy,

Grandchild of Anloga Agodomatu
Adeladja and Fia Sri

ancestor chiefs of the South-Eastern part of Ghana. He was indeed, according to the poet, the grandchild of all ancestor chiefs of Ghana, individually and collectively. The extent to which this was genetically or historically valid was irrelevant to the poet.

Despite the national base of Nkrumah's appellations, however, the appellations of the eight traditional Akan states or clans were the most exploited; for in addition to the proud history of most of these Akan states, their appellations were themselves in the Akan language, the medium of the Nkrumah's appellation performances. Added to this was the fact that Akan is the most dominant language in Ghana; and for a national leader exploiting a traditional institution to mystify his ego, this seemed strategically valid.

But the strategy was significant in another respect. For the period Nkrumah adorned himself with the appellations of other chiefs (1960 onwards) was at the same time, the period Nkrumah had diminished the immense power of chiefs, through amendments in the independence constitution. The reduction of the power of the chiefs after independence was indeed expected; for prior to independence in 1957, he had vehemently protested against the immense powers given to the Asantehene by the colonial authorities. In later years, Nkrumah is quoted several times as saying, if they chiefs do not co-operate with the people, "they will run away and leave their sandals behind."

The chiefs, of course, did not run away; but they became less significant in local administration, and they shared with Kwame Nkrumah, appellations that otherwise related to their unique ancestries. But the technique eventually worked in a manner that pleased both sides; for while Kwame Nkrumah was enjoying "borrowed" traditional titles and appellations, the chiefs, according to Nkrumah's poet, were also bathing in the joy of hearing their appellations sounded on the state radio, for the first time in their lives.

Nkrumah did not historically belong to the Adanse traditional state, but according to the poet he was,

> Osagyefo, the root of state is Adanse
> Wirenkyemadu Akoten, where God created things
>
> Long long long ago.

He was also,

> Grandchild of Aferi Keseku of Dwaben
> Who prides in the ownership of a golden horn
> Grandchild of the earliest of the Asakyiri clan.

If these were historically untrue, they were still significant; for just as the Adanse state was considered to be the earliest of the Akan states, Ghana was also the first African state in sub-Saharan Africa to attain independence, through the ingenuity of Kwame Nkrumah. Neither was the ancestral association of 'golden horn' with Nkrumah, completely irrelevant—for the immense gold potential in the soil of Ghana had been reflected in the earlier name, Gold Coast, which was changed to Ghana on the attainment of independence.

More directly, however, Nkrumah's personal poet referred to him as,

> Osagyefo, it's you who by your contrivance
> Have pushed afar the English flag,
> Planting in its place the flag of Ghana
>
> Osagyefo, the fearsome Gyan Adu,
> Whose presence is sniffed in the entire village
> Even though he was sighted at the outskirts.
> It's Atoapem the Ever-ready-shooter.
> The landmark, dufokye tree, lying across the path of Africa;
> When England sat on it, it wetted her bottom.
> When France avoided it, she lost her way in the woods.
> When Belgium passed beneath it, it fell on her
> Scaring cowardly Portugal to take to her heels.
>
> Osagyefo!
> Grandchild of Otutu and Otu, the Extinguishers,
> The extinguisher of fire who has extinguished fire in
>   the hearthstone.
> The hearthstone has cooled off, giving Africa a place
>   to sleep.

Whenever Kwame Nkrumah returned from a meeting in Europe or America, his bold criticism of the Big powers found expression in such appellations as,

> Shaker of the brave
> Shaker of the mighty
> Shaker of the brave, Kwame, the Ever-ready All-Embracing
>   Protective Hyde
> You shook the big crowd in America
>   and received approbation
> And you shook the fearsome one in Southern Africa;
> He fled leaving his troops in peril.

The efforts of Kwame Nkrumah in forging African Unity were also expressed in traditional poetry.

> Osagyefo!
> The axe of Otieku
> The axe of Gyamenampon
> The axe of Gyaakye
> When three axes combine
> To fell a tree, it falls.
> You ordered the Takwa state to fell it,
>   she could not.
> You said Breman should try it,
>   she was ill-prepared.
> Osagyefo Kwame, the Ever-ready All-Embracing
>   Protective Hyde has felled it,
> Forcing Takwa and Breman to bow down their heads
>   in shame.

But just as Nkrumah's achievements overseas were being extolled in hyperbolic terms, so were internal matters that were firmly under Nkrumah's control. The spread of false rumor against him to which he alluded in a dawn broadcast in April 1961 as well as the several assassination attempts on Nkrumah's life were all highlighted and couched in traditional phraseology. In one of the assassination attempts by one of his own bodyguards at the Flagstaff House in Accra, 5 bullets missed Nkrumah, though they did kill one of his guards. In this incident, Nkrumah was supposed to have run after the assassin and overpowered him, receiving in the process a scar under his left eye. This is beside several bomb attempts, particularly one in Kulungugu, in Northern Ghana (See Marais 1972:116–126). These had all failed, but had succeeded in thickening the air of mystery surrounding Kwame Nkrumah. To Kwame Nkrumah's poet, Nkrumah was

> Osagyefo,
> The cluster of palm nuts, when you aim at it,
>   you waste your bullets.
>
> Osagyefo Kwame Atoapem, the Ever-ready,
> The arrogant snake who left his trail on the
>   big rock in Kulungugu
> The hunters and their sensitive dogs searched for
>   him in vain.

Osagyefo!
When you trap him, you trap him in vain
When you let him off, you are in trouble
    into a frog
Playing games in the puddle

The performance of Nkrumah's appellations in public, in parliament and on national radio, evidently uplifted his ego. Through the use of traditional channels, Kwame Nkrumah had thereby strengthened the link between himself and the people, applying to himself traditional appellations that were of immense evocative appeal to the people. The use of the oral-aural channel had an added advantage over the projection of Nkrumah's image in visual designs; for in spite of the evanescence of oral poetry, its very existence in acoustic space signals present actuality, an ongoing phenomenon, or rather a personal presence (Ong 1967:111–112). The phenomenon of Kwame Nkrumah was thus ever present, and had registered itself firmly in the lives of Ghanaians.

But being a double-pronged tool, oral poetry can make and break. It had indeed helped in crystallizing the mystery surrounding Nkrumah; it had extolled his virtues and uplifted his ego, but like all appellations, praise need not be the primary objective. Appellations, indeed, seek to telescope and define the socio-cultural relevance of its subject in nominative terms, relegating the theme of praise or condemnation to a secondary position (See Yankah 1983). A close look at the appellations applied to Kwame Nkrumah affirms this. For rather than explicitly praising Nkrumah, the bard sought to highlight events and attributes that instilled fear in the opponents of Nkrumah. Perhaps, Nkrumah's appellations would have been less meaningful if political events in Ghana at the time were different. But under such peculiar circumstances, when to many observers Nkrumah had turned a tyrant, clamping political opponents in detention without trial in the name of the Preventive Detention Act, under circumstances where the dismissal of public officers was believed to be politically motivated, where many of this opponents had fled the country for fear of detention, the appellations, depicting the imagery of intimidation, were bound to be increasingly significant. Observe the following examples,

Osagyefo, Agyen the Uprooter, feared by children
    and elders.
Osagyefo,

> The Valiant Kokofe Kwako, when you share farm
>   boundaries with him
> You harvest your yams prematurely.
>
> Osagyefo, the valiant warrior, playing games
>   with jaw bones.

Beside these appellations that were not altogether complimentary, part of Nkrumah's appellations by accident or design were not different from those the Akan normally apply to the Supreme God. One such example is Atuapem or Atoapoma (literally, he fires and it is loaded), the Ever-ready shooter. This is the appellation of the Saturday born, which Nkrumah was. But it is also that of the Supreme God, who Akan believe is God of Saturday (See Danquah 1944:43–57). But there were other related images in Nkrumah's appellations such as

> Osagyefo, the long sprawling root and helper
> Whose ancestry is from Heaven

In a Christian country like Ghana, such appellations were construed by many as a challenge to the omnipotence of God. But there were other strands of evidence that were invoked to support this. Kwame Nkrumah had introduced the Ghana Young Pioneers Club, whose youths had been charged through rumour with heathenism and Godlessness. According to this charge, Nkrumah had been projected as God to the youths, and it was unto him that the children directed daily prayers. Whether this latter charge was valid or not, the fact remains that part of the recitals of the Ghana Young Pioneers included such lines as

> Nkrumah is our leader
> Nkrumah is our Messiah
> Nkrumah never dies

Such slogans and appellations combined with the general deification of Nkrumah to justify a charge of Godlessness against Ghana's first president. Indeed Nkrumah deported leading churchmen for criticizing the deification of his personality by his followers, who also called him Redeemer. And after his overthrow, churches throughout Ghana held thanksgiving services for 'deliverance' (See Timothy 1981:197). The charge of Godlessness on Nkrumah may seem ironical; for Nkrumah was not only baptized in the Catholic Church, but he also taught at a Roman Catholic Seminary in his early years, and took a degree at Lincoln

University in Sacred Theology. In Nkrumah's own words in 1957, "Today, I am a non-denominational Christian, and a Marxist socialist, and I have not found any contradiction between the two (1975:12)."

But the debilitating influence of appellation poetry and its ambivalent signification was not the end of the use of traditional poetry to comment on President Nkrumah. The song medium was also exploited in various ways. There were, of course, songs of adoration by guitar bands as early as 1950 when Nkrumah was imprisoned by the British, and also on his release from prison (Collins 1976); there were choral songs such as the following composed in Akan by J.T. Essuman,

> Dr. Nkrumah has achieved a lot for me,
> Who is his equal?
> It's he who will speak and fight for us
> Africa, is calling you
> Africa is calling you, Nkrumah
> He will fight for us
> He will speak for us
> He will arrive, Osagyefo, the Savior-at-war.

Such songs were explicitly laudatory, so were such party songs that depicted the flamboyance of Nkrumah, sung in English

> Nkrumah, alas!
> Nkrumah (the) Show-Boy
> I want to see you
> Kwame Nkrumah (the) Show-boy.

Even after Nkrumah's death in 1972, laudatory songs on him continued to be composed and sung, such as the following recorded in Akan by Ani Johnson, a highlife song artist, entitled "Osagyefo Kwame Nkrumah":

> "Alas alas proceed you all
> Proceed, . . . unite minds
> And ponder over affairs of the state
> Proceed, . . . Unite your strengths
> And collect together your scattered treasures
> One and two make strength
> One and two make a blessing."
>
> Those are the words of the public announcer
> The advocate of African unity, those are his words.

Kwame Nkrumah,
He came to the world with a single aim,
To unite all of Africa
It's the message of unity he brought and worked for
Till he died for Africa.

Children of the future
Shall with their ears
Hear your good name
With their eyes
They shall see your illustrious works
And with their tongues
They shall sing songs of Allelujah
Glorifying your name as follows:
"It would have been better
Had Osagyefo lived."

This song continues with a citation of some of Nkrumah's appellations and his famous speeches.

If the people were yearning to see Kwame Nkrumah, the flamboyant leader, and were even on his death, perpetuating his name in explicitly complimentary lyrics, was the song medium exploited also by Nkrumah's critics and opponents?

To begin with, on Nkrumah's overthrow in 1966, parades and demonstrations supporting his downfall explicitly condemned and ridiculed Kwame Nkrumah in brief songs such as,

I would have been wealthy
I would have been wealthy
I would have been richer
But for Nkrumah's misdeeds.

The tone of critical lyrics during Nkrumah's rule was, however, different.

As a backdrop to this, it is worth mentioning that the opponents of President Nkrumah's rule, generally, had very few or no channels to project their viewpoints in Nkrumah's one-party state. The newspapers were under a close surveillance, and in 1962, for instance the *Ashanti Pioneer,* an outspoken newspaper, was banned. In 1963, the Newspaper Licensing Act was passed, requiring Newspapers to obtain a license in order to publish or renew their publication. By 1965 the mass media was under very close control.

Under these conditions, where dissentful sentiments could only be bottled up for fear of retribution, traditional lore provided another escape route; and Ghanaians found themselves nationally participating in the poetic tradition of slandering without mentioning names. Reference to this literary phenomenon is indeed made by Captain R. S. Rattray, who in the introduction to his *Ashanti Folktales* (1930) relates the use of folktales by the Ashanti to satirize the misdeed of elders, who could not be mentioned by name. In Akan, the relevant expression is *bo akutia*—to chide or scold one publicly without mentioning his name. In homes co-habited by two rival wives, *akutiabo* (oblique slander) is a common phenomenon; and a safe one at that. For art being what it is, it may effectively give an unkind cut, and when confronted by the danger of the law, recoil into the cyst of artistic immunity.

In Nkrumah's Ghana, an extra dimension was given to this device; for while the real motives of song writers were never known, some songs played on the radio became more and more imputed with political signification by the authorities, and were banned from air play accord-ingly. A song performed by E.K. Nyame's Band, "Nsuo beto a mframa dikan" (The storm is a foreshadow of rain) was interpreted by Nkrumah as forecasting the end of his rule. Another song performed by the same band, though written by Joe Eyison, entitled *Ponko Abo Dam* (A crazy-horse), was stopped from air play, for it could be a proverbial recap by Nkrumah's opponents referring to the maltreatment which was being meted out to them by Nkrumah's regime. The lyric runs as follows:

> Brother,
> I will say not a word
> About your sinister deeds.
> For God will provide the sacrificial lamb
> Do unto me what you deem fit
> The horse may be crazy
> But its owner remains sane

In 1964, another highlife song performed by K. Gyasi's Band was banned. It carried the title *Agyima Mansa,* and was a prayer to a deceased mother to return, for her children on earth were suffering. Was this an allusion to the suffering of Ghanaians? This was not clear; but like all proverbialisms, the potential for such connotations loomed large, to the mind of the authorities. The lyric runs as follows:

> Mansa, your children are struggling
> Agyima Mansa I speak of

Comes from Agona Asamang
She is riddled with disease
Mansa your children are calling.
Come, for often times we inspire pity.
Sensiaso, the aquatic bird
My foot prints are ill-fated
When I went to cut the reed
It's a python I saw
When I bent to sit down
I had sat in a thorny yam pit
When I stood up
A bee hive fell on me

When I took a step back
My foot landed in a trap
The iron trap and me together
We both landed in a thorny trench
The have-not in the midst of trouble
Who will speak on my behalf
Agyima Mansa, your children are struggling
Often times we inspire pity
Mansa your children are struggling.

The theme in this song, in which the singer communicates with a dead mother is under normal circumstances an unmarked one. Indeed, in the Akan society, there is a specialized method of communication, libation pouring, in which the help and blessings of the ancestors are solicited through the pouring of drinks alongside a rigidly structured spoken prayer. The same theme is evident in Akan dirges and laments; and even in the vein of highlife songs, in which the above song was expressed, artists sometimes solicit the blessings and occasionally the return of a dead one to help solve problems confronting them (See Yankah, forthcoming). Indeed the Akan, and several cultures in West Africa believe in life herafter. However, in a politically charged situation such as in 1964 when Ghanaians were experiencing political and economic hardship, traditional themes had to be used with caution (See also Geest and Darko 1982; Anyidoho 1983).

The banning of these politically suggestive songs form air play and public performances, did not mean the artists themselves were in deep political trouble; neither did it mean artistic creativity had been stiffled out of existence. It only meant that, the artist in fashioning his diction, should be guided by the wider semantic scope the spoken word had acquired in the circumstances. But it was the power of the spoken word that had deepened the mystery surrounding Kwame Nkrumah. Through the medium of traditional appellation, it had given more meaning and greater mystical essence to Nkrumah's own rhetorical wit, sharpening his credo, and embellishing his charisma.

But while it mystifies by establishing an effective presence, folk poetry has also a mechanism for loosening the mystery it builds. Kwame Nkrumah had asked for it, but had underrated the multiple signification of the traditional weapon he wielded.

NOTES AND ACKNOWLEDGEMENT

This paper is partially based on interviews with President Nkrumah's personal poet, Okyeame Boafo Akuffo while he was appointed as traditional and cultural consultant in the Linguistics Department of the University of Ghana, from 1974–1976. Some of the appellations cited here may also be found in Okyeame Akuffo's book, *Kotokohene Dammirifua due,* a book of clan appellations written in Akan. The translations here are my own. I am very grateful to Okyeame Akuffo for granting the interviews; I also appreciate suggestions on this paper offered by Jonas Yeboa-Dankwa, a graduate student of the Folklore Institute of Indiana University.

REFERENCES CITED

Anyidoho, Kofi. "Mythmaker and Mythbreaker: The Oral Poet as Earwitness," Paper delivered at the ALA meeting in Urbana-Champagne, 1983.

Akuffo, Boafo Okyeame. *Kotokohene Dammirifua Due,* Accra: Ghana Publishing Corporation, 1975.

Collins, E. J. "Ghanaian Highlife" *African Arts* 1:4 (1976), pp. 30–34, 101.

Danquah, J. B. *The Akan Doctrine of God.* London: Frank Cass Co., 1944.

Finnegan, Ruth. *Oral Literature in Africa.* Oxford: Clarendon Press, 1970.

Geest, Sjaak Van der and Asante-Darko N. K. "The Political Meaning of Highlife Songs in Ghana," *The African Studies Review* XXV:1 (1982), 27–35.

Marais, Genoveva, *Kwame Nkrumah: As I knew Him,* Chichester: Janey Publishing Co., 1972.

Nkrumah, Kwame, *The Autobiography of Kwame Nkrumah.* London: Thomas Nelson and Sons, 1957.

Ocran. *A Myth is Broken.* Essex: Green and Co., Ltd., 1968.

Oinas, Felix J. ed. *Folklore, Nationalism and Politics,* Columbus: Slavica Publishers, 1978.

Ong, Walter, *The Presence of the Word.* Yale University Press, 1967.

Rattray, R. S., *Akan-Ashanti Folktales.* Oxford: Clarendon Press, 1930.

Timothy Bankole, *Kwame Nkrumah, from Cradle to Grave.* Dorset: The Gavin Press, 1981.

Yankah, Kwesi, "To Praise or not to Praise the King: Akan Apae in the Context of Referential Poetry," forthcoming in *Research in African Literatures,* 1983, 14:3.

———. "The Akan Highlife Song: A Medium of Cultural Reflection or Deflection?" forthcoming in *Research in African Literatures.*

POPULAR LITERATURE

COMIC OPERA IN GHANA

E. J. Collins

Since the Second World War, one of the most vital folk arts in Ghana has been the concert party, a contemporary roving comic opera. Like many features of Ghana today, this theater can be considered a syncretic fusion of Western and indigenous elements, created out of the impact of Western musical and dramatic influences on the traditional performing arts.

The "party" is a professional organization composed of a central core of founding members and an ever-changing periphery of band-boys. The concert play is a slapstick musical comedy containing a prominent moral tone, performed in the Akan language. Music punctuates the speech of the actors, and song lyrics are relevant to the plot of the play. Highlife is the primary music used, itself a syncretic fusion of West African and European music. The concert actors portray in a humorous and exaggerated fashion situations and stereotypes familiar to their audience; the audience responds with a great sense of participation.

The early history of the concert party is closely tied to traditional West African performances in which the music, enactment, and dance are blended together and the distinction between audience and performer is limited. Traditionally the drama is not a discrete event here as it is in the Occident; in West Africa it is generally found encapsulated within a whole range of rites and ceremonies. It would be incorrect, however, to assume that there has been no specialization within West African drama. In the savanna regions there is a long tradition of professional historicans-cum-entertainers (the *griots*), and in the forest areas, drama has been developed to a high degree within the masquerades of the secret societies and in association with the art of storytelling. The latter tradition is particularly important as a formative agent on the Ghanaian concert party, for it was in the Akan-speaking areas of southern Ghana, with its wealth of spider stories *(Anansesem),* that the concert party evolved. In these *Anansesem,* the narrator has traditionally used different voices for the various characters and has sometimes dressed up as well.

Western dramatic influences, introduced to coastal Ghana from the turn of the last century, also contributed much to the formation of the comic

61

opera. As the name "concert party" suggests, the genre originated from the school concerts performed on Empire Day. Many prominent concert actors began their careers by acting in these shows. The idea of a stage (i.e., a physical barrier separating performers from the audience) was introduced to the concert party through these school plays, as well as through Cantatas, church-organized morality plays. A third foreign influence on early concert was silent films, which started appearing in Ghana around the First World War. After World War I, Afro-American music, dance, and comedy were brought to the port towns by Black American seamen and comedians.

Ghana's first concert actor was Teacher Yalley, the headmaster of a Sekondi elementary school, who began acting in his school's Empire Day concerts in 1918. In these, he used to joke, sing, and dance, wearing a fancy dress, wig, false moustache and the white makeup of a minstrel. His shows were in English, and tickets were expensive; consequently the audience consisted mostly of the educated Black elite. The show opened with a hired brass band that campaigned around town and ended up outside the theater. Inside the theater, Yalley performed his comedy sketches with the assistance of a trap drummer and a harmonium player, who provided an assortment of then-current popular Western dance-music, such as Black American ragtimes, and ballroom styles like the foxtrot, quickstep, and waltz. The famous Fanti comedian Bob Johnson was a boy at this time and recalls the Yalley's shows lasted three hours and that the audience consisted of "official people and gentlemen," including a small number of Europeans.

Bob Johnson's own acting career started at shows performed at his Sekondi Methodist school, after the Empire Day parade around town. His group became known as the Versatile Eight, the main characters being the joker, the gentleman and the lady impersonator. Bob Johnson played the joker, and did it so well that this concert role has since been known as "the Bob." This character, a central one to concert, usually wears bizarre and often ragged clothes and used the white makeup of the minstrel. Although he clowns around mischievously, the audiences adore him as he is really a theatrical continuation of Ananse the spider, the popular but self-centered hero of Akan folk stores. Ironically, the "Original Bob" Johnson's real first name is Ishmael. He told me that he obtained the nickname "Bob" from the Afro-American seamen who visited the Optimism Club opposite his home in Sekondi. He used to hang around that place watching and listening to Liberian sailors singing sea-shanties and highlifes to the accompaniment of guitar and musical saw, and Afro-Americans performing comedy sketches and singing foxtrots and ragtimes. It was they who called him Bob; in fact, he recalls that the Black American sailors seemed to call everybody Bob.

Another Afro-American influence on Johnson was the shows performed between 1924 and 1926 by the Black American couple Glass and Grant who were brought to Accra by Mr. Ocansey, a film distributor and cinema-hall owner. Johnson saw them in Sekondi and was impressed by their boldness on stage (i.e., their professionalism). Their shows, high-class affairs like Yalley's, began with a silent film before the comedy act and a dance afterwards. The act was vaudeville, with Glass the minstrel and Grant his wife, joking, tap-dancing, and singing ragtimes. This pair also influenced Ga actors like Williams and Marbel so that when the Americans returned to the United States, the "Accra Vaudeville" continued. By the mid-twenties, concerts had separated into two distinct variations: the upper-class shows of Yalley and the Accra Vaudeville on the one hand, and Johnson's sixpenny shows on the other.

In 1930 Johnson went professional when he formed The Two Bobs and Their Carolina Girl. Their shows were publicized by a masked bell-ringer wearing a billboard, and they commenced with a half-hour introduction consisting of an "Opening Chorus" of quicksteps, danced and sung by the three comedians, followed by an "In," during which one of the Bobs sang ragtimes, and closing with a "Duet" of joking by the two Bobs. Music was supplied by the group's trap-drummer, who was usually helped by members of a school orchestra hired for the night. The play proper, or "Scene," that followed the introduction lasted an hour and was performed in English, with an occasional translation into Akan; this concert audience was less educated than its high-class counterpart. Yet another difference between the two varieties of concert was that Johnson incorporated, in addition to popular Western songs, a few highlifes sung in pidgin English.

In 1935 Johnson became the joker for the Axim Trio, the concert party that eventually became a prototype for succeeding parties. E. K. Dadson played Susanna, their lady impersonator, the Charlie Turpin was the gentlemen; they acted to the accompaniment of harmonium and drums. Their first engagement was a tour of Nigeria, during which they were joined by the 22-strong Cape Coast Sugar Babies dance-orchestra. The Trio's normal practic in Ghana, however, was to supplement their two musicians with a brass band, or Konkomba group, hired for the night. (Konkomba was a choral highlife popular in southern Ghana between the thirties and fifties.) Their shows consisted of an Opening Chorus, In and Duet, followed by a two-hour long play. The plays they performed between 1935 and the mid-fifties (when the Trio dissolved) included: *The*

Coronation of King George the Sixth; The Bond of 1844; The Ten-Foot Man; The Downfall of Adolph Hitler; Kwame Nkrumah Will Never Die; Love is the Sweetest Thing; and *Kwame Nkrumah is a Mightly Man.* In the course of its career, the Trio conducted two trips to Nigeria, extensive tours of Ghana, and also visited Liberia, the Ivory Coast, and Sierra Leone.

The high-class concerts died out before the Second World War. In contrast, the Axim Trio became so popular that by the early forties, five other concerts had modeled themselves after it. In 1937 Bob Cole formed the Happy Trio in the Western Region. Cole had played the piccolo as a boy and became leader of his school band; he started his group after seeing the Axim Trio perform. Like the Versatile Eight, this was a schoolboy affair, playing for pennies and sticks of plantain. About the same time the Dix Covian Jokers and West End Trio were formed; they, too, were from the Western Region. In fact, the only concert not based in this region was the Keta Trio, formed by Ewes from eastern Ghana.

World War II had its effect on the concert profession, as several concert actors performed for the troops. Concerts were even held for the African troops in India; between 1943 and 1946 an African theatre was set up within the West African Frontier Force based there. Bob Vans was the leader, and with six other Gnanaians they played at camps and hospitals. The language they used was pidgin English and the music Konkomba. Vans was influenced by Black American comedians he met and when he returned to Ghana he formed, along with other Ghanaian ex-servicemen, the Burma Jokers. Due to nationalist sentiment, his group was later renamed the Ghana Trio.

This brief history of the concert party would be incomplete without a discussion of the growth of highlife music, for these two syncretic art forms have merged together. The high-class concerts included highlifes in the dances that closed the show; the Axim Trio even used an occasional one in the play itself, but this music never became fully integral to the acting until E. K. Nyame formed his Akan Trio in 1952.

Like concert, highlife music grew up around the turn of the century in the coastal Fanti area. It was based on the acculturation of traditional recreational music with Western musical influences; the resuling syncretic dance-musics, the most important being Osibiasaba, became known collectively by the 1920s as "highlife." By that time, three varieties of this music were in evidence: that played by the brass band; that by acoustic guitar bands; and that prestigious dance-orchestras. The orchestras created a very Westernized variant of the music aimed at a wealthy audience, and it was out of this milieu that the term "High Life" was coined.

It was the guitar-band style of highlife, however, that became particularly associated with the concert play, an innovation pioneered by E. K. Nyame. Nyame was the leader of a guitar band for some years until 1952 when, encouraged by the Axim Trio's popularity, he formed the Akan Trio from among his bandsmen, taking the role of gentleman for himself. His synthesis of highlife and concert, plus the fact that the Akan Trio was the first to perform exclusively in Akan, made his group an instant success, and within a few years most of the other guitar bands followed suit. Conversely, concerts already operating expanded their small musical section to a full-scale guitar band.

The Akan Trio has become the prototype for the present-day concert, of which there are now at least fifty in Ghana. Their immense popularity and relevance to contemporary life has recently led to an upsurge of interest in concert parties by film directors, television producers and academics. In the latter part of 1973, the Arts Council of Ghana presented a ten-day National Festival of Concert Parties, the first of its kind in the country.

The evolution of the concert party has seen continual multiplication and diffusion of groups, and a consequent change in the performances. Early concert parties were formed in coastal towns. Apart from the schoolboy Versatile Eight, they were performed for a literate and affluent urban audience; it was not until the Axim Trio that concert spread into the rural hinterland. By World War II, the vaudeville concert had died out and there were a handful of groups modeled on the Axim Trio; by 1954, there were ten. In 1960, when concert actors and musicinas organized the Ghana National Entertainments Association, there were thirty concerts, all staged in the Akan language and employing guitar bands. the change from the early concert to the present one can be attributed to the three groups that served as prototypes for their successors; Teacher Yalley's, the less-Westernized Axim Trio, and the post-war Akan Trio.

Feedback of ideas from Black American theater and music has been a major influence on concert history. The most direct source of this influence was Glass and Grant. Less direct were the cinema minstrels such as Al Jolson; here one finds the ironic situation of Ghanaian actors copying white actors who in turn were copying the humor, dress, music, and dialect of Southern plantation slaves of the United States. Even ragtime, the music of early Ghanaian concert, orginated form the Black American slaves.

In addition to a causal relationship, there are also parallel features present in Black American theater and Ghanaian concert which are illuminating to compare. Both are low-brow comedy performed without script and both provide humorous satire for a newly-urbanized and polyglot audience. (Black theater, that is, minstrelsy and its derivative, vaudeville, originated in mid-nineteenth century North America, a period of high immigration and rapid urbanization.)

Also significant to comic opera history is its relevance to social change. Politcal involvement and criticism in the form of musical and dramatic satire, which has a long tradition in West Africa, has been carried through to contemporary syncretic theater. For instance, during the 1945 Nigerian general strike against the British, Yoruba Herbert Ogunde wrote a play for his concert called *Strike and Hunger*. A later play called *Yoruba Ronu*, with its allegorical plot based on the 1964 power struggle in Western Nigeria, was considered so inflammatory that it was banned (Adedeje 1967). In Ghana, there were a number of concert plays that came out in open support of the independence struggle. The Axim Trio's *Nkrumah Will Never Die* and *Nkrumah is a Mighty Man* have already been mentioned. Another play taking a politcal stand was *Kwame Nkrumah is Greater Than Before*, which they staged in 1950 and then donated part of its proceeds to the Convention Peoples Party fund (*Gold Coast Evening News*, July 5, 1950). In 1952 S. Sackey presented a concert called *Bo Hu Ke Ono Aba* (Wait Until Your Turn Comes), which defended Nkrumah's constitutional reforms (*Daily Graphic*, December 7, 1952). Indeed, the government-financed Worker's Brigade bands and their concert parties, formed in the late fifties and sixties, became organs of C.P.P. propaganda. In the latter part of Nkrumah's rule, when disenchantment set in, concerts became less inclined to support the government, although none were overtly critical. In fact, openly political plays have been rather the exception in Ghana, their reflections on the existing order being more in the form of social criticism and morality tales. For instance, Osofo Dadzie, one of the most popular concerts today, specializes in plays about corruption and inefficiency in high places—such as a hospital.

These roving theaters, bringing new ideas and the attractions of city life to even the most remote areas, have contributed to the process of urban pull. Their importance has been appreciable, for television and rural cinema are only fairly recent in Ghana. Comic opera is, of course, also popular in the ever-expanding towns and cities; but rather than catering to a high-class audience as they did in the twenties, they are now aimed predominately at newly-arrived rural immigrants, i.e., first generation city-dwellers. In the ethnically heterogeneous urban areas, the plays and songs act as a humorous mechanism for releasing psychological-cum-social tensions—a dramatic lingua franca. The concert shows, in portraying stereotypes and situations found in city life to both rural and urban audiences, are agents of urban socialization, as they educate the audience to the complex multiple roles met within modern Ghanaian life.

In order to illustrate the workings of contemporary concert parites, the second half of this article will examine the history, strucutre, and plays of one particular concert party, the Jaguar Jokers, with whom I have worked for six years as a musician and researcher.

The leader of the Jaguar Jokers (J.J.'s), Mr. Bampoe, began his acting career at eleven years old performing in his elementary school plays based on Ananse and Bible stories. About the same time (1946), influenced by the Axim Trio who regularly lodged at his home in Suhum (40 miles north of Accra), Bampoe and some of his school friends formed the Yanky Trio. After completing elementary school and spending a short period as a tailor, Bambpoe joined the City Trio. In 1954, he and two other Fantis, the Hammond Brothers, formed the Jaguar Jokers. The band's name was chosen because Jaguar (pronounced Jagwah) was a word that was popular in Ghana in the 1950s that represented the quintessence of modern urban life.

A major difference between the J.J.'s and the earlier Yanky and City Trios was that the J.J.'s modeled itself after the Akan Trio and therefore staged in Fanti and Twi (both Akan languages), rather than in English. Also, in stead of hiring out Konkomba groups for the night, the J.J.'s established their own guitar band. At the beginning, they played highlifes, foxtrots, quicksteps, ragtimes, and West Indian calypsos, the last being very popular in Ghana during the 1950s. In the 1960s the band incorporated into its repertoire Western pop music (Elvis Presley, the Beatles, James Brown, Wilson Pickett, etc.) and Congo music, a syncretic form that grew up in the Congo after World War II. The latest addition is Afrobeat, a sort of African soul music, pioneered by Nigeria's Fela Ransome Kuti since 1970.

The J.J's have reached an enormous audience in twenty years; besides extensive tours of Ghana and parts of the Ivory Coast, the group has been making radio broadcasts since the late fifties (Radio Entertainment in Akan) and regularly appears on television today.

Like other concert parties, the J.J.'s are a professional group composed of an executive committee and wage-earning artists. The J.J.'s executive committee numbers six (all actors) including a secretary (Bampoe), a chairman, and a treasurer. The other performers are paid between thirty and sixty dollars a month (1974 wages), and after all expenses have been settled, the remainder of the group's income is divided among the executive members.

In 1974, the band consisted of 23 members, plus a driver and mate. Most had received an elementary education, and their previous occupations included cobbling, house construction, electrician-work, farming and pharmacy. There were 13 actors, 9 musicians and a pioneer-man (the band's own promoter); two were Ewes from Southeastern Ghana and the rest were from the various Akan-speaking areas. Members ranged in age from their early twenties to their late thirties.

The J.J.'s have unwritten rules and practices. Bandsmen can be fined and expelled by the executives for fighting and drunkenness on stage or other misconduct. On the other hand, if a member becomes sick, the band pays his hospital fees; if one of his family dies, the J.J.'s contribute toward the funeral expenses; and if a member himself dies, the band will supply the coffin.

The group travels in a hired mini-bus and makes seven or eight major tours (treks) a year, covering the entire country. Each trek begins on payday (the end of the month) and lasts three weeks, during which time the band moves from town to town playing every night. During the rainy season (May to August), they make a series of short local treks, with long periods of rest and rehearsal at their base town of Adoagyiri, twenty miles north of Accra. The theaters used by the band vary from place to place: they may be cinema halls, night clubs or, in a village, a private compound-house containing a crude wooden stage in the courtyard.

The J.J.'s prefer that their treks be planned by their own pioneer-man, who goes ahead of the group to advertise, hire theaters and obtain police permits and chiefs' permission. Most treks, however, are arranged through private promoters who pay all the costs, take all the gate receipts, and pay the band an agreed price. The J.J.'s, like many other concerts, are often forced during the quiet rainy season to borrow money from these promoters, who then bond them during the lucrative Christmas cocoa season. The huge profit-making by the promoters of the concert business has stimulated the formation of a concert union. (Mr. Bampoe played a role in the formation of the Ghana National Entertainments Association, and since its collapse after the 1966 coup, he has been involved in several attempts to revive the union.)

When the J.J.'s arrive at a town or village, some of the musicians campaign around the area in the mini-bus, making announcements and playing music through a battery amplifier. When they return, the musical equipment and lighting are made ready; in the areas where there is no electricity, a portable generator is used. An anteroom is curtained off behind the stage to provide a place for the actors to change and make up. Mr. Bampoe has told me that many bandsmen put magical potions in their face-powders to increase their popularity on stage, while others have taboos against eating specific foods when "on trek."

The show itself begins at about 9:00 p.m. with a dance for which the band plays a cross-section of currently popular Ghanaian dance music: highlifes, Congo numbers, Afro-beats, rock-and-roll, soul, and reggae.

The play starts when the theater is full, usually around 11:00, and lasts three hours. After this, the band plays again for a short while, the night's show rarely finishing before 2:00 a.m. The bandsmen sleep on the floor of the theater and are up early in the morning to travel to their next station.

The concert audience varies from place to place, although it always embraces both men and women, the old and the young, including babies slung on their mothers' backs. In the rural areas, the audience is composed primarily of farmers and their families; in the cities, poorer urban dwellers, often first generation migrants from the countryside, attend. Because of its audience, concert is considered by the more sophisticated and wealthy urbanities to be rather "bush," even though fifty years ago it started off as a posh affair. Mr. Bampoe has told me that the low esteem in which his profession is held creates many problems. Concert actors and musicians are treated as rascals, and occasionally a school even forbids its pupils to attend a show. This situation is fortunately beginning to change as Ghanaians are coming to realize that this folk theater is a legitimate part of their country's cultural heritage.

The plays performed by the J.J.'s consist of an Opening, followed by a Scene, the play proper. The Opening was originally on hour long, and, like the Axim Trio's, was composed of an Opening Chorus, In and Duet, in which the actors, with whitening around the mouth and eyes, tap-danced and sang ragtimes. The Opening today is only twenty minutes in length, but still contains many features borrowed form the Axim Trio, including one of its songs. It is within the Opening that the early vaudeville influences have been retained.

The Scenes, of which the J.J.'s had fourteen in 1974, are each about three hours long, although in the group's early days they were shorter. Music for the plays is supplied by four musicians on drums and guitars. The plays are basically morality stories with a pronounced religious content, an influence from the cantata. They also have many traditional features, including performance in a vernacular language, indigenous music and dance, and the portrayal of traditional figures such as chiefs, elders and priests.

The characters in the plays represent a cross-section of stereotypes found in Ghana today: rural figures such as the illiterate farmer and the village elder; and urbanites such as doctors, lawyers, and teachers. The young urban literate is also depicted, wearing the latest stylish clothes and speaking contemporary urban slang. Some of the lady impersonators (there have never been actresses in the J.J.'s) play the role of the adventurous "high-time" girls who leave their villages for the cities. Different ethnic groups also appear: the northern policeman speaking a mixture of Hausa, Twi and pidgin English; Lagotians with strong Yoruba accents; and Accra marketwomen speaking Ga. Mr. Bampoe always clowns in the role of Opia, an Ananse-like imp loved dearly by the audience.

As with traditional Ghanaian performing arts, there is a great deal of audience participation in the form of applauding, weeping, jeering, and throwing food or coins on stage. Sometimes spectators are so moved by an actor's portrayal of an unfortunate character that they will go up to the stage with food and money; or they may stick coins on the moist forheads of popular actors and musicians.

The importance of these plays bringing new ideas to the rural population must be stressed, for the performances give a glimpse of urban life and its problems to rustic audiences. Themes of sociological interest that recur in the stories include the following: 1) *Urban migration*. At some point, the plots usually describe the plight of young, single men and women who leave home to go to the cities. They turn to crime, drunkenness and prostitution and return with no respect for the old ways. 2) *Social stratification*. Unemployment and poverty in the cities is portrayed, and the humble, hard worker is contrasted with the avaricious man who destroys friends in his scramble for money and position. 3) *Cash crops*. New wealth has increased divisive tensions within the extended family system (especially among the matrilineal Akan), manifested in inheritance disputes. The plays often contain themes of the witchcraft accusations and poisonings resulting from such disputes within a family group. 4) *Changing sexual norms*. Women are becoming increasingly emancipated; they are rejecting polygyny, obtaining a Western education, experimenting with family planning and becoming wealthy traders. Consequently the authority of the husband in being undermined, a topic treated humorously in the plays. 5) *Generation problems*. The ever-changing influx of new ideas on the youth is graphically portrayed, and loss of respect for traditional authority criticized.

To illustrate how these themes are handled and what type of music is played, printed below are synopses of two plays performed by the Jaguar Jokers during 1973 and 1974.

OPIA HIA MMOA (MAN NEEDS HELP); 2 hours, 25 minutes

Kofi, a farmer's son, has been educated and goes to Accra to find work, followed later by his wife, Comfort. After he settles in a job, Kofi's parents come to visit and he gives them gifts. He also gives a small gift to his Aunt Amakom, who is so ungrateful that she curses him. Kofi falls to the floor in agony and Comfort calls in three fetish-priests. They perform a wild dance, strip Kofi of his clothes and leave Comfort with medicine to rub into his body. After some weeks, Comfort's friend Selena, a high-time girl, persuades Comfort to leave the still-sick and helpless Kofi. He is left in the care of his mother and his friend, Opia. Because the traditional medicine does not work, they bring a Christian priest to the sick man. The priest, through prayer, drives out the evil spirit and obtains a repentance from the aunt. After Kofi's recovery, one of the fetish-priests is seen wearing the clothes taken from Kofi and never returned. The unfortunate priest is drilled around the stage by Opia and taken away by Corporal Bobo, a Hausa policeman. Opia, pointing at the disheveled aunt, gives a long soliloquy on how witches in a family can cause barrenness, drunkenness, debt, and general bad luck. Kofi naturally divorces Comfort and then remarries. He does so well for himself that the spoiled Selena and Comfort decide to visit him, both at the same time. They fight and are thrown out by Opia. The play ends with Kofi's father advising the new wife on her duties and Kofi on his need to be humble and involve himself in the community projects of the town in which he has decided to settle.

The 32 songs played during the course of the show included: 23 *highlifes,* ranging from slow, sad renderings to a fast song accompanied by crazy and scatty dancing; one *calypso,* sung in English; two *"swing" songs,* both in English, one of which was invented for the play, the other entitled "Chattanooga Choo Choo"; four *traditional songs,* including music of Akan royalty (the Adowa), one traditonal drunkard's song, one traditional Akan lament, and one song played on conga drums and gong during the fetish scene, accompanied by a full-scale fetish-dance; and two *Apostolic hymns,* sung in the Akan (the Apostolic Church is nominally christian but has many African features like spirit healing and possession; in other words, like highlife and concert, it is syncretic).

A WISIA YI WO ANI (ORPHAN, DO NOT GLANCE ENVIOUSLY); 3 hours, 15 minutes

Mr. Johnson is a building contractor who works away from home most of the time. He has three children, one by his dead wife, and two by his domineering second wife, Comfort. Whenever he is away Comfort favors her own children, the arrogant King Sam and the high-time daughter, Dansowa, over the unfortunate and humble orphan, Kofi Antobam. Opia is brought to the house as a servant to help Comfort, but she feeds neither him nor Kofi. Finally she decides to remove Kofi altogether by sending an evil spirit to him, but he is saved by three angels singing Apostolic hymns. Mr. Johnson is so disturbed by his wife's actions that he sends Kofi to

Kumasi to complete his education out of harm's way. Some years pass, and while Dansowa and King Sam waste their lives in beer-bars listening to pop music, Kofi is working hard at school and is rewarded by passing the Common Entrance Exam. He becomes a postmaster, marries and travels home to introduce his wife to the family. He arrives to find King Sam harassed by women and expelled from school. Kofi's wife gives advice to girls about how they should go about looking for husbands. The couple then distributes gifts to everyone and promises to help Sam continue his education, if he changes his ways. Mr. Johnson sings the closing highlife, in which he points out the problems of having children by different wives, referring particularly to preferential treatment of children by their own mothers and maltreatment by their stepmothers. He also advises young people to respect their elders and, if unsuccessful in life, to move on and try their luck elsewhere.

This show had 40 songs in total, including: 29 *highlifes;* one *Akan funeral song,* sung in Fanti, an Akan language; one *quick step,* called "Cry Baby Cry," sung twice in English; two *Apostolic hymns,* sung in Akan; two *Presbyterian hymns,* sung in Akan; one *rock-and-roll* song, not sung but danced to by King Sam and Dansowa, graphically demonstrating how spoiled they are; one *soul song,* called "Funky Funky," sung and danced to by King Sam and later parodied by Opia; and one *Congo number,* not sung but danced to by Dansowa at the opening of the play.

THE CHARACTER OF POPULAR FICTION IN GHANA

Ime Ikiddeh

Hardly noticed, Ghanaian popular literature in English has come of age, and placed alongside similar literature in Nigeria, it reveals traits acquired during the period of character formation different from those belonging to its famous West African prototype, the "Onitsha market literature."[1] In Ghana most of the practitioners in popular writing have been people with considerable formal education armed with secondary school and journalists' certificates. And they have generally approached their "art," if not their trade, with a sophistication unequalled by their Onitsha counterparts. Their books when published are not peddled at lorry stations—with all the advantages of that method—rather, they go into competition in university bookshops and leading department stores with Agatha Christie and Edgar Wallace. (I have seen them sold alongside the classics in English.) Whereas Nigerian popular literature includes a sizeable amount of experiments in drama, the Ghanaian product, except in one or two cases, has been exclusively prose fiction.[2] Nor does it exploit political and other topical issues of the day except very remotely. In one respect at least, however, it has kept to the tradition of all popular art: cooked to the taste of large numbers, finished and served out fast and consumed while it is still hot. If Ghanaian popular literature has shown nothing of the profusion of Onitsha writing—and you can almost count off the number of available titles on your fingers and toes[3]—part of the explanation must be that the bulk of this literature has a comparatively short history dating back only a few years.

Among the reasons for the late rise of popular fiction in Ghana, indeed of written literature generally, one of the most plausible is the corresponingly late rise of indigenous printing enterprise. Writing, in spite of the elusive concepts of art and inspiration, *is,* by and large, enterprise, and even if other forms of it are not, popular writing by its very nature is. For the pamphleteers who crowded the streets of Onitsha before the Nigerian war, setting up a small press and getting a marketable book out of it was as much a business as retail trade in cloth, the spirit that guided it, if not the methods, being that which charles Jenner satirizes in England of the late eighteenth century:

> Why not engage with Noble or with Bell,
> To weave thin novels that are sure to sell?
> Thrice happy authors, who, with little skill,
> In two short weeks can two short volumes fill.[4]

As far as I know, nowhere in Ghana was the commerical spirit ever translated into an accumulation of indigenous printing and publishing enterprise—as one found in Onitsha, Aba and Port Harcourt—to promote literature on a popular level. Even now, although initiative in the field has risen considerably, most of the country's popular literature is printed by the public-owned State Publishing Corporation. In spite of our ideals, literary history would be inclined to the view, that the economic motive in writing and the writer's well-known urge to express or communicate need not be mutually exclusive. Indeed, they quite often discover art too in their company! In any case, the importance one claims for popular literature in Onitsha or Accra would be more a functional than a qualitative one.

Among the titles of popular fiction extant in Ghana, those by J. Benibengor Blay must rank among the earliest.[5] (One of the younger writers has fondly described Blay to me as "the father of us all.") Blay's *Emelia's Promise* first appeared in 1944 and went into three editions, followed "at the request of several readers" by the conclusion of Emelia's story, *After the Wedding* (two editions). Recently, the two works have been combined into a neatly bound volume under the title *Emelia's Promise and Fulfilment. Be Content with your Lot,* 1947, and *Love in a Clinic,* 1957, are little more than short stories, each booklet being less than thirty pages long. Benibengor Blay is a versatile writer who has published works of fiction, as well as several travel books, a history, some poetry, essays and memoirs.[6] Once junior Minister of Education in Ghana, Blay now lives in retirement, seemingly reprinting his books for a living.

If *Emelia* is representative of his work, then Blay stands for an old and past order of Ghanaian fiction. His narrative ability is considerable, his English idiom is near-perfect, yet in telling this conventional love story of an all-virtuous woman, the writer shows a lack of realism in setting, character, and attitude that must shock present-day Ghanaian audiences. Everything from the lush diction to the unrelieved moral earnestness is guided by the standards of eighteenth-century England.

As a character Emelia is as implausible as the basis for her attachment

to Joe Kellon is unconvincing. A kind of shallow Pamela, she is hailed in
the novel as "though human, [having] all the qualities of an angel." Such
is her virtue that in spite of all the cruelty of her husband, and humilia-
tions from his mistress, "like Job she underwent those hard tests and kept
her faith alive." The setting of the novel is supposed to be a town in
Ghana and the characters to be Ghanaians, but Emelia's father receives
one of his daughter's suitors after dinner in "the drawing-room," and one
of the winning qualities he must display is that of "a good conversational-
ist!" The names of Emelia's five suitors in themselves declare where they
belong: Joe Kellon, Karl Milton, Jones Mellor, Thomas Byron, and Jack
Doe.

Blay stands apart from the younger writers he has helped to inspire, the
pathetic example of talent warped to ruin by the facts of history. His
sincerity notwithstanding, the values he holds out to his public bear little
relationship to reality, least of all the reality of his own soil. If Canadians
and New Zealanders have been stunned by what they now recognize as
the colonial slavishness of some of their early writers, then Blay perhaps
deserves more than pity.[7] Besides, his later work, for example, *Love in a
Clinic,* shows that his fiction is moving towards naturalization in Ghana.
Perhaps political independence in the same year has something to do with
this? Perhaps too, it is of significance that *Love in a Clinic* is printed by
Graphic Press, publishers of a national daily, and *Emelia* is done by the
Presbyterian Press?

In any case, it is in direct opposition to the puritanical morality of
Emelia, that in the fierce debate on social evils that makes up Kobina
Nortey's *The Man with Two Wives* a character can utter the conclusion:

> It's therefore a fact that the drinking of distilled alcohol is
> merely an artificial means of supplementing what nature had
> already prescribed to the well-being of the human body.

In the debate on marriage, Albert Busa, described as "a debater capable
of parliamentary behaviour," sees monogamy as "an imported form of
marriage with all its hypocritical aspects," and polygamy as

> a form of marriage native to us and as a historic institution
> nursed on the same cradle with the hills.[8]

And is it any surprise that in Nortey the man with two wives wins the
day?

As in Western literature, the man-woman relationship inside and outside marriage is a dominant interest in Ghanaian popular fiction. But

although it keeps alive the romantic tradition of wild dreams, sentimental protestations, tears, and heartbreaks—and the convenience of the epistolary form is fully exploited here[9]—the positions in the man-woman tangle are often reversed. In Ghanaian fiction, the woman is almost invariably the cause of friction and disruption. The man becomes a powerless victim of her extravagance, greed, duplicity, or unfaithfulness. Invariably too, it is the man's wealth or status that attracts her into any relationship. Wealth, the corrupting mammon, is condemned, and with it, the acquisitive attitude, but there is undeclared admiration for the man who has got his loot without trouble; the respect he commands, the influence he exerts, and the pleasures open to him in his community are all too lavishly emphasized. As for the woman in these novelettes, usually somewhat educated and domiciled in the town, she is condemned by standards both traditional and Christian which are contrary to her acquired urban values. In the end she ruins herself and sometimes her man as well:

> Akua Brenya's insatiable lust for easy money and expensive living had driven her . . . to marry an elderly Nzima rich man . . .

So begins Nsiah-Bota's *Love in a Tragedy.* The story ends with the insanity of her first husband and the deaths of the second and of Akua herself. Konadu's *Shadow of Wealth, Don't Leave Me Mercy, A Husband for Esi Ellua,*[10] and Donkor's *Pretty Betty Sent Me Crashing*[11] are all in this cycle. But by far the most corrupt woman, portrayed in her most sinister aspect, is to be found in E.K. Mickson's *Who Killed Lucy* series. It leads logically to his severest verdict on her in his latest volume.

> Truly, woman is poison. And the moment you begin to move with a woman, you must know you are moving with poison.[12]

In one instance only, in the only work in my collection designed for the stage, is an author entirely on the side of the woman. Skot, the writer of *The Tears of a Jealous Husband* protests in the preface:

> Some husbands do not permit their wives to talk to anyone— be that one a man or a woman. Is the wife to be cut off from society because she is married? No.!

The action of the play takes place in court where Kwesi Maniawu is standing trial following a mistaken arrest for housebreaking during one of his spying missions on his wife. One of the play's most dramatic qualities is the hilarious rendering in pidgin English of the evidence of an illiterate policeman.

The most prominent popular fiction writers in Ghana today are Asare Konadu and E.K. Mickson. Between them they share about a dozen titles, the major part published during the last two years. Together they dominate the fiction market in Ghana. Both are young: they are in their thirties. Both started writing through journalism—Mickson is editor of the weekly, *Ghana Pictorial*. Each has set up his own publishing business: Konadu, the Anowuo Educational Publications; Mickson, Micky Publications. It is to them that one must look for the trends of contemporary Ghanaian popular fiction.

By far the best known of Mickson's fiction is the *Who Killed Lucy* series. *When the Heart Decides* came out early in 1966, and following its popularity, Mickson added the main title of the series in 1967 which was easily followed by the concluding part *Now I Know* in August 1968. A month after came his latest, *The Violent Kiss* and *Woman is Poison,* and in the making is another to be called *God is Suffering*.

When the Heart Decides explains why Frank Ofosu decides to write the dramatic letter that opens this novelette to "his own Sweetie," Lucy. Part of the letter reads:

> I have therefore been compelled to go against the very dictates
> of my heart to ask you to let us put an end to our love affair as
> from 8 p.m. this fateful Wednesday.

From this point we are led through the story of Frank and Lucy in retrospect. Over the years the innocent Frank has been the victim of Lucy's duplicity in love, "double-crossing" (rather more than triple here!) as it is locally known. While Lucy is loudly professing love, there are in fact four other men in her life including a "tight" friend of Frank's, and Frank's office boss. In each case Frank has discovered the trickery and his Sweetie has promised to be a good girl. But not Lucy. The instincts that drive her into unfaithfulness seem to lie outside her control. The author, however, takes little advantage of the psychological (or is it pathological?) possibilities inherent here, nor can he make Frank into anything but a weak, sentimental lover who goes on forgiving and loving the unlovable.

But Mickson's narrative technique is more complex than his characters might suggest. Frank is telling the story to confidants: his friend, Seth, and Lucy's friend, Lily. Seth in turn is reporting the story to us straight from Frank's mouth, with his own interjections of the shock of the Lucy story to himself and Lily. (The method reminds one of *Wuthering Heights* and some of the tales of Conrad.) The intervention of the two friends is too late, as Frank's heart has already decided. In part two the letter is delivered. Lucy, a mixture of pride, regret and more "double-crossing" involving her other lovers, is later back with Frank—thanks to the persistent efforts of Seth and Lily. But for Frank it cannot be the same again, however good Lucy tries to be. In the end Lucy is stabbed in circumstances which tend to incriminate Frank, and she loses a leg in the hospital as a result.

Part three is a mixed bag. It starts off with Lucy's great suffering, remorse, and repentance, continues into a ghost story in which Frank features under an assumed name, and ends as a piece of detective exercise. But the author manages to tie them all together. Lucy dies a wretched cripple. Frank, once thought dead, reappears to be cleared of police charges. By turning the screw of suffering a little too tight on Lucy, this last part has the effect of directing the reader's sympathy towards her, for Lucy becomes a kind of Moll Flanders denied salvation. For Mickson, the strong moral purpose of the Lucy story dictates that poetic justice must work full cycle. Lucy ends up in the grave just as Janet in *Woman is Poison* walks out of court to begin a life sentence with hard labour.

The moral remains the writer's primary assignment in these stories, persistent and undisguised. And why not? In the Introduction to *Who Killed Lucy* he explains he is telling the story as "a forewarning to many a young man desperately in love, against heartbreaks." He goes on:

> because it will serve as a reprimand and perhaps a "purgative"
> to those of our ladies who, flattered by their beauty, popularity
> or positions in life, make not only folly but also donkeys of
> themselves by remaining rolling stones in the hands of men.

Women have firmly but good-humouredly protested to Mickson against his strictures but many men have congratulated him. (A minister of religion used the Lucy story for a sermon with tremendous effect.) Was *The Violent Kiss* designed to appease the wounded women? There, Princess Serwaa deserts an eligible young man at the church door, but it is to marry her own choice even though he is a slave. The concluding sentence is significant:

> I am adding that: There is always a way where there is true
> love, and that in all sincerity, love knows no bounds.

In Konadu's work, responsibility for the breakdown in relationships is often more evenly shared between the man and the woman. Only Mercy comes near to being "poison" but she is not as sinister as any of Mickson's women. Mercy tricks Owusu into marriage but only because of the man's naivety. After heartache and separation, the two are re-united.

Naivety and reconciliation come up again in *Shadow of Wealth*. Here the partners are victims of circumstance. Independent, but rural and simple, Alice arrives in Accra in search of a job and easily becomes the mistress of Frimpong, Managing Director of the big business which employes her. But Frimpong is wrong in thinking that money alone can guarantee the young woman's contentment. The novel traces Alice's naive fascination with wealth, her subsequent disenchantment and fight to free herself; Frimpong ruins his business but gets reconciled to his wife.

A significant feature of Konadu's fiction is its abundant use of Ghanaian customs as the basis for plot—a far cry from Benibengor Blay's drawing-grooms. Konadu has personally undertaken research into certain customs of the Akan, and evidence of it is to be seen particularly in *Come Back Dora, Night Watchers of Korlebu* and *A Woman in her Prime*.[13] The first of these is from beginning to end an exposition of Akan customary funeral rites, but the novel unfortunately does not gain much by it. Boateng is a lifeless character who is there only to enable the author to conduct us through an episodic ritual. Neither he nor the Church is powerful enough in their opposition to the rites to effect any intended conflict in the novel. Boateng's insistence that he has "killed" his wife and the remorse he is supposed to be living through remain unconvincing. (I am not one of those who want nothing of anthropology in our creative literature, but if the African Studies Centre of a university reprints a novel presumably for anthropological studies, then I know where it rightly belongs.)[14]

Yet Konadu is the most talented among Ghanaian writers of popular fiction and the one who, like Cyprian Ekwensi before him, could become a major figure in West African writing.[15] The fact that already he has had a novel published internationally must be seen as a recognition of his potential. Versatile and enterprising, Asare Konadu devotes all his work-ing time to writing, publishing, and allied businesses. He has successfully run an Ideal Home Exhibition and soon he is bringing overseas publishers to a Book Fair in Accra. Part of Konadu's present ambition is to provide Ghanaians with more to read, and in this connection, his Anowuo Educational Publications is obtaining rights from foreign publishers to reproduce locally a selected number of books popular among his country-men. In a country where prices of books are rather high and their importation has to be covered by a licence, the advantages of such an arrangement are only too obvious.

Mickson shows tremendous inventive ability. His sentimental love scenes are the type that will appeal to a great many young readers—a typical letter in *Who Killed Lucy* begins:

> My Sweet Sweetie,
> In fact life without you is lifeless . . .

And ends:

> . . . keep loving, till we meet, in our dreams under our usual "forget-me-not" tree.

But he is yet to develop the creative insight and the sensitive approach to characters and situations which Konadu is capable of. Here is the opening paragraph of *A Husband for Esi Ellua:*

> There had been no rain in Eshiem for some time now. The river running north of the village was dry. The bed of sand and small pebbles was dug to yield water for domestic use. Women waited several hours for the water to fill the holes and with little calabashes scooped it into long-necked earthenware water-pots. The sun came up early. The red fiery ball rose from the east, blotting up every drop of dew before it. And the tall grass which stood round the village dried up and danced with the dry winds. There were the trees too, which stood out majestically above the grass and at first seemed not to take notice of the wind and sun. Then, as the sun continued to burn everything before it and the water holes dried up, all their leaves turned brown.

That could come from the work of the most sophisticated novelist. The writer's evocation of drought is in itself excellent prose, but in this community the phenomenon described is a sign of something gone wrong, for when the evergreen "nyamedua" tree in the goddess's grove begins to shed its leaves the villagers of Eshiem know for certain that some unusual disaster is around the corner. And that disaster which the novel goes on to describe in the life of Abaka and his village is the beginning of the Second World War. *A Husband for Esi Ellua* is far from being a great novel, though a very readable one. Like others of Konadu's works it is uneven in quality.

The question of unevenness could form a study of its own. For teachers of English the area of anxiety centres around the language of these works, as Mickson and Konadu, both with a large clientele in schools and colleges, are subject to crude journalese, cliches, grandiloquence and such-like evils, the former rather more so. And both not infrequently suffer from Tutuola-esque grammatical lapses, among the commonest in Konadu being the omission of essential pronouns:

That is what I have been trying to get Dad to see and wouldn't (i.e., *he* wouldn't). But there is a dance at Adibo tonight and would want you to take me there (i.e., *I*).[16]

There is in addition the gamut of West African (Ghanaian) English and personal coinages—which means that lovers in Mickson write to "themselves" not to each other, and Lucy's love affair with a certain young man ends with her "bringing forth by him"; Konadu's postal agent looks "askantly" at customers, and Boateng is the first man to build a "sand crete" house in his village.

No doubt a problem does exist here but it should not be exaggerated. The West African teacher of English must admit that of the factors that militate against his classroom efforts popular fiction by no means provides the greatest threat. Besides, although language is central to literature it can not be the only consideration in it, certainly not what the great majority of young people will read popular fiction for. The will of language to change—particularly in a new home—is well known. West African coinages and other innovations which do not necessarily offend against idomatic English will, for example, continue to press for recognition of the type accorded their more prolific American cousins.[17] A closer look at some of these writings might reveal that their untidiness is not a reflection of the writer's expressional handicap. Popular fiction by its very nature flies out of the writer's pen with supersonic speed. In Ghana, where the writer is often his own editor, publisher and distributor, a ready loaf may be only half-baked. And this is where teachers of English, critics, and experienced writers come in.

Is there any reason why the works of the more promising of these practitioners should not on publication enjoy local reviews? Surely some of the writers would benefit from comments. There are those who would appreciate help in editing. The State Publishing Corporation, no doubt with a record to be proud of in this field, cannot afford, for the sake of its own reputation, to be mere printers without the services of trained proofreaders.

For me, the most startling facts have been in the sales figures of these books, and with them, the readership. The summary is as follows:[18]

Shadow of Wealth	25,000	Has had fourth printing
Don't Leave Me Mercy	30,000	Reprint imminent
Come Back Dora	30–45,000	Still selling
Painful Road to Kadjebi	15,000	No reprint
A Husband for Esi Ellua	10,000	
Night Watchers of Korlebu	8,000	

When the Heart Decides	40,000	Has had third printing
second printing of	10,000	Sold out in 2-3 weeks
Who Killed Lucy	40,000	Fourth printing imminent
Now I Know	10,000	Sold out within a month
The Violent Kiss	10,000	Sold out within a month
Woman is Poison	10,000	Sold out within a month

Only a few hundred ever go outside Ghana. These figures are in spite of the fact that *Woman is Poison,* a pamphlet of 78 pages, sells at the equivalent of five shillings. My inquiries revealed that although the readership may be highest among people with minimal formal education, large numbers of lawyers and university people read popular fiction, even if they complain about the standard. Young women form a high proportion of readers.

After those disclosures we may have to re-state our opinions on the absence of a reading public in West Africa, and we shall be indifferent to these writings only at our own risk.

A BIBLIOGRAPHY OF GHANAIAN POPULAR FICTION

Bediako, K. A.
  Don't Leave Me Mercy, Anowuo Educational Publications, 1966.
  A Husband for Esi Ellua, Anowuo, Educational Publications, 1967.
Blay, J. B.
  Emelia's Promise, 1944.
  After the Wedding, published with *Emelia's Promise* as *Emilia's Promise and Fulfilment,* Waterville Publishing House, Accra, 1967.
  Be Content with your Lot, Benibengor Book Agency, 1947.
  Love in a Clinic, Benibengor Book Agency, 1957.
  Parted Lovers
  Dr Bengia Wants a Wife
  Operation Witchcraft
  Stubborn Girl
Darko, D. O.
  Friends Today Enemies Tomorrow, Bureau of Ghana Languages, Accra, 1959.
Donkor, Willie
  The Troubles of a Bachelor, Liberty Press, Accra.
  The Weals and Woes of a Certain Scholarship
  The Forbidden Taste, Facts and Fiction Agency, 1968.
  A Stab in my Heart
Hihetah, R. K.
  Painful Road to Kadjebi, Anowuo, Educational Publications, 1966.
Konadu, S. A.
  The Wizard of Asamang, 1963.
  The Lawyer who Bungled his Life, 1965.
  Shadow of Wealth, 1966.
  Come Back Dora, 1966.
  Night Watchers of Korlebu, 1967.

Mickson, E. K.
  When the Heart Decides, 1965.
  Who Killed Lucy, 1967.
  Now I Know, 1968.
  Woman is Poison, 1968.
  The Violent Kiss, 1968.
Nortey, K.
  The Man with Two Wives, 1964.
Nsiah-Bota, K.
  Love in a Tagedy, no date.
Skot
  The Tears of a Jealous Husband, 1965.
Wamek, Uncle
  The Love Letter Writer, no date.

NOTES

1. Several articles have appeared on this subject. My comparisons are based on Donatus Nwoga's under this title in *Transition,* Vol. 4, 1965.
2. I have on record only one play and a Love Letter Writer.
3. Largely oral and in Ghanaian languages, the popular theatre of the Concert Parties is not considered here. Some of the titles in the bibliography of Ghanaian popular fiction at the end of this chapter are not available.
4. Charles Jenner, *Town Eclogues,* 1772; quoted in J. M. S. Tompkins, *The Popular Novel in England 1770–1800,* Methuen, p. 1.
5. The possibility exists of much earlier fiction: the blurb of Nortey's *The Man with Two Wives,* 1964, credits the writer with works "mostly fiction . . . published in the Gold coast some thirty years ago."
6. For a full list of Blay's fiction, see the bibliography at the end of this chapter.
7. Compare John Matthews, "The Canadian Experience," and W. H. Pearson, "The Recognition of Reality," in *Commonwealth Literature,* Heinemann, 1965, pp. 21–31; 32–47.
8. For a similar debate on this subject, see Obi Egbuna, *Wind Versus Polygamy,* 1964.
9. See J. M. S. Tompkins, op. cit., chapter on "Theory and Technique."
10. Asare Konadu also uses the name K. A. Bediako. For convenience only the name Konadu is used in this paper.
11. Donkor's story appears in his volume, *The Troubles of a Bachelor.*
12. E. K. Mickson, *Woman is Poison,* last sentence.
13. Asare Konadu, *A Woman in her Prime,* Heinemann, 1967.
14. African Studies Centre, UCLA, is reprinting this novel. Also republished by Heinemann under the title *Ordained by the Oracle,* 1969.
15. Cyprian Ekwensi's first "novel," *When Love Whispers,* was published in Onitsha in 1947.
16. *Don't Leave Me Mercy,* p. 75; *Shadow of Wealth,* p. 121.
17. For more of my views on this, see Ime Ikideh, *Drum Beats,* E. J. Arnold, 1968, p. 13.
18. The system of sales facilitates the reckoning of figures though approximate. The writers themselves are my source.

POETRY

KOFI AWOONOR AND THE EWE TRADITION OF SONGS OF ABUSE (HALO)

Kofi Anyidoho

INTRODUCTION

This essay attempts to demonstrate one significant case of what Kofi Awoonor has referred to as "tradition and continuity in African Literature."[1] This view of literature as a creatively continuous art is reflected in current trends in criticism and research in African literature. The theme of this very conference and the subjects of various papers testify to this point.[2] However, we need to remind ourselves that it is not enough to point in the right direction; we must be sure we are pointing the right things out. The critic's contribution to our understanding of this process of creative continuity could be most effective if he isolates and analyzes the specific aspects of oral tradition a particular writer may be drawing upon.[3]

Richard M. Dorson suggests three tests for establishing the relationship of a given written work to oral tradition: *biographical evidence* that the author has enjoyed direct contact with oral lore; *internal evidence* indicating the author's familiarity with folklore; *corroborative evidence* "that the saying, tale, song, or custom inside the literary work possesses an independent traditional life."[4] But there is a problem with Dorson's third test as it stands. Perhaps we do not have to hunt for evidence of folklore as borrowed *items* only. We may not find a traditional Ewe proverb or fragments of songs in every Awoonor poem or novel, but can we discount the evidence of traditional Ewe styles and techniques of poetic composition? It seems that a writer's ability to adopt and adapt oral *styles* and *techniques* is a far more significant case of creative continuity than the incorporation of fragments of folklore into written literature. After all, the good writer is an artist, a creator, not a mere dealer in borrowed items. And when most people talk of African writers being influenced by Western literary traditions they think more in terms of style, technique, and genre rather than "borrowed" passages.

Our biographical evidence places Awoonor firmly within the fertile soil of a living oral tradition: "Born into a community of drummers, dancers,

87

and singers, my earliest recollections of Ewe oral poetry became the basic inspiration of my earliest writings."[5] It has been suggested that partly because of this influence, especially from the dirge poetry of the poet-cantor, Akpalu Vinoko, Awoonor's poetry is dominated by a tendency towards the elegiac. Jawa Apronti, for instance, concludes that "the final impression of Awoonor is of a predominantly sad poet, hooked almost to the elegiac, calling from the brink of the underworld to the community of the living."[6] This may be largely true of much of his early work, but we find that he has often changed tunes, giving up the slow rhythm of songs of sorrow for the brisk and taunting voice of combat. For this new kind of poetry, Awoonor finds a ready precedent in the Ewe tradition of songs of abuse, known as *halo*. The rest of this paper discusses the main features of *halo* and establishes parallels between this traditional oral genre and the lighter side of Awoonor's writing, focusing on verbal aggression as a source of satire and humor.

THE *HALO* TRADITION

An early mention of *halo* in ethnographic literature was by the Ewe musician S. B. Gadzekpo who described *halo* as "songs of insult (which) deal with the shameful history of individuals among the opponents."[7] Philip Gbeho, another noted Ewe musician, described *halo* songs as one of the more elaborate types of folk song in the then Gold Coast.[8] Both writers leave the impression that *halo* was mainly an inter-village contest. This was not always the case. Many instances of halo involved rival sections of the same town or village, a point made by G. K. Nukunya in his assessment of the "ward" as a significant unit of the Ewe socio-political system.[9] Somewhat fuller accounts of *halo* are offered by Awoonor in sections of *The Breast of the Earth* and in *Guardians of the Sacred Word: Ewe Poetry* where we find genuine *halo* texts from living poets. He provides very useful insights into both stylistic features and the social and psychological implications of this tradition:

> The Ewe *halo* poetry was a regular feature of Ewe drumming for a long time. Its essence is its verbal agility, exaggeration, and elaborate use of imagery. *Halo* became the instrument through which rival villages settled outstanding differences. Each side commissioned its poets to dig into the history of the other group for all the scandalous details about their leaders, true or false. The ingredients constitute the material for verbal

assault on the ugliness of the opponents' leadership, juicy bits
about whose grandmother was a whore or whose great-grand-
father built a wealth on stolen goods . . . This poetry tends to
dramatize intragroup conflicts and dissipates these in words.
Its recitation works at a cummulative level; it indulges in sheer
verbal overkill.[10]

We are especially concerned here with its use as an instrument of satire
and humor, and the great demand it makes on the poet's inventiveness in
order to ensure victory over opponents. Awoonor reminds us that "what
receives great emphasis is the comic and the humorous aspect. Other
skills that are called upon are also expected from poets of other traditions
and styles—e.g., good voice, verbal skill, excellent drumming, and superb dancing."[11] Halo is an excellent instance of the use of insult as
entertainment. But such entertainment is meaningful only within a formal
artistic framework with clearly defined aesthetic and social norms. Ordi-
narily, no one takes insult without a protests, and reaction to insult may
range from violent physical action to legal suits, verbal rebuttals, or
apparent indifference. Indifference to insult could be a counter insult to
the violator, a positive way of rising above his meanness of spirit. Charles
P. Flynn in his *Insult and Society* talks of insult as a violation of a person's
self-regard and self-esteem and points out the significance of particular
reactions prescribed by socio-cultural systems.[12] The case of *halo* tells us
that it is even more significant that the tradition prescribes not only
response to insult but also the need for insult as a legitimate reaction to an
individual's disregard for society's norms. It is as though society is saying
that we know insult hurts, but we would respect your self-esteem only
when you respect ours, you insult us with your deviant behavior and we
shall appoint our poets to throw your shame back in your face. In doing
so, however, the tradition takes care to convert a potentially disruptive
situation into a mechanism for inducing laughter in spite of hurt feelings.

Here, then, is an excellent opportunity for the functionalist theoretician
to indulge his logic to its inevitable conclusion. Alan P. Merriam makes a
fair recommendation in urging that we investigate poetic insults such as
halo for the psychological processes of the people.[13] However, the
investigator should not hasten to take *halo* song texts much more seriously than the facts may warrant. One crucial fact is that *halo* is an
organized game governed by aesthetic norms which mingle reality with
fantasy. Many songs may be based on embarrassing facts about an
individual and his family, but as Awoonor correctly points out, "The fact
remains, however, that *halo* also depends on inventiveness, and an insult

may be based on sheer fiction."[14] This is an important reminder of what I call the primacy of the creative aspects of *halo*. A recognition of the fictive contents of songs makes it easier for them to be accepted in the spirit of a game; those being ridiculed can hid their shame behind the common claim that "poets are liars." Their dignified contempt creates the impression that it is all lies and should not amount to anything but a joke. Indeed, to react with anger is to concede defeat and admit that the poets may, after all, be telling the truth.

Halo is also a poetry of dramatic confrontation. We see this in the tone of combat which permeates the song texts and especially in the performance situation. As a dramatic enactment, *halo* achieves its total effect only in the combined arts of singing, drumming, and dancing. The stage proper is the village public square. The performance reaches a climax in what is called *hatsatsia,* the "recitation" or "song chain".[15] At this point the drums yield the stage to the slanderous voice of poetry. To the syncopated rhythm of the gong and the *toke,* a boat-shaped iron instrument, the cantors follow one another in a circle, stamping their feet to reinforce the background rhythm, twisting and turning their bodies as they sing through a chain of songs. Every care is taken to ensure maximum clarity of the song texts. At intervals the circle is broken, and each cantor confronts a section of the audience and gives a personal rendition of the songs, drawing heavily on verbal agility and body language to ensure maximum communication of meaning and feeling. The extensive and skillful use of gestures for dramatic interpretation of songs is known as *hamekoko* (literally, "cutting the song open to lay bare its entrails"). In one particular performance I witnessed in Wheta in the mid-nineteen-fifties, the drama received a special impact with a sudden display of a horrible sculpture alleged to be the exact image of the person being attacked in the song.

On the performance arena the climactic nature of the *hatsatsia* sometimes receives a double thrust with the presence of members of the opposing group. Their presence enables them to determine how best to answer back when their turn for performance comes on another day. It also adds a special dimension to the aesthetic appeal of the songs. For instance, when a particular song is about someone present in the audience, he may be obliged to step forward and face the poet-cantors as they publicly celebrate his shame in song, directing the song and gestures to his face. Such confrontation generates great excitement among spectators and creates a tremendous feeling of suspense as everyone looks forward to the next performance when today's harrassed spectator will in turn take the stage and launch a counter-offensive.

TYPES OF INSULT USED IN *HALO*

For our limited purposes we may identify three broad categories of insult used in *halo:* those dealing with physical appearance, those directed at deviant behavior, and the somewhat special class of "obscenities."[16]

Physical perfection is an ideal about which most people can only dream, and the Ewe recognize that no one may be blamed for having been born ugly. Parents of a particularly ugly child may console themselves and the child with such a name as *Yihame* (She too is a human being: *Eya ha amee.*) Despite all this, however, society in its search for the aesthetic ideal is often reluctant to accept ugly specimens of humanity without protest. This may been seen in the extensive use of insults about physical imperfections. In the context of *halo* an ugly opponent may find himself exposed, item by item from forehead to toe-nails. He is expected to appear unimpressed even if the audience greets his misfortune with loud applause and laughter.

Awoonor's translations of the *halo* poets Ekpe and Dunyo in *Guardians of the Sacred Word* give us some excellent samples of insults about ugly looks. We have, for instance, Dunyo's portrait of the whore:

> Come and hear the voice of slander.
> You clutch the earth like a leather bag.
> On your stem you stand like a porcupine in clothes.
> You run like the bush rope.
> Your back caves in rising like the hillock.
> Beneath your stomach is the hyaena's ravine.
> Your chest is as short as the red monkey on the corn barn.
> Will this too insult the poet? (p. 57)

In another song Komi Ekpe, like Dunyo, attacks a woman who has apparently provoked him into song:

> She with the jaw-bone of a cow
> Falling upon her chest like sea-egret's beak
> Her waist is flat, earlobes hanging, oversize intestines.
> It was you who took my affairs to Sokpe
> and asked him to sing against me. (p. 91)

Both poets excuse their use of insults by suggesting that they are only fighting back under extreme provocation. Their portraits often amount to a distortion of the reality, especially through the constant use of imagery,

91

exaggeration, even obvious fabrications. To state that Kodzo has a badly cut figure, bad eyes, and a long mouth, may be interesting but nothing special. So the poet adds some color to the portrait and in the process creates a spectacle worth remembering with laughter:

> his backside runs into a slope
> his eye twisted like the sun-inspector,
> he has many supporters in Tsiame
> his mouth as long as the pig
> blowing the twin whistle. (p. 84)

Moral excellence, unlike physical excellence, is not just an ideal for society at large but an obligation. Thus it is no surprise that some of the most serious *halo* insults are about loose morals. Unacceptable behavior may range from lack of personal hygiene to the most outrageous crimes punishable by death. At one end is the recognition that a man may be excused for his ugly looks, but lack of personal hygiene cannot be blamed on the gods. At the other end is the understanding that the presence of incorrigible rogues constitutes an intolerable threat to social harmony.

Many insults about immoral behavior are directed against elders. It is often said of African societies that respect for elders borders on religious awe. What is not always added is that such respectability goes with responsibility: "Old age automatically confers honor and elicits respect. Increase in years brings increase in responsibility, in the number of offices held and the exercise of leadership."[17] The elder's leadership role obliges him to show exemplary behavior. Indeed, at his death a stupid and worthless elder is sent to his grave with the warning that he should never reincarnate with such abominable behavior. He may not even be mentioned much when ancestors are remembered in prayers and other religious ceremonies.[18] Memory of such people is an eternal shame to kinsmen, which is why *halo* poets like to heap insults on the living by digging into their family history for the stupidities of their forebears.

In one song Ekpe threatens to bring down Kodzo's house. Kodzo's crimes include three very serious ones: theft, chronic indebtedness (often seen as a sign of laziness, wastefulness, or greed) and adultery. Dunyo's poem concentrates its venom on another serious kind of immoral behavior—prostitution—advising all those who give birth to a whore to kill her before she ever has the chance to ruin homesteads. Earlier in the song Dunyo tells us how loose and stupid the whore could be:

> The whore was forgetful; she walked
> like a wandering duck into my song.
> She thought it was a matter of opening legs. (p. 57)

This last line on the whore leads directly into the extensive use of obscenities in *halo* insults. Reinhold Aman has pointed out the widespread use of *maledicta* ("bad words") all over the world and in every sub-group of culture.[19] And Flynn points up sex and obscenity as a cultural universal deployed in insult behavior.[20] Perhaps it is the paradox of shock and pleasure induced by obscenities which makes them so effective as materials for songs of abuse. In their use the poets stretch their license to its limits. In his essay "Art and Mythology: A General Theory," George Devereux postulates a close connection between art and etiquette, "in that (art) prescribes polite ways for saving impolite things, it provides ways for expressing the inexpressible."[21] Devereux suggests that society accepts the inexpressible in art form because "artistic technique transmutes truth into beauty."[22] This may be true of *halo* but only to a point, especially when we remember that although the *halo* poet may be playing games with words, it is a game in which goals are scored through shock and the rules allow "foul play." Owusu Brempong reminds us that "in contrast to proverbs and folktales, the goal in using insults in not subtlety but shock and surprise."[23]

In its proper *halo* context the obscene and the profane is invariably linked to moral transgression in those being insulted. This juxtapositon of obscenity and immorality tends to transfer our shock form the obscene to the immoral. When Ekpe tells us that Kodzo is an evil animal,

> His penis has wound a rope around his waist
> pulling him around and away, (p. 84)

we are shocked not so much by the poet's "foul mouth" as by the revelation that this indecent penis is an instrument of moral transgression, for Kodzo "fucks others' wives fatteningly."

From the limited samples available to us, we find a major stylistic difference between songs or sections of songs dealing with the first type of insults and those dealing with the second type. Insults on physical appearance draw heavily on metaphor and simile and exaggeration for their poetic effect. this is perhaps no surprise since the goal in such insults is to create fantastic verbal pictures. On the other hand, insults about deviant behavior tend to register their effect through declarative statements, sometimes with a dose of irony or sarcasm. In the use of obscenities there is no clearly dominant technique. Sometimes fantastic images are created, like the above example about Kodzo's penis. Sometimes we find blunt statements of accusation to which our response may be shock, but often shock received with hilarious laughter.

One other significant technique favored by *halo* pets is boasting. This is in tune with the spirit of combat in which *halo* thrives. The poet seeks to impress upon everyone that his opponent should blame himself for provoking his superior into a contest. We see this boastful self-justification in both Dunyo and Ekpe. Dunyo announces that his song "came from the Creator's house simmering in his head," but he would not use it without serious provocation:

> Please, I say gently,
> there is something beyond
> whose leg is larger than the hippo.
> I will be mute; let someone abuse me
> then I will tell it to him. (p. 57)

Unfortunately for the forgetful whore, she walks like a wandering duck into Dunyo's song, so he lets it loose on her, concluding with a word of advice and a boastful challenge:

> If my song hurts you,
> Go on a journey. Travel for to Kedzi.
> Bring with you the poets there.
> They and I will wrestle on the ground
> The whore knows me not
> So her insults climb the air
> My songs are beyond a million; I've cut and
> kept the overflow. The harlot opens the door
> and my song floows like the river
> flows like the turbulent river. (p. 58)

Halo is indeed an art form, but is an art whose aesthetic is governed by a sense of justice and morality. To ensure total victory the poet strives not only for poetic excellence but also lays claims to moral superiority.

AWOONOR'S USE OF INSULT

An initial point of connection between *halo* and Awoonor's use of insult is offered by this piece of autobiographical evidence:

> Then I wrote some songs of abuse. In the Ewe tradition we
> have something called poetry of abuse, or *halo*. When I was
> growing up, if there is a quarrel among two sections of the
> village, the poets will sharpen their instruments, and will come

out, and they can throw a lot of mud. I was doing field work in
1970 and came upon, I sort of unearthed, a lot of this poetry of
abuse, just incredible stuff. There was a guy who was referred
to as "He had ears so big that whenever he took a canoe, the
canoe had no need of sails." (laughter) I'll read to you poems
of abuse I did following this particular tradition.[24]

We are often told that the African scholar or artist educated in Western
tradition cannot but suffer alienation. Some say that having once drunk of
alien wines, the African scholar or artist must forever remain intoxicated
and lost. Indeed, we do know of some who may drink themselves to
death, but we also know of others who indulge their thirst but only for
awhile. They eventually wake up somewhat sober and head for home.

Awoonor clearly admits to having been drunk on alien wines, but he
insists that his initial intoxication with poetry was with Ewe oral poetry.
He speaks of a second period of the divided allegiance, torn between his
people's traditions and alien ones. But he survived into a third stage
where he sees triumph of harmony and "can switch backwards and
forwards without any conflict with any of them."[25] Significantly, it is to
this period that his own "Songs of Abuse" belong. Following his rediscovery of the *halo* poets in 1970 his own songs appear in *Ride Me,
Memory* (1973).[26] What he has given us so far is a rather meager harvest,
but rich with the inheritance of *halo*.

In five short pieces, Awoonor sharpens his instruments of satire and
humor against the alleged provocations and transgressions of five per-
verted individuals. For him the performance arena has extended beyond
the wildest dreams of the old *halo* poets. Each of those he must insult is a
man of the world, so the poet broadens the scope of his references to
embrace most of our contemporary world, moving away from shameful
family histories and petty domestic theft to the large canvas of revolutions
of the world. These are international criminals parading as revolutionary
heroes, and herein lies the poet's justification to expose them to ridicule
and scorn. Besides, each one has provoked him through personal attacks.
Stanislaus stole his spring overcoat; the eminent scholar and meddler
slandered him and later insulted his mother; uncle Jonathan is now
walking his beaches and cursing his sacred name.

Awoonor's techniques closely parallel those of the *halo* poets. However, he makes minimal use of insults about physical imperfections. The
few instances we find hardly ever develop into the extended metaphorical
portraits common to traditional *halo*. From the phrase "dirty face" we
may go to the statement "Your red nose is covered with fifty ugly warts,"
but nothing more elaborate. The poet seems to be particularly concerned

with lack of personal hygiene. the piece "To My Uncle Jonathan" opens with the abrupt declaration: "Sir, you stink," and later we are told of Jonathan's stinking daughter: "that lean-assed whorelet you sent to my home the other night/the bitch temptress, smelling of mayonnaise and pastrami." (p. 22) In "To Stanislaus the Renegade," we have a rare case of bad smell:

> The jail you occupied in Poonaville, Tennessee
> Was burnt down after you escaped; they could not eradicate
> the smell. (p. 20)

These poems are primarily concerned with private and public morals. Stanislaus is accused of cheating and stealing. He is now settling down to drug-trafficking. Yet, for all his ill-gotten wealth, he cannot even buy decent clothes:

> Verna wrote the other day, you remember Verna,
> the lean-assed girl whose rent money you stole in Detroit,
> she wrote to say you are still running around in her underpants.

The Eminent Scholar and Meddler excels Stanislaus as a master of scandal and obscenity:

> You joined the revolutionaries of Azania
> only to betray them for multi-colored blankets
> and a battered copy of the *Pilgrim's Progress*.
> You were caught eating hog in a synagogue in Rome,
> uttering profanities during a rain dance in Navajo country,
> screaming the sacred name of the Buddha across the Punjabi plain
> taking a shit in a shinto shrine in Kyoto. (p. 20)

And Uncle Jonathan surpasses them both in sexual indiscretion:

> You fucker of sheep and goats
> a pederast in bloomers
> a whiskered fool with an obscene mouth

No wonder he even schemes to trade off his own daughter for a few favors from the poet, but this poet is too good to stoop so low:

> I threw her out, for I am a man of dignity and respect.
> If you don't respect my name, others do.

Like traditional poets of *halo,* this poet too lays claim to moral superiority. Like them, he also makes use of boasts, challenges, and threats. We see this in his concluding message to Stanislaus:

> I will be waiting for you; for every gun you buy
> I shall command a thousand assegais, for every sword
> a million Ashanti matchets and Masai spears
> I am not afraid of you anymore. Those days are past
> when you stole my school fees and my catapult
> and fled into the cove beyond bird island
> I too came of age.

My earlier claim that insults is a widely used technique in Awoonor's writing needs to be qualified and substantiated. In his earlier collections *Rediscovery* and *Night of My Blood* we find only occasional use of insult functioning within a pervading mood of lament for neglected homestands and ancestral shrines, and it is directed mainly at the colonial establishment, the church, and the *mis*educated African such as we meet in "We Have Found a New Land":

> The smartest professionals in three piece
> Sweating away their humanity in driblets
> And wiping the blood from their brow.
> (Night of My Blood, p. 28)

In lines such as these the blow of an intended tirade is softened by a sense of loss and pity. In others, however, the poet's vehemence suffers no mitigation, as for instance, when in "March, Kind Comrade, Abreast Him," he diagnoses "the diseased socialists/That walk the bank pavements with gold/in their teeth." The tone sometimes is surprisingly mild, but the satiric intent is nonetheless biting:

> He studied law in Dublin
> His spectacles glinting
> as he wrote decrees for every regime;
> disqualification, forfeiture and seizure
> of property, rumours and rumour-mongering;
> wars and rumours of wars
> That is his talisman of hope. (p. 84)

There is also the occasional blashemy: "O, come all ye faithless," or "Our Father who art in heaven/do whatever pleases you." And in "I Hold the Dreams," the poet dreams of "purple paradises,/of the laughter of naked virgins in the arms of buffoons."

In *Ride Me, Memory,* the use of insult is much more extensive than in the earlier works, and it is not limited to the "Songs of Abuse" discussed above but may be found in at least sections of most poems except the last group, "African Memories," in which the poet returns to the theme of lament for kinsmen and a lost childhood. In "America," the first poem of the volume, the poet celebrates the American Indian chieftain Geronimo and in doing so, lashes out at those "despoilers, half-starved immigrants from a despoiled Europe." On the occasion of the Cambodian invasion, American academics come in for some tongue-lashing:

> What other grounds shall they hallow
> with their gutless cynical blunderings,
> these fools dancing at their own execution?

Probably the best satiric piece in the section called "Long Island Sketches" is one which "celebrates" empty academic qualifications:

> The proclamation came first
> in pencil. You must address me doctor.
> Puzzled beyond words I send polite inquiries
> doctor of what? Of letters, words,
> oral examinations, course works
> brilliant essays on Hopkins and Eliot, a masters thesis
> on Pound the renegade, and above all
> a dissertation on the elaborate and unconventional
> use of the comma in the poetry
> of C.C. Razoogakool the poet laureate of Togaloo
> who in 1864 single-handed defected to the liberal side
> and saved the country and his letters for the world
> of tomorrow and the day before tomorrow:
> Long live all Ph.D.'s. They are the salt of the earth.

There is a light-heartedness in this piece and the poet's laughter is echoed in the obvious play on the long drawn-out sound [oo]. The mock-praise of the last line is an appropriate sarcastic conclusion to this announcement.

Even in verse devoted to "praise, celebration, and prayer," the poet villifies those he holds responsible for war and suffering in south-east Asia:

> Yahya Khan's nose is Nero's fiddle
> played upon by scents of burning incense
> and Krishna swore Mohammed was a bigot,
> a felonious war-monger in women's clothes,
> a holy assassin in the name of Allah . . .

This may be both insulting and blasphemous, but the poet takes care to put such blasphemy in the mouth of Krishna. In the poem "To the Anonymous Brown-Skinned Girl in Frisko," we find a singular case of obscenity neatly packed into one line:

> even the hairs in your ass-hole have been eaten by the termites.

Awoonor's latest collection, *The House By The Sea*,[27] also offers scattered instances of insult. They very first poem contains a reference to "miracle workers in rented clothes." The third has a sketch of "the Russian frauds who know nothing,/Brodsky with his deadly ignorance/ Voznesesky and his motocycle jacket/believing the world and its half-truths." The poet comes closest to the rhetoric of *halo* in "Requiem for Pablo" where we encounter Memory personified, "soiling his pants before the forced trip into the ovens." His anger bursts upon the impiety of pretenders who "sing the obscenities of Jerusalem":

> They cannot move in the manner of God
> who fucks other people's wives
> and leaves cash payments on the dresser
> with a note promising
> just promising. (p.8)

The use of verbal aggression extends even into Awoonor's prose work, *This Earth, My Brother*.[28] This is especially true with his description of characters. The very first lines introduce us to some unnamed pretenders, "casting furtive glances, and withdrawing their eyes like hawks that give not to their offspring, averting their eyes. As if I wanted something off their asses." The village elders are introduced as greedy, lazy, and "stupid-looking old men." One of them is singled out for special dishonor: "Topa, his head like a Kuli water pot, eyes flaming like a parrot's tail feather. Never did an honest day's work. All he knew was to sit in judgment on others and get a drink out of them." This damnation of the elders and their traditional claim to respect is presented indirectly as the angry thoughts of the town crier, Kodzo, who has been fined for negligence of duty. Chapter Two begins with a close-up on a "a long line of lawyers, sweating freely in their black coats and their pin-stripe trousers." These are the caricatures of White Europe and we remember having met them before as "The smart professionals in three piece." Some of these sketches are so pathetic and yet so humorous, like the half-hungry lottery girls (with) legs like spindles in badly fitting clothes." (p.21) The satire in such insulting characterization reaches heights as we move into the National Club where decadent bureacrats indulge their animal passions to the full. The whole place stinks with their foul words, their lousy attitude to national problems, their immoral acts. Very appropriately, this ridiculous gathering is thrown out by an entertaining duel involving the wife and the harlot girl of one of these rotten men:

> the women had swung into a verbal match in which they hurled all kinds of abuses and slanders at each other. They named whose mother was a whore, a witch, a thief, who was a prostitute, and a dirty slut, who stunk. (pp. 32–33)

Awoonor's satire in this novel is largely aimed at the elite for their various failings. The academics are found guilty of "the ignorance of the learned," the common crime of those like the "Ghanaian boy who spent five years in England learning Old English and Transformational Grammar. A few friends he had known had glittering careers in Oxford studying Herodotus. The ignorance of the learned." With such training in apemanship for the "leaders" of state institutions it is no wonder that this nation soon degenerates into "a revolting malevolence." We begin to see why the school teacher we meet at Deme Primary School (Chapter 3) can teach only stilted English and bits of the Bible in parrot fashion and is unable to understand why his pupils so happily forget his lessons, though he insults and curses them" "Good, next time don't forget, you silly goat, hopeless cow."

CONCLUSION

It has been my aim in this study to demonstrate creative continuity in African literature, using Kofi Awoonor's debt to the Ewe *halo* tradition as an example. But to demonstrate that Awoonor follows the tradition in not to argue that his poetry is true *halo* poetry. We may only see him as an extension of that tradition, an extension which seeks to apply old styles and techniques to new and wider dimensions of life. The expansion of his stage beyond the narrow confines of the village square calls for new

references and possibly new value judgments. But a much more fundamental way in which Awoonor departs from the tradition is the fact that
he works in a written rather than an oral medium. the great benefits of this
new medium have often been celebrated, but we may also count some of
the losses that go with them.

A major advantage of oral tradition that is lost to the writer is the living
experience of the performance. For a poetry of abuse, this is a major loss,
especially when we consider the extent to which the spirit of combat and
of satiric humor achieves dramatic realization in face-to-face encounters
fully backed by music, dance, gesture, and an active audience. The
impact of the satire and the humor is more sharply defined for the *halo*
poet. His opponents are known individuals whose presence in the audience or the community adds a whole new dimension to the appreciation of
his songs. *Halo* is defined by both text and context of creation and of
performance. This context is at once immediate and homogeneous. There
is a context to Awoonor's work as well, but it is somewhat diffused. His
opponents must of necessity remain anonymous lest he suffer a strict
application of one rule of written tradition—libel. There are severe
restrictions on his poetic license.

Perhaps we need not argue primary differences between oral and
written cultures in terms of a profit and loss theory. Those who see
ambiguity of meaning as a positive feature of our literary experience may
suggest that Awoonor's songs of abuse are the richer for leaving their
referents open to the judgment of each reader according to his or her own
experience. The written word may function somewhat differently from
the spoken, but each in its own way makes its point when used effectively. And laughter at man's incurable failings may be equally heart-
warming, whether it is drawn out by words on the printed page or words
from the lips of a poet-cantor.

NOTES

1. See Karen L. Morell, ed., *In Person: Achebe, Awoonor, and Soyinka* (Seattle: University of Washington, 1975), pp. 133–160.
2. The 6th annual meeting of The African Literature Association, Gainsville, Florida.
3. For a closer look at some of the issues involved see Bernth Lindfors, "Critical
   Approaches to Folklore in African Literature," in Richard M. Dorson, ed., *African
   Folklore*, (Doubleday, 1972).
4. "Folklore in Literature: A Symposium." *Journal of American Folklore* 70 (1957): 1–8.
5. Kofi Awoonor, *The Breast of the Earth*, (New York: Doubleday, 1975), p. 202.
6. "Ghanaian Poetry in the 1970s," in Kolawole Ogungbesan, ed., *New West African
   Literature*, (London: Heinemann, 1979), p. 35.
7. "Making Music in Eweland," *West African Review* 23 (1952): 819.
8. "Music of the Gold Coast," *African Music* 1 (1954): 62.
9. *Kinship and Marriage Among the Anlo Ewe* (London: The Athlone Press, 1969), p. 14.

10. *The Breast of the Earth,* pp. 86–87.
11. *Guardians of the Sacred Word: Ewe Poetry* (New York: Nok Publishers, 1974), p. 7.
12. Charles P. Flynn, *Insult and Society* (Kennikat Press, 1977), p. 10.
13. Alan P. Merriam, *Anthropology of Music* (Northwestern, 1964), pp. 200–01.
14. *The Breast of the Earth,* p. 123.
515. See Awoonor, *Guardians . . . ,* p. 18, and also Nissio Fiagbedze, *The Music of the Anlo,* Ph.D. dissertation, University of California at Los Angeles, 1977, p. 129.
16. For an attempt at insult classification according to the criterion of deviation from the norm, see Owusu Brempong, *Attacking Deviation from the Norm,* unpublished M.A. thesis, Indiana University, Bloomington, 1978. Also D. M. Warren & Owusu Brempong, "Attacking Deviation from the Norm: Poetic Insults in Bono, Ghana," in Maledicta 1, 2 (1978), pp. 141–67.
17. Nukunya, *Kinship and Marriage,* p. 153.
18. For a comparable situation among the Akan of Ghana, see Kofi Asare Opoku, *West African Traditional Religion* (Accra: FEP International, 1978), p. 36.
19. *Maledicta* 1, 1 (Summer 1977), p. 3.
20. *Insult and Society,* p. 16.
21. See Carol F. Jopling, ed., *Art and Aesthetics in Primitive Societies* (New York: E. P. Dutton, 1977), p. 205.
22. Ibid., p. 210.
23. Owusu Brempong, *Attacking Deviation from the Norm,* p. 1.
24. Morell, *In Person,* p. 159.
25. Lindfors, Munro, Priebe, and Sanders, eds., *Palaver* (Austin, 1972), p. 53.
26. Greenfield Review Press.
27. Ibid., 1978.
28. Doubleday, 1971.

KOFI AWOONOR'S POETRY

L. R. Early

Kofi Awoonor is a name that reappears with some frequency in discussions and anthologies of contempory African literature. He has published two volumes of poetry, *Rediscovery* (1964) and *Night of My Blood* (1971); a novel, *This Earth, My Brother* (1971); and two plays in *Short African Plays,* edited by Cosmo Pieterse (1972).[1] His essays and poems have appeared in a number of magazines, and he has been interviewed in a series on African writers. *Night of My Blood* and the paperback edition of *This Earth, My Brother* have introductions by two of Africa's outstanding contemporary writers, Ezekiel Mphahlele and Chinua Achebe. While Awoonor's published work is relatively slight in volume, it is a substantial achievement in recent African writing in English, and promising in its development and versatility.

The facts of Awoonor's life may in part explain this accomplishment and promise. He was born in 1935 near Keta in Ghana, and attended Achimota School and the University of Ghana, where he later worked in the Institute of African Studies, specializing in vernacular poetry. He edited *Okyeame,* a literary magazine which appeared irregularly in the early sixties, and served as an associate editor of *Transition.* More recently he has co-edited with G. Adali-Mortty an anthology, *Messages/ Poems from Ghana* (1971). In the mid-sixties Awoonor was Director of the Ghana Film Corporation. He took an M.A. at the University of London in 1968 and subsequently became Visiting Professor in African Literature at the State University of New York, Stony Brook, and Chairman of its Comparative Literature Program.

Awoonor's diversity of interests and the cosmopolitan pattern of his life have produced a poetry of considerable complexity which presents several difficulties, especially for readers like myself of a non-African background. Among the most interesting of these problems is his use of the oral tradition in the poetry of his Ewe ancestors. I shall attempt to make an assessment of the influence of traditional genres, structures, and rhythms on Awoonor's work. The details of certain tribal customs, especially those of funeral ceremony (which recurs as a theme and metaphor in *Night of My Blood*), and the implications of certain local

103

notions such as "the man of huge testicles" (in "What Song Shall We Sing," p. 27), may also perplex the Western reader.[2] There are some specifically autobiographical references in Awoonor's poetry, though I find these less a difficulty than the cultural material. Some footnotes in *Night of My Blood* clarify his allusions to personal relationships, and these are also illuminated by a brief reminiscence published among contributions to an African-Scandinavian Writers' Conference in Stockholm, in 1967.[3] At any rate, Awoonor, like Yeats in his references to Maud Gonne and MacBride, generally makes the allusion serve the poem, rather than the other way around. There remain, however, difficulties in Awoonor's work which may be attributed not to the critic's limitations but to the poet's: the lapses of craft to which writers of any culture are liable.

While he shows a deep interest in the oral tradition of African poetry, Awoonor has also enriched his work through his understanding of Western literature. Excerpts from Dante form an important motif in *This Earth, My Brother,* and many poems in *Night of My Blood* owe something to English writers from Shakespeare through T. S. Eliot. Awoonor has himself remarked on the convergence in his work of Ewe oral tradition and the English language: "I have always felt, perhaps involuntarily, I should take my poetic sensibility if you like the word, from the tradition that sort of feeds my language, because in my language there is a lot of poetry, there is a lot of music and there is a lot of literary art, even though not written, and so I take my cue from this old tradition, and begin to break it into English, to give it a new dimension as it were."[4] Awoonor's poetry is exciting because it offers (at its best) the creative fusion of two cultures.

His poetry is also exciting because it transcends particular cultures. This universality is especially expressed in the recurring archetype at the core of *Night of My Blood,* the journey, which as quest for meaning and identity is a pattern implicit in Western poetry since Homer. Awoonor develops the motif in several ways. There is the historical migration of the Ewe people chronicled and mythologized in "Night of My Blood," and there is the recent traumatic journey of the African people out of a technologically primitive culture of their own into the welter of modernization and Westernization. This development is viewed as a journey of the dispossessed in "Exiles" (p. 23). Conversely, there is the journey of "rediscovery" undertaken by those Africans who (like Awoonor, in "Desire," p. 24) seek to regain the wisdom of their ancestors. The most important refinement in Awoonor's use of the motif involves the journey as voyage, with its cluster of associated symbols, the canoe, the river, the estuary, the sea. The boat as a symbol of the journeying soul is an archetype in the works of such English Romantics and Moderns as Shelley, D. H. Lawrence, and Malcolm Lowry. We don't need to invoke the European tradition, though. The symbolism of the Ewe mythology of death and beyond is clearly the source of the boat image in many of Awoonor's poems:

The Journey Beyond

The howling cry through door posts
carrying boiling pots
ready for the feasters.
Kutsiami* the benevolent boatman;
when I come to the river shore
please ferry me across
I do not have tied in my cloth the
price of your stewardship.

*Kutsiami: In Ewe mythology Kutsiami is the ferryman on the river that divides the dead from the living. He ferries those who die into *avlime*. He must be paid for his services. That is why money is put in the dead person's coffin to enable him to pay Kutsiami. If the dead person carries no money and is therefore unable to pay him, his spirit will wander on this side of the river forever. (p. 41)

One of the most arresting things about Awoonor's poetry is its music, the quality which first interested me in his work, and which is signified in the dedication to *Night of My Blood:*

To the memory
of my grandmother
Afedomesi;
who set me
on the way of songs

Awoonor's heritage includes the oral tradition of African village songs, with their various communal forms, themes, and functions. A few of the poems in *Night of My Blood* seem to be faithful versions of the oral songs which Awoonor's people performed on ceremonial occasions. "The Purification" (p. 39) records a sacrifice to the sea-god in a time of poor fishing, and "A Dirge" strikes the authentic communal note:

Tell them, tell it to them
That we the children of Ashiagbor's house
Went to hunt; when we returned
Our guns were pointing to the earth,
We cannot say it; someone say it for us.
Our tears cannot fall.
We have no mouths to say it with.
We took the canoe, the canoe with the sandload
They say the hippo cannot overturn.
Our fathers, the hippo has overturned our canoe.
We come home
Our guns pointing to the earth.
Our mother, our dear mother,
Where are our tears, where are our tears?
Give us mouth to say it, our mother.
We are on our knees to you
We are still on our knees. (p. 63)

Awoonor's countryman and co-editor, Geormbeeyi Adali-Mortty, has written that Ewe song in general has a "vague, all pervasive sadness," which he attributes to the harshness of Ewe life.[5] Elegiac and ritual rhythms are a powerful presence in Awoonor's work, but so is the sound of ocean. He was born, he tells us, "at Keta (Ghana)—the flood town, with the sea in my ears."[6] And his rhythms also echo those of certain English poets, especially T. S. Eliot, with whom he shares an ear for cadences so memorable that even lines of obscure meaning haunt one's mind by virtue of their sound. Whatever their lineage or source, an impressive number of Awoonor's lines do sing, a quality which often makes the difference between good and mediocre poetry.

The structure of many of Awoonor's poems resembles certain features of traditional oral verse. Images, phrases, even whole passages in his poems of the early sixties are repeated in later works, especially in the two long poems which mark the main stages of his development, "I Heard a Bird Cry" and "Hymn to My Dumb Earth." His radio play "Lament" (in *Short African Plays*) is essentially a reassembly of passages from these and other poems. His practice, therefore, resembles that of folk art, which is liable to catalyze traditional pieces at each new performance. "I Heard a Bird Cry," in particular, achieves the effect of improvisation common to folk song, in the way it accumulates fable, refrain, proverbial folk wisdom, and ceremonial utterance. Many commentators on the oral traditions of Africa have noticed the random progression of tribal songs. Thus Kwabena Nketia on the recitative style in Akan poetry: "The delivery is usually fast, the emphasis being on the continual flow of utterances which need not be linked by an apparent intellectual thread, but which are united by their cumulative emotional effect."[7] Awoonor's poetry often achieves the illusion of this kind of spontaneity and a logical movement; in fact, it is usually intellectually coherent, having a sophisticated unity of symbol and theme. In his latest work, however, he has abandoned the linear (if apparently random) movement of "I Heard a Bird Cry" for the complex collages of "Hymn to My Dumb Earth" and *This Earth, My Brother.*

Song is not only the mode of much of Awoonor's poetry, it is also a theme and a value. One infers that the *act* of singing is in itself a triumph over adversity. The first poem in *Night of My Blood* establishes this view of the value of singing and relates it also to the prevailing theme of modern African literature (and of Awoonor's early work): the dispossession of Africans of their social heritage, and the forced implanting among them of European institutions and ideas:

My God of Songs Was Ill

Go and tell them that I crossed the river
While the canoes were still empty
And the boatman had gone away.
My god of songs was ill
And I was taking him to be cured.
When I went the fetish priest was away
So I waited outside the hut
My god of songs was groaning
Crying.
I gathered courage
I knocked on the fetish hut
And the cure god said in my tongue
"Come in with your backside"
So I walked in with my backside
With my god of songs crying on my head
I placed him on the still.
Then the bells rang and my name was called thrice
My god groaned amidst the many voices
The cure god said I had violated my god
"Take him to your father's gods"
But before they opened the hut
My god burst into songs, new strong songs
That I am still singing with him. (p. 22)

In this poem the old culture remains for Awoonor a source of renewed vitality despite the disappearance of mediating priests and beliefs.

Another feature of Awoonor's work illustrated in "My God of Songs Was Ill" is the communal voice which is created in most of his poems. This is another obvious influence of his heritage of oral song, and distinguishes his poetry from much that has been written by Western poets in our century. One of the characteristics of modernism in poetry is the introversion of the speaker, his sense of isolation (or alienation) amid the complexity and disorder of modern society and recent history. It has been remarked by more than one observer that whereas the Western writer speaks for himself, out of his own experience, and often with great difficulty, the African writer, like his ancestors, often speaks for his community. Today, though, he too has difficulty because of the shattering of communal traditions through the advent of modernism in Africa. Awoonor has defined this as the essential problem of contemporary Africa and of its writers: ". . . one invariably returns to a certain basic aspect, which is the technological advancement of Africa, and all the things that are added on to it: what are we going to do with some of the basic traditions of African life, African communal life, the general spirit that did motivate African societies long before the white man came? . . . one has to adjust oneself to the thinking, the way of life which has almost died, to marry it to this new technology."[8] The communal impulse informs much of Awoonor's verse and issues in a voice to which Ezekiel Mphahlele has attributed "the aura of a sage's words."[9]

It is interesting that Mphahlele, who has been one of the most persistent adversaries of negritude in African writing, has written an admiring and sympathetic introduction to *Night of My Blood*. Revulsion from the European influence in modern Africa, and a search for values in traditional African culture, form the subject of many of Awoonor's poems, as they formed the basis of the negritude movement. But his disgust with modernism and his yearning after the sustaining ethos of the shattered traditions seldom harden into doctrine and precept in Awoonor's work. Far from making the prescriptive statements of a negritude manifesto, Awoonor's is essentially a poetry of questions, indeed of *quest,* which is precisely the theme on which Mphahlele's introduction focuses. Awoonor's songs express some of the deepest agonies of recent African experience and while they may at times suggest the attitudes of the negritude school, they generally sustain their intelligence and quality as poems. In any case, we should entertain the critical axiom that one can disagree with the viewpoint implicit in a poem while continuing to admire the excellence of its poetry.

One of the European institutions superimposed on Africans, towards which Awoonor does maintain a well-defined attitude, is the Christianity purveyed by missionaries and their converts. Some of the best of Awoonor's early poems are powerful rejections and critiques of the Christian view. "Easter Dawn," one of the few poems from *Rediscovery* which I think Awoonor errs in excluding from *Night of My Blood,* rebukes the neglect of his ancestral gods as set against the flourishing of Christian ritual.[10] An early poem that *is* reprinted in the later volume says much about Awoonor's reaction to Christian teaching:

In My Sick Bed

> This flesh shall melt in the melting pot
> Of receding clay and the flesh shall peel off
> And be used to muffle the funeral drums.
> The lights are grey and the voices faint
> The buzzing flies ask soul searchers' questions
> Expecting answers
> Liars and hypocrites
> Who says there is a resting place elsewhere?
> It is here with us,
> Here with us in the sound of the fall of
> dust on coffin
> And in the priestly prayers of the communicants
> Not beyond, not beyond O Lord. (p. 26)

Here the imagery of a distinctly African scene is combined with echoes of the kind of medieval Christian meditation on sickness and death which reaches its finest expression in poems like Nashe's "Litany in Time of Plague" and Donne's "Hymn to God, My God in My Sickness." But the characteristic attitudes of the Christian meditation are significantly qualified. While the speaker acknowledges his mortal frailty and evokes the sense of despondency and squalor that attends sickness, he rejects the idea of an after life where all manner of things shall be well. "The priestly prayers of the communnicants" are valued as rituals of reverence and communion among the living mourners, not as a communion with a deity. Prayer—supplication—is a pervasive attitude in Awoonor's poetry, but rather than any abiding faith in God or gods it reflects the intensity of his distress, and his articulation of his people's anguish. Other powerful poems on Christianity and its influence in Africa include "The Cathedral" and "That Flesh is Heir To."

Two long, fine poems that followed *Rediscovery* represent the culmination of Awoonor's interest in the precolonial culture and history of his people. "I Heard a Bird Cry" is a poem of symbolic subtlety and considerable beauty. By turns mournful, prophetic, and hortative, it seems to move forward, twist, double back, leap forward again, conveying its meaning through motifs and gnomic utterance. The singer weeps for the desolation among his people and decides to seek regeneration in the neglected gods and rituals of his fathers. A vision of corruption in the modern African scene (which will be portrayed with greater bitterness in *This Earth, My Brother*) is followed by the account of a ceremony of sacrifice and supplication to the ancestors. The central motif of the bird is developed, and then a variation of Awoonor's familiar symbolism of canoe-river-quest is introduced. The general meaning of the symbolism of birds involves war, anarchy, and destruction in the prophet's country:

> There was a tree which died in the desert
> Birds came and built their nests in it.
> Funeral songs reached us on the village square.
>
> I shall weave new sisal ropes
> And kill two white cocks
> Whose blood will cleanse the stools. (p. 42)
>
> The desert river was dry
> Before the harmattan came
> And the storm wind does not
> Frighten the eagle. (p. 44)
>
> The swooping eagle does not give to its child.
> So the child must turn a beggar in the market place. (p. 47)
>
> The heroes, where are the war heroes?
> Did they smear themselves
> With the blood of fowls
> And are bellowing, bellowing
> Like wounded hippos? (p. 49)
>
> The swallow says
> It is the harmattan wind
> That chased him into the rafters of the rich (p. 49)
>
> Weaver birds came and ravaged my corn-field (p. 50)
>
> A cock has laid an egg by the river side
> But a hawk came and snatched it.
> What shall we do? (p. 51)

The key passages are exchanges between the crows, westernized mockers of those like the speaker who seek for nourishment in the dead past, and the vulture, who represents the latter:

> Those who stood around the ring laughed
> And said my feet had blundered
> And our hands have lost the cunning of the drums.
>
> We answered them, answered them
> That the crow asked the vulture
> You are an uneatable bird
> Why are you so full of your own importance? (p. 45)
>
> The vulture, it says
> Because helpers are not there
> That is why
> I have shorn my head
> Awaiting my funeral.
>
> My heart, be at rest
> For the vultures that came
> Shaking the rafters of your house
> Have flown away, flown far away,
> Towards the land of my forefathers.
> It was in the season of the burning feet,
> And the feast is ready for us. (p. 53)

Ultimately, I think the poem suggests the inadequacy of any of the birds (including the vulture) as menders of the torn society. Some are predators, some victims, other scaverngers. A true healing of the prophet's wasted country requires a steady focus on the realities of the present. (The refrain "Hush! I heard a bird cry" commands alertness at the same time that it directs our attention to the symbolism.) The poem accumulates more and more perceptions of violence, poverty, suffering, venality, gullibility, as it moves towards the resolution quoted above.

"Night of My Blood," which follows "I Heard a Bird Cry" in the volume to which it gives its title, is Awoonor's attempt to render a mythology of his people's past, of their origins and experience. The recounting of the Ewe migration many centuries ago from the interior to the coast of West Africa is elaborated in a vision of their character, their sufferings and yearnings. There are distant echoes in this poem of "The Journey of the Magi," and it is perhaps his interest in Eliot's work that led

Awoonor to use the Christian symbolism which startles one in "Night of My Blood," a poem whose theme is the dimly recalled past of a pagan people. Nevertheless, this technique issues in some lines of concentrated power and nuance:

> We walked from the beginning
> towards the land of sunset
> We were a band of malefactors
> and saints. (p. 54)

And the poem conveys a sense of the enormity of great historical movements—of the anonymous multitudes who suffered and vanished into the earth. In the European tradition, melancholy is an aberration of the individual. In "Night of My Blood," Kofi Awoonor evokes a tragic melancholy as the prevailing condition of his people.

The shape of Awoonor's work as it develops in *Night of My Blood* is through the early poems from *Rediscovery* towards the two long poems I have just discussed. I think that there is then some decline in quality in a number of the succeeding lyrics, until Awoonor's talent crests again in three more long poems at the end of the volume. There is also a shift form his interest in the ancestral traditions to a concern with events in West Africa in the late sixties, a movement towards present realities which is already implicit in "I Heard a Bird Cry." One assumes that Awoonor would assent to this last remark, given the biographical note in *Messages,* the anthology of Ghanaian poets which he co-edited:

> Kofi Awoonor's early poetry—published under the name of George Awoonor-Williams—marks his apprecenticeship as a poet; this period saw him using and translating traditional poetry. The poems of this period—some of which are included in Beier and Moore's *Modern Poetry from Africa*—capture the songs and the funeral dirges of the Anlos. What may be described as the second phase of his development is marked by the poetry of *Night of My Blood,* and the poems which are included in this volume. He says of this phase: 'I have gone through the trauma of growth, anger, love and the innocence and nostalgia of my personal dreams. These are beyond me now. Not anger, or love, but the sensibility that shaped and saw them as communal acts of which I am only the articulator. Now I write out of my renewed anguish about the crippling distresses of my country and my people, of death by guns, of death by disease and malnutrition, of the death of friends

whose lives held so much promise, of the chicanery of politics and the men who indulge in them, of the misery of the poor in the midst of plenty . . .'[11]

Awoonor's less successful poetry includes not only some of the "apprentice" poems from *Rediscovery*—such as several wordy love lyrics—but also some later, shorter imitations of "I Heard a Bird Cry." Poems such as "More Messages" (p. 65) and "At the Gates" (p. 68) rehash the themes and motifs of earlier works without achieving the earlier intensity and coherence. In these poems and a few others, I think that Awoonor abuses two elements of his style which he practices elsewhere to good effect: his musical facility and his taste for oblique utterance. Occasionally he indulges in sound without regard to substance, and he is sometimes gratuitously cryptic.

Three of the last poems in *Night of My Blood* show, however, a renewed and increased strength in Awoonor's abilities as a poet. "Lament of the Silent Sister" is an elegy for Christopher Okigbo, the Nigerian poet who was killed in 1967 while fighting on the side of the Biafran forces. "This Earth, My Brother" and "Hymn to My Dumb Earth" are also concerned with the recent violence and despair in West African nations. The last poem, especially, resembles Awoonor's novel, *This Earth, My Brother,* in technique as well as in its pessimistic interpretation of the current West African scene. Donatus Nwoga has accurately described the mood of Awoonor's recent work: ". . . he still carries a tone of tragedy and confusion born of his long-distance look at himself and his home. The poetry of West Africa has deepened its mood of dismay, of fearful concern for communities that appear to have no way out of a catastrophic future, in spite of harsh experiences already undergone."[12] The pity, the terror, the dismay of Awoonor's reaction to the present condition of his homeland, seem to have renewed his creative energies, for the long poems toward the end of *Night of My Blood* are among the best in the volume.

In "Lament of the Silent Sister" the persona is female, one of the chorus, evidently, from Okigbo's poem "Lament of the Silent Sisters." She experiences a visitation, as though in a dream, from the slain man (perhaps on the night of his death). Okigbo appears to her as a Christ-figure, sacrifice and redeemer. The opening movement of the elegy is rich in images of youth, fertility, birth, and death, in tones of awe and grief:

> That night he came home, he came unto me
> at the cold hour of the night
> Smelling of corn wine in the dawn dew.

> He stretched his hand and covered my forehead.
> There was a moon beam sparking rays in particles.
> The drummer boys had got themselves a goat.
> The din was high in the wail of the harvest moon.
> The flood was up, gurgling through the fields
> Birth waters swimming in floods of the new blood.
> He whispered my name in a far echo
> Sky-wailing into a million sounds
> across my shores. His voice still bore
> the sadness of the wanderer.
> To wail and die in a soft lonely echo
> That echo I heard long ago. (p. 74)

The speaker remembers the living man and her previous immaturity in relation to him. Imagery of birth and of sexual initiation merges with the symbolism of canoe and river as she recalls an incomplete experience of redemption in her acquaintance with Okigbo:

> Into the bright evening I rushed
> Crying I have found him I have found him.
> He stood there rustling in the wind
> The desire to go was written large upon his forehead.
> I was not ready for his coming.
> I was not ready for his loneliness,
> for his sad solitude against the rustling wind. (p. 75)

The arousing of love and vision in her were insufficient, falling short of the commitments of speech and action that Okigbo made in the "howling wind" of the Nigerian debacle. The poem then returns to the visitation described in the opening lines, and new the speaker's redemption is consummated, again in sexual imagery:

> He was erect like the totem pole of his household
> He burned and blazed for an ending.
> Then I was ready. As he pierced my agony
> with his cry, my river burst into flood.
> My shores reeled and rolled
> to the world's end, where they say
> at the world's end the graves are green. (p. 77)

The evidence of the speaker's redemption is the breaking of her silence into the eloquence of the elegy itself, the first fruit of her achieved sense of total relation to the world.

"This Earth, My Brother" is in several respects a poem of extremities. Anguish and bitter despair take the poetry at times to the verge of incoherence. The modern warfare in post-colonial Africa is linked to the tribal slaughters of the past. Ritual sacrifice is understood as an expression of sexual impulse. Even the attitudes of hope and prayer are considered potential sources of violence. As if in rejection of the prospect of redemption envisioned in the preceding poem, the figure of a redeemer is conjured up only to give way to a graphic account of a massacre of prisoners:

> They led them unto the mound
> In a game of blindman's bluff
> They tottered to lean on the sandbags
> Their backs to the ocean
> that will bear them away.
> The crackling report of brens
> and the falling down;
> a shout greeted them
> tossing them into the darkness.
>
> and my mountains reel and roll
> to the world's end. (p. 81)

Upon the beauty and affirmation of "Lament of the Silent Sister," "This Earth, My Brother" follows hard like a shriek of the damned.

Awoonor's novel of the same title is a study of squalor and injustice in contemporary Ghana. *This Earth, My Brother* portrays impartially the ignorance and corruption of the British colonial officials before Ghanaian independence and the ignorance and corruption of the African government and people since. It is merely a question of whose ignorance is most damaging and whose corruption sustains some semblance of social cohesion. Sexual and marital failures among the characters mirror the larger social deterioration of the country. Awoonor's technique in this novel—interspersing the fictional narrative with symbolic and highly lyrical prose-poems which record the protagonist's memories and dreams—resembles after a fashion his technique in "Hymn to My Dumb Earth," the last major poem in *Night of My Blood*. The themes of the two works are also similar.

"Hymn to My Dumb Earth" is a poem of even larger dimensions than "I Heard a Bird Cry," and also incorporates pieces of shorter lyrics. The intricate symbolic movement of the earlier work has been replaced by an extraordinary collage of voices and images. Among the voices are those of the clown, the prophet, and of Awoonor himself as, variously, the cosmopolitan African, the self-conscious poet, the adult recalling his childhood. Ghanaian "cultural activists" and turncoats are juxtaposed with American Black Power radicals and jazz musicians. Nkrumah himself appears, as do Okigbo (again) and a number of less famous persons. Scriptural phrases and Marxist slogans, Sunday School hymns and tribal folk proverbs—all are presented as implicit comments on one another. Snatches of English poetry appear. The influence of Eliot which can be discerned for better and for worse in Awoonor's work, is finally brought completely under control:

> Oh Son of man.
> The brigade major held a conference;
> fear death by guns. (p. 90)

The ominous esoterica of the English poet is simultaneously parodied and converted into a pointed remark about the sad facts of West Africa in the late sixties. Indeed, "Hymn to My Dumb Earth" seems more like a chronicle on ruin than a shoring of fragments. Awoonor's lyric eloquence is toughened and extended in this poem through a new skill at irony:

> What has not happened before?
> An animal has caught me,
> it has me in its claws
> Someone, someone, save
> Save me, someone,
> for I die.
> What a wounded name.
> At the Central Committee today
> a vote was taken on democratic centralism.
> It will be written next week
> into the Constitution.
> Everything comes from God. (pp. 86-87)

The refrain of "I Heard a Bird Cry" was a signal of revelation. The refrain of "Hynm to My Dumb Earth"—"everything comes from God"—is a pious cliche that becomes an increasingly bad joke as the poem piles up its exhibits of sorrow, sordidness and death in a kaleidoscope of irony and lyricism.

Night of My Blood shows a development of craft, of scope, and of thought in Kofi Awoonor's poetry. His work achieves an extraordinary fusion of traditional African and modern English cadences, techniques, and themes. I hope that his talent survives the devastation of the society to which he feels such a deep relationship. While the earth is dumb, the singer delivers his song, however bleak and painful.

NOTES

1. *Rediscovery* was published under the name George Awoonor-Williams; his later books bear the name Kofi Awoonor.
2. Page numbers refer to *Night of My Blood* (New York: Doubleday, 1971), from which all my quotations of Awoonor's poetry are taken. *Night of My Blood* reprints as about a quarter of its volume, about two-thirds of the poems in *Rediscovery*.
3. "Reminiscences of Earlier Days," in *The Writer in Modern Africa*, ed., Per Wästberg (Uppsala: The Scandinavian Institute of African Studies, 1968), pp. 112–18.
4. "Kofi Awoonor," in *African Writers Talking/A Collection of Interviews*, ed., Dennis Duerden and Cosmo Pieterse (London: Heinemann, 1972), p. 30.
5. "Ewe Poetry," in *Introduction to African Literature*, ed., Ulli Beier (Evanston: Northwestern UP, 1967), p. 4.
6. Note in *Rediscovery* (Ibadan: Mbari, 1964), p. 4.
7. "Akan Poetry," in *Introduction to African Literature*, ed., Ulli Beier, p. 25.
8. "Kofi Awoonor," in *African Writers Talking*, p. 30.
9. "Introduction" to *Night of My Blood*, p. 9.
10. "Easter Dawn" is probably more readily available to Western readers in *Modern Poetry from Africa*, Revised, ed. Gerald Moore and Ulli Beier (Harmondsworth: Penguin, 1968), p. 103.
11. *Messages/Poems from Ghana*, ed., Kofi Awoonor and G. Adali-Mortty (London: Heinemann, 1971), p. 183.
12. "West Africa," *The Journal of Commonwealth Literature* 7 (December 1972), p. 29.

KWESI BREW: THE POETRY OF STATEMENT AND SITUATION

Edwin Thumboo

Most of Kwesi Brew's principal interests are retailed in "Our Palm-Tree Strength"[1]

> And still I sit here in the dust
> Struggling to understand
> The world and its words
> And so I have sometimes cast
> A hopeful glance over the shoulders of those
> Whose hoes have helped
> A friend to till a thorny ground
> And wondered whether to look
> In fear upon the past or to rejoice;
> To rejoice that we have achieved so much
> That so much has escaped
> The eyes of the gods who hold
> The rod of punishment;
> That the red-clay kitchens
> Of our ancestral homes still
> Teem with the feasts of the year. (p. 62)

While the writing is not notable, we are nevertheless struck by a certain old-fashioned dignity much in keeping with the virtues adumbrated: a strong desire to understand, to follow the example of those who are charitable, and an abiding "faith in humanity." Brew is conservative, and though this reduces the excitement of his poetry, it saves him from excesses. As we shall see, even when his language sins, the sins are of a predictable kind, falling close to the diction of the Hymnal.

"The Shadow of Laughter" which not only provides the title for his collection, but stands as the introductory poem to the volume, is less declamatory. The start is dramatic:

> No—do not frown at me,
> while these sweet words tumble . . . (p. 1)

119

Brew seeks ancestral dispensation for his new freedom and individuality.[2] It is out of freedom that joy shall emerge, shall have the strength to break through "the stupid restraints of a decent world." He believes the world has taken after "saddened men" and is therefore hostile to the true impulses of life. As a consequence of the restraints

> We fear the looks in the eyes of our old men,
> Where they sit in the corners
> Of their crumbling huts
> Casting tremulous looks
> At the loud crashing waves.
> For in their hearts
> Rages a storm of tossing surfs,
> And the battered canoes

These attitudes define Brew's position. While they don't wholly explain the main business of his poetry, they tell us what not to expect. Modern life is non-heroic. The old battles with the elements, the unflinching sacrifices are absent, perhaps because the same opportunities do not exist, or if they do, no longer offer the same uncomplicated challenge. Perhaps, again, some acceptable malaise has crept in. Brew is unusually honest and doesn't pretend the twentieth century didn't happen, or that the past can be recovered intact, or that it was glorious. (You never catch him wearing his African heart upon his modern sleeve.)

The essential elements of traditional belief remain. The characteristics of the African personality have not been disturbed. The continuum between life and death persists. "Ancestral Faces" (p. 52) is a specific instance.[3] It is "the god of my fathers" who calls the poet in "Through the Forest," where the physical presence is unmistakable.

> Through the forest
> Whitened by the moon
> Come the distant rattles;
> The pulse of the night,
> The pulse of the day.
>
> I hear them
> The rattles;
> Masculine vibrations
> Centuries old. (p. 53)

Brew, however, does not surrender to the past, an awkwardness difficult to avoid were the past resurrected too vigorously. The case of Awoonor-

Williams amply demonstrates what can happen when a poet is denied responsibility by having themes thrust upon him.

The respect for ancestors has other rarifications. Their role is not purely spiritual. "The wisdom of our fathers' is a familiar phrase. It represents a whole set of values which exercise an unusual tyranny. Wisdom is a subtle kind of precedence, a most persuasive form of moral or religious injuction. It is the application of principles proceeding from accumulated experiences. When you come to think of it, wisdom is really impersonal. Brew warns us:

> So look not for wisdom
> And guidance
> In their speech, my beloved.
> Let the same fire
> Which chastened their tongue,
> Into silence,
> Teach us—teach us.   ("The Search," p. 26)

While the last line is over-insistent, even shrill, the message is clear. Wisdom has to be personally acquired, without outside help. Incidentally, it is interesting, though not surprising, that wisdom is associated with chastening, a shaping of powers through punishment, the imposition of discipline. It would be a pretty simple business to suffer for a period and then reap the benefits. But the grip on reality constantly threatens to slip.

> When we dream of what has gone before
> And what is to come after;
> When the sun comes up over the hills in the mornings
> And sets the way it rose with the moon and stars;
> When at last we hang up our weapons upon our mud walls
> And weep with joy because the battle is over and won . . .
> Do we know indeed what has gone before
> And what is to come after?   ("Questions of Our Time," p. 64)

This stress on the individual's need to renew his conviction, to re-establish his certitude, is responsible for the concreteness of Brew's poetry. It leads to the almost relentless disclosure of his subject. His poems do not have the transparency of Okigbo's or the mercurial escape of thought into image we occasionally notice in Okara's. Brew's poems are, with few exceptions, related to specific situations.

Moreover, his mind is essentially sympathetic and gentle, and civilized, animated by a near-Christian charity. His vigour is of an unusual kind, powerful but non-violent. Few of his images startle or flash. Their effectiveness derives from an apt illumination.

This fits the view of poetry implicit in his work. Brew's is the poetry of situation. He is confident that if disclosed properly, the elements of a situation have their own convincing power. A poet chips away and so lays bare the situation, as a first requirement, and then proceeds to generate out of the other sinews of language, important, but supplementary, meaning.

> When your call came
> I was not at home:
> I had gone abroad
> To look for herbs,
> Not for today's happiness
> But for the troubles of tomorrow.
> Back home I am now blamed
> That I was not here
> When your call came.   ("When Your Call Came," p. 10)

Here the poetry is in the anticipation gradually built up by the unfolding event. We feel that things are heading for a climax of sorts, though there is little in the phrasing itself to contribute tension. The language is pared down, left in essential simplicity.

The strategy of allowing the situation to come through forcefully, is based on a special attitude to language. Each word remains firmly denotative. "When Your Call Came," reads like a translation into English, as if demonstrating the truth of Okara's claim that the cultural impediments of language are not easily translatable, that one gets only a basic, as against a restlessly suggestive, meaning. We feel that we can trust the words to stand firmly in line, without the slightest danger of mischief. The syntax is simple, though the simplicty is, paradoxically, a kind of sophistication.4 It is there to supply a particular version of things, solid and faithful. There are no procedures to discuss or explicate, no unusual features, no metaphor or simile. If we need to probe, it is into the situation, the emotional content, and not the language. Once the poet's general approach is known, the kind of criticism suitable for concentrated poetry has little to offer. Post-Empsonian readers have come to expect ambiguity, levels of meaning, parallel responses to denotative and connotative meanings, a poetry in which the whole exceeds the parts, because a whole range of elements belonging to words are brought into significant relationship. Brew's poems generally neglect these elements. With few exceptions, his interests are served without them. He sacrifices a number of powerful agencies, the use of sophisticated syntax and the intensities provided by images, just to name two. I am not suggesting that Brew invariably ignores the connotative possibilities, or that he is a *simple* poet; merely that at times he successfully does away with them. And when he does so, the "normal" expectations of what a poem should be, how it should work, will not help us understand the life of the poem. The power in "When Your Call Came" depends firmly on the non-aggressiveness of language. Poetry ceases to be a raid into the inarticulate, ceases to throw up metaphors to clutch new areas of experience.

Brew returns to this method in a number of poems, and to suggest what was added to this basic procedure is to provide a description of his mature style. I propose to examine "The Two Finds" (p. 21) and "The Heart's Anchor" (p. 56). The first of these poems depicts a situation of pure, uncomplicated feeling.

> I pursued her through the forest
> And along the lonely paths of my heart,
> At last I found the aggrey beads
> I gave her, thrown carelessly
> On the banks of the River Volta.
> I wept for the memories that had
> Been cast away.
>
> I came back home, and found her,
> Lying fast asleep
> On my bed!
> Did she know I had pursued her?
> Was my effort worthwhile, I asked,
> And bent to kiss her on the lips.

This is not even confessional. Freed from restless associations and reduced to their fundamentals, the worlds function directly. This influences the way we treat the lines. We do not impute any untoward sexuality, nor find cause for discomfort. Brew discloses feeling—"I wept" he says—without shame or shudder. That usual, and at times hypocritcal, division between public and private, between feelings displayable and those considered *infra dig,* fails to erect itself. We get a direct conversion of feeling into words and gestures.

But neither "When Your Call Came" nor "The Two Finds" are outstanding poems of their kind. Only in "The Heart's Anchor" does the mode achieve a remarkable success. The language aids the drift of the poem by gathering a dignity, an austerity reminiscent of the Psalms.

> I have arrived at last, O my Lord
> At your shrine;
> The songs you asked me to sing
> I have sung them all
> On the desolate sands of my journey.

The tone indicates prayer, incantation even, a direct and nobly simple address of deity. The eventual drama is contained in "I have arrived *at last* . . ." He has performed the tasks, sung the songs "On the desolate sands of my journey" and received signs of coming fulfilment, but soon realizes that the peace so fervently sought is still beyond his reach. There are no hints of hysteria—Brew never shakes his fist—though the disappointment is all the more heavily felt by not being made much of. The difficulty of securing an abiding faith recurs in "Lest We Should Be the Last" (p. 51) and "Unfaithful Faith" (p. 58). The procedure, substantially that of direct statement, describes a quest in the first poem while the second is a lament for enlightenment withheld.

But Brew, in "The Heart's Anchor" at any rate, does not deny himself the contributions of connotative meaning, or the metamorphoses of key words. It is "shrine" that dominates the movement in stanza one. We recognize and without hesitation accept its exclusively religious meaning. And this conditions our understanding of "arrived," "journey," "songs," and "desolate sands," leading us to the religiousity in stanza two.

> The morning dew filled
> The chambers of my hair
> And I felt the crown of your hand on my head.

The dew, a conventional image of spiritual agency, brings blessing; this *"crown* of your hand" in the last line is, universally, a blessing. We have, then, a clearly established religious context to provide for the doubling of significances.

> I have arrived O my Lord at your shrine.
> I have done the penance you ordered;
> But the peace you promised me stays
> In your heart—beyond my reach.

He has "arrived" by completing the journey, but also, what is important for our appreciation of the final disappointment, attained to a higher spiritual state. The whole tone and structure of the first two lines require them to be read as statements of fact. He has fulfilled what was prescribed. We are at the dramatic heart of the poem. The disappointment, as noticed earlier, is all the more acute for its quiet implicitness.

The comprehensiveness of such poetry is limited. While he draws our attention to things we may otherwise miss, the emotional range is narrow. This poses certain dangers and problems. It is not always possible to decide whether the failure of a poem is on account of its language or feebleness of material, or Brew's failure to distinguish the ordinary from the profound.

> I am now too old to look back.
> The urgent future faces me
> And cuts from my sight the end
> That should inevitably come.
> The task that has been assigned to me
> Remains unfinished and almost insurmountable.
> Is it fear of the wasteland at my back
> That keeps me looking ahead,
> Or the lame struggling will to do the work?
> Am I past the middle of the river
> And therefore must go on?   ("The Middle of the River," p. 42)

There is little of interest here. The whole situation is a cliche and Brew does nothing to dispel its triteness. The language fails to shape itself and, consequently, remains pretty ordinary, innocent of any feeling of tragedy, of large undertakings unresolved. The second and concluding stanzas with its "fitful yearning," lacks the crisp force of Tennyson's "Ulysses"—though in that poem the means utilized are clearly of a different order. In Brew's piece the tension, the heoism is limp. The lines read like notes and speculations for a poem. Another case of the simple-obvious is "Nickname": it need not have been written at all.

One other limitation is the degree to which the approach loses its virtues when dealing with a complex relationship. When the drama ceases to be located primarily in the situation, or where it is no longer possible to identify it with a situation, Brew is less successful. This is the case with "The Harvest of Our Life" (p. 43) in which the action is focused on the changing, developing consciousness of man.

This, Brew's biggest poem, is meant to carry his central reflections. But it is nowhere near an incisive statement. The start of the poem does suggest the basic movement.

> If this is the time
> To master my heart
> Do so!
> Do so now!
> As the clouds float
> Home to their rain-drenched
> Caverns behind the hills.

The clouds retreat, an imagistic confirmation that the movement is propitious. We feel in the presence of an important beginning, of what proves to be the heart's initiation into disciplines and adult intimacies.

The second stanza contains a similar emphasis. What matter, from the point of thematic development, are the first four lines.

> If this is the time
> To master my heart,
> Let me fall an easy victim
> To the pleasures that you hold to my lips
> When the duiker
> Lingers along the pool to drink
> And the ailing leopard
> Turns its dry unbelieving snout away;
> When the dew-drops dry
> Unnoticed on the sinews of the leaf
> And the soft paddling duck
> Webs its way
> Through the subtle
> Entanglement of weeds
> Along the river Prah.

The surrender is expanded and invested with a mixture of tender, severe, and explosive images to reflect the duality of the moment, its gentleness as well as the surprise it has to store. The "ailing leopard" is evocative, one of those images which somehow continues to fascinate and expand both within context and when contemplated alone. But thematic continuity is affected by images which prove too successful and superior. They draw our responses without including a renewal of contact with the main business of the poem. The greater the fascination, the surer the dislocation. The contrast they offer to Brew's low-pressure poems is vivid. Brew hasn't the technique to mix the two "styles."

The second movement commences with stanza three.

O, I remember the songs
You sang that night,
And the whirl of raffia skirts;
The speechless pulsations of living bones.
O, I remember the songs you sang
Recounting what has gone before
And what is ours beyond
The tracks of our thoughts and feet.

Obviously the song and dance recount tribal lore. But clarity is not forthcoming. Either Brew's language has changed its mode of operation or he fails to achieve control. We do not have quick accesses to the poem. The voice of the poem, the "I," is unable to arrange a fluent accommodation of theme and language. We want, but are not able, to enter into the world of the poem. Apart from this, the fourth line proves puzzling. Why "living bones"? The picture evoked of skeletons dancing, is hardly rhythmic or edifying. Why, again, *"speechless* pulsations"? Brew requires one narrow quality of the word and gets it, but leaves a number of other painful associations unsuppressed.

The fourth stanza offers in miniature the knowledge provided with initiation.

You sang of beautiful women
(The kangaroo-jumps of their youthful breasts)
Flirting with sportive spirits
Red-eyed, with red-lips, hoary-red
With quaffing of frequent libations;
You sang of feasts and festivals . . .
And the loading of the dice;
Why the barndog barked
At the moon as she sang
And why the mouse dropped the pearl-corn
From its teeth and stood forced-humble
With the soft light of fear in its eyes.

It seems hardly possible for a poet as sensitive as Brew to allow that link between kangaroo and breasts. But even discounting that, we still have a curious mixture of sloppy phrasing—"sportive spirits," "hoary-red"—with some pretty interesting stuff.

In the stanza that follows, the initiate reaches a higher state of "consciousness." He sees "a sheen of light" and becomes aware of her with

127

"hair like the dark eyes of an eagle/over the affairs of men." From this point the reader finds it hard to keep in touch with the poem. We suspect some symbolic impact but are unable to identify it. The poetry, to a large extent, defeats itself by excluding our understanding.

> And yet the river rolled on
> And passed over rocks;
> While sand in the bed
> Bearing the burden of rotten wood
> Twigs, grass—a flower—the breath
> Of the soul and the bones of thousands
> Who should have lived
> To fight a war for this or that,
> And this or that a ruse
> To deceive the mover of the move,
> And the mover of the move
> Always moved by an uncertainty.
>
> And yet to fight
> And yet to conquer;
> This was the badge we bore
> On the pale texture of our hearts.
> And yet to fight
> And yet to conquer.
>
> The sea-gulls blow
> Like paper-pieces over the hard blue sea
> And yet we live to conquer.
> So we talked of wars
> With their women
> And they wept at the foot of the hills.
>
> And the waters rolled on.
> And what was old was new
> And what was new never came to stay.
> But to skim the gates of change;
> Forever new; forever old and new;
> Once-upon-a-time,
> Never the same,
> Always at last the same.

Unless we provide a specific value for "river," we are hard put to get any meaning going. And it is difficult not to be arbitrary. Moreover, what does the "war" relate to? Who is the "mover"? These are crude questions, crude but necessary. The compression is too severe, links are suppressed, and ideas remain embryonic. Despite the Keatsian echo, the last six lines do suggest, however unsatisfactorily, the reservoir of power and renewal available to the initiate. The apparent paradox of an ancient yet potent cultural force which each generation has to rediscover is something we understand. But this does not mean that the foreground of ideas leading to it can be sketchily developed or taken for granted. Without them the poetry remains inaccessible.

This section is the metaphysical core of the poem. It comes between the appearance of the dark lady and the battle for her possession. Had the poetry not locked its meaning so severely, we might have risen to the climactic, almost sexual resolution. Perhaps the "lady of situations," represents a life-force, a completion to experience, a final encounter to round off the initiation. The structural arrangement of the poem points to this.

> But those who slept with her in those mud huts
> (Arrows in their grips
> And bows on their shoulders)
> Have crawled away soft-bellied,
> Into hollow chambers
> Along the road;
> Lined their walls
> With smooth white stones;
> Abandoned the shade
> That sheltered their peace
> And call that peace of mind
> Now floating away with the clouds
> As peace—
> That passes understanding.

The initiation, understandably, brings change. Sheltered peace is abandoned in favour of positive action.

Brew knows the importance of linking the various movements, especially in a poem of some length. The evidence is there. Lines and phrases recall earlier parts. But this is not really helpful as these parts themselves are imperfectly enunciated. What we miss is inner organization of the kind of Okigbo's poems, where aspects of the themes develop usefully within a framework. We are able to correlate our responses. "The Harvest of Our Lives" lacks this firm structure. There is little hope for a reader unless he is willing to devote an excessive amount of time to expand a phrase here and there and generally get the lines going. But many would say this exceeds what can properly be expected of readers, or that it would be altogether an impertinent undertaking.

Brew is capable of shaping his intentions imagistically, a technique essential to the long poem. Images can be developed, patterned, syncopated, used judiciously, to reinforce statement. Not merely by telling us more about what is happening, but by bringing in cogent implications. An example from Brew is "Waiting":

> When I came to you;
> The door was shut
> I knocked;
> And you opened the door.
> For a shimmering moment
> That stars shone
> Over our heads
> The grass swayed in the wind;
> For they knew
> You and I
> Have touched the rims of the sun together
> In the waters of the Black Nile.
>
> You uttered the word
> And the sun told me
> It was too late in the day,
> So you must leave.   (p. 24)

The full emotional explosion accompanying his lover's opening the door, that "shimmering moment," is imaged in the marked upheaval of star and wind. Nature bestows her approval, providing a cosmic grandeur, the immensity of some unutterably profound communion of synoptic powers. The performance indicates an imaginative capacity of a high order. We feel compelled to understand, to receive the quickly multiplying life.

"The Sea Eats Our Land" (p. 41) contains a further example. Erosion gradually destroys Keta, a town "built on a narrow strip of land between a lagoon and the sea." (See *The Shadow of Laughter,* p. 41). The destruction, also seen as punishment for some spiritual ommission, is conveyed simply.

> Here stood our ancestral home:
> The crumbling wall marks the spot.
> Here a sheep was led to slaughter

130

To appease the gods and stone
For faults which our destiny
Has blossomed into crimes.
There my cursed father once stood
And shouted to us, his children,
To come back from our play
To our evening meal and sleep.

The clouds were thickening in the red sky
At night had charmed
A black power in the pounding waves.

Here once lay Keta.
Now her golden girls
Erode into the arms
Of strange towns.

The foreboding is carried by the middle stanza. It is the waves which
destroyed Keta. They have been strengthened by the gathering power of
darkness. The image itself is carefully placed to prepare us for the
destruction.
  Brew's images can be very fetching

    Gamilli's arm has broken into buds . . .

or have a certain telling precision:

    . . . these tribal marks of the world.

or manage a terrific capture of feeling in

    O there are flowers in Tamale
    That smell like fire.

But there are also disastrous lapses:

    But a vision of your lyrical bosom
    Floats like a ship on the storm
    Of my delirious mind.

Even the suspicion of Freudian undertones fails to retrieve the picture.
Heroic proportions do not always secure plain sailing. Brew is guilty of

exaggeration, as when in the lines preceding those quoted, he calls the eyes "Oasis of ecstasy."

The flow of his poetry is at times disturbed by a "softness" of phrasing. We find, in "The Lonely Traveller," (p. 33) for instance, "sweet energy," "priceless peace," "ethereal bliss," "shores of eternity," and "genial mists of courage," all within seven lines. The two final lines are, "Meandering his weary way/On the green and golden hills of Africa!" These vestiges of weaker impulses of English poetry, include:

> With his faith as his spear
> And his past as his shield
> He battled the bondage of bludgeons.   (p. 33)

It is not easy to decide whether the defect is one of sensibility or sentiment. Ghanaian poets frequently suffer a lapse in vital creative usage by trusting the surface of a phrase, taking its power for granted. Is it because their longer familiarity with the language bred the kind of contempt which results in an inability to suspect the obvious? It is too prevalent to be explained away as loss of creative pressure.

Brew's style does of course include other contrivances. The most interesting ones are based on syntactical structures and a diction close to proverbial expression. A simple instance is furnished by the following lines from "Through the Forest":

> Through the forest
> Whitened by the moon
> Come the distant rattles;
> Come the beat of a pulse
> The pulse of the night,
> The pulse of the day.   (p. 53)

The pairs of common structures help to concentrate the elements they gather. The first evokes a feeling of the earth alive, rolling in "her diurnal round," and "distant rattles" which are akin to Wordsworth's "ghostly language of the earth." The pairs are linked by "pulse" to suggest, in combination, the primal life of the earth.

A more calculated use of structure is the balance of alternatives:

> You sang of beautiful women . . .
> The red blood-line across the necks
> Of sacrificial sheep;
> Of acceptance and refusal of gifts;

> Of sacrifice offered and withheld.
> Of good men and their lot;
> Of good name and its loss; of the die cast
> And the loading of the dice.   (p. 44)

The repetition concentrates our attention on the fights which come with initiation. But "The Harvest of our Life" is a long poem. Extensive use of the device can prove boring, and give the impression of the same point made repeatedly.

Brew sought suppleness in order to achieve a comprehensive poetic statement. It was, moreover, essential to the life of his staple line.

> And soon, soon the fires,
> The fires will begin to burn,
> The hawk will flutter and turn
> On its wings and swoop for the mouse,
> The dog will run for the hare,
> The hare for its little life.   ("The Dry Season," p. 38)

The common syntactical structures and the repetition of words across the lineation, condense phrase and line to produce one dominant suggestion to conclude the poem: this is the dry season and nature is at her most cruel. The repetition of "soon" and "fires" carries a suppressed sympathy. And the rhymes "burn" and "turn" connect their subjects: "fire" and "hawk," both mercilessly destructive. The developing tragedy is epitomized in the hawk's flutter, turn and swoop. The fittest survive, the strong consume the weak.

It was suggested earlier that "The Vulture" read very much like an expanded proverb. Brew frequently pitches his diction in such a way that we feel he is either translating out of traditional sources or modifying them.

> The broken bone cannot be made whole!
> The strong had sheltered in their strength
> The swift had sought life in their speed
> The crippled and the tired heaped out of the way.
> Onto the ant hills . . .

These lines give, in quick firm strokes, the recent state of things in Ghana. The first tells of despair, the second selfishness, the third a loss of courage, the fourth, death of charity. That proverbial ring supplies a solid basis to the dissatisfaction.

133

Kwesi Brew's work has not received the attention it deserves. His poetry is neither flamboyant, nor does it provoke spectacular analysis. Nor is it readily enlisted to support large and urgent purposes. The poetry is seldom hurried, preferring to move with a confident patience. Few of his poems are memorable in the way that some poems are, staying in the mind as an incantatory whole, independent of the printed text. Their virtues are on the quiet side. These are perhaps reason for the absence of any really serious discussion of his work, which is a pity, as it is close in spirit to much traditional poetry and could provide insights for a possible rapprochment between English and what the vernaculars have to offer.

NOTES

1. Quotations from Brew's poems are taken from *The Shadow of Laughter* (London 1968). The number in brackets after the title gives the page reference.
2. Lewis Nkosi has a useful comment on the growth of "individual vision":
    > In many areas of Africa the destruction of traditional African values by European imperialism and the concomitant Christianization of Africans has drastically reversed the role of the poet or artist in the community.
    > First there has been a change in the social organization which has resulted in more emphasis being placed on the individual rather than the communal. Hence the art of communal celebration is being replaced by lonely artistic creation—by an individual vision, so to speak. For the first time the African Artist is confronting the community as an individual (even an alienate individual) whose vision may not conform to that of the statesman, the political or the religious leader. (*Home and Exile,* London 1965, p. 104).

    "The Search" (p. 26) is a poetic statement of a similar conclusion.
3. Both George Awoonor-Williams (in the interview by Robert Serumaga reported in *Cultural Events,* No. 29, April 1967, p. IV) and Ezekiel Mphahlele ("The Language of African Literature, English Poetry in Africa," *Africa: A Handbook,* p. 400) maintain that Brew "helps us visualize the various elements that are in ancestral worship and which symbolize a whole way of life."
4. Gerald Moore in reviewing Okyeame, No. 1 (1961) in *Black Orpheus,* No. 10, p. 66, says "Kwesi Brew's language has weight and a kind of held-back rhythm which keeps the reader's attention." Moore adds that Brew has a "vivid descriptive gift" and quotes the opening lines of "A Plea for Mercy" (p. 55) in support:
    > We have come to your shrine to worship—
    > We the sons of the land.
    > The naked cowherd has brought
    > The cows safely home,
    > And stands silent with his bamboo flute
    > Wiping the rain from his brow

    We need to qualify the vividness by saying that it results from carefully picked and accurately described details.

ATUKWEI OKAI AND HIS POETIC TERRITORY

Kofi Anyidoho

I, Oshamraku Atukwei, standing
   before your shrine declare
   myself by appointment the
   organ-grinder to God and Man.
Reality is responsible for my subconscious . . .
your songs are responsible for my
inner tensions . . . my dreams
are in pain . . . though you hear no
screams.[1]

In these words Atukwei Okai announces his arrival upon the poetic scene in Africa. He seems to be in no doubt about his qualifications and the nature of his calling. He is ordained by the creator-god. He is not just a poet but a poet-cantor with a priest-like function. His songs may start from his subconscious, but their burden is founded on reality, and it is a disturbing reality which fills his soul with inner tensions. Part of the reality, he suggests elsewhere, consists in a breakdown in communication between God and man:

> The switch-board in God's chamber is jammed!
> Walls. Walls. Please, be still . . .   (*Oath*, p. 74)

But the poet does not seek to blame his people's loss of social balance on any negligence on the part of God. As a poet-cantor, he sees in himself a source of inspiration for his fallen race to rise again to reach out for their pride and their god:

> My brothers,
>   my people,
>   my brothers:
> Fontomfrom! ....Fontomfrom!
> I am
>   the Fontomfrom—
>   listen!

135

> Of you the living,
> I am
>   the Fontomfrom—
>   listen!
> Fontomfrom! ....Fontomfrom! (*Oath,* pp. 20-21)

In "Prelude," Okai, poet, organ-grinder, and Fontomfrom, anticipates the reactions of some of his own brothers to his song and his authority:

> You ask:
> Which is
> My territory
> I reply
> This is my song. You ask: By whose authority,
> I reply
> Who says
> I am wrong   (*Oath,* pp. 70-1)

This reply raises two central questions about Okai's poetry in particular, and African poetry in general. What is the validity of this type of poetry? By what criteria must it be judged? These questions have been thoroughly discussed in the general context of African literature and it might seem tedious to take them up again. But they are particularly relevant to Okai's poetry and an essay on him might well start with a brief look at these same questions.

Atukwei Okai is an important poet in the recent history of the development of African literature. His importance derives mainly from the nature and scope of the linguistic experimentation that goes on in his poems. Most African critics as well as some writers have declared that the African writer's task is complicated by the fact that he must use a borrowed language to record experiences which are mostly native to his own culture. Okai does not seem to be troubled by any such supposed complication. Rather, he defiantly flings his poetry in the general direction of his audience, as if to say, "See, the white man's language is not my burden, I can handle it well enough and in my own way." He is not the first or only African writer engaged in this type of thing, but he is certainly the boldest in the scope of his experimentation. This is not to say that he is automatically the greatest poet in Africa today. One could be important in any field of human endeavour without necessarily being great. Okai is important for the daring nature of his linguistic experimentation. The question of his greatness is another thing, to be settled with reference to the extent of his success with the experiment. This question will be taken up in the rest of this essay.

Reaction to Okai's poetry has been varied and contradictory. Some greet him with cheers and generous praise such as appear in the blurb of *Lorgorligi Logarithms:*

> the "enfant terrible" of the Ghana Cultural scene; the new Guy Warren of Ghana who can put the old wine into new bottles; one of the foremost African poets; a first-rate craftsman whose poetry of arresting, startling imagery is the music of Africa; the Picasso of modern African poetry.

Others, however, have little difficulty in dismissing Okai's poetry as "mere verbiage." A particularly disparaging assessment of Okai's standing as a poet comes from K. K. Dei-Annang in his review of *Oath of the Fontomfrom and Other Poems*. The following concluding paragraph sums up Dei-Annang's reactions to Okai's verse:

> . . . unlike his non-African comtemporaries, John Okai's path is beset with the insidiously fatal trap in the fact that, as an African poet, he may wish to write "African" poetry. Whether there is any legitimately distinguishable form of the art which is entitled to such a name is not a matter that can be adequately discussed here. What is important is the embarrassing fact that the recent history of writing in Africa is littered with literary skeletons of countless would-be writers whose unrecognized (and therefore unchecked) hubris led them from writing poems *in* Africa into the fatal wish to write *"African"* poetry.[2]

Thus Dei-Annang dismisses Okai for the very reason that others admire him: that his poetry is distinctively *African*. Dei-Annang quotes a portion of Okai's "Prelude," and declares: "Well, this, at least, is *not* English poetry, nor even poetry in English." But it is a strange somersault in logical reasoning to move from this statement to a position that denies the existence of such a things as "African" poetry. Dei-Annang falls victim to the prescriptions of what he calls "serious students of literary aesthetics" or "contemporary connoisseurs." In Africa the poetic art still exists in oral form, and poetry has not as yet "liberated itself form both the drum and the dance." Okai's poetry clearly and boldly seeks to establish a link between written and oral poetry and it is not very helpful trying to evaluate it strictly "on the chaste witness of the printed page." It calls for a readjustment of critical approach, of the kind suggested by the Nigerian critic, Abiola Irele:

> . . . the very differentiation that marks the two frames of reference of this literature imposes upon the critical function important adjustments of those principles worked out in the Western tradition, to the peculiar modes of sensibility which feature in the African works, and which derive from the African background, of which the uses of language, both conditioned by and conditioning the traditional modes of feeling and apprehension, constitute a distinct social reality.[3]

The forgoing remarks are not meant to be an apology for what might be genuine flaws in Okai's craftsmanship. The very nature of his approach to poetry carries with it a fundamental burden. There is a constant need to reconcile the peculiar nuances of two distinct linguistic media, each with its own artistic traditions. This is a troublesome burden for any poet and Okai may not always handle it with success. For example, the "Fifth Ofruntum, Gong-Four: Chain Gang—Soul Autopsy" of the long poem "Tinkongkong! Ayawaso" (*Longorligi,* pp. 63–81) is a strange song, a curious experiment in linguistic stylistics. It is meant to be a lament on the death of Kwame Nkrumah, but it is a very unusual lament. On the surface, it is a jumble of familiar tunes and echoes from diverse linguistic-cultural backgrounds. There is the Christian preacher's voice linked to the nostalgia of Negro spirituals and to political catch-phrases from the lips of street-boys; in the background we hear a chorus of Akan voices invoking ancestral gods. They sing to the rhythm of the talking drums, and at intervals the mournful tone of the hornblowers' dirge is captured in appropriate poetic expression. There are also voices in Hausa and Ga trying to comfort us by saying "Baalefi" (It's all right) and "Efee noko" (It doesn't matter). Other voices in Ga and Nzema bid us farewell while we receive greetings in Mampruli from folks at home saying "Pusiyini."

In this poem we see most clearly the eclectic nature of Okai's art. There are no linguistic boundaries to his poetic territory. We see also what difficulties such a method may run into if not handled with craft: a jumble of voices (and sounds) each striving too loud to be heard above the others. If carried to the extreme, its effect could be bewildering. Only with much homework and cross-references could some of the details be made to fall into place in the overall sense-scheme. Perhaps the poet does not need to put his readers and hearers to all that trouble, and there is also the danger that the poem may lose its artistic and imaginative balance and crumble into a confused heap. In the end what saves this poem from total chaos is the underlying unity of theme and mood. The real failure in this poem, however, is not that the reader-hearer is bewildered by a babble of tongues, but that, too often, the essential poetic voice flags, losing the pith appropriate to the mood of the lament. The poet gives way to the radio announcer or town-crier or even to the master-of-ceremonies at a mad political rally. There is also a little too much of the

> lead kindly light
> lead kindly light
> AMID THE ENCIRCLING GLOOM.

This makes portions of the poem drag with the tediousness of an overused processional hymn. But the poem is not a total failure. If it is weak and trite in portions, it is redeemed by moments of artistic excellence, like the lines on the *mmenson,* in which we find balance and beauty in the coalescence of sound and sense:

> the seven horns of the solemn *mmenson*
> mourn and moan their dirge upon the dead
> the memories of the *mmenson* haunt the dawn
> the memories of the *mmenson* haunt the morn
> (*Lorgorligi,* p. 69)

While this poem provides evidence of some of the worst dangers of Okai's poetic craft, it also points to some of the possibilities that exist for a poet with diverse linguistic-cultural resources to draw upon.

Most critics of Okai's poetry, admirers and detractors alike, are agreed on at least one point: that much of his poetry exhibits a certain imbalance in the adjustment of sound to sense. Okai himself once, at a public recital, reacted to this objection by declaring that it does not make sense to insist on separating the sound qualities of words from their meaning. But this is beside the point. The objection is not that his poetry is only sounds but rather that he sometimes gives much of it which does not create any sensible impression. As a poet consciously working out a link with the oral medium, he needs to make maximum use of sound effects. But surely there must be a limit to even this maximum, in spite of Nwoga's observation that in Okai's poetry sound is more important "as a means to sense than the meaning of words."[4] Too often Okai oversteps the boundaries of sound-sense and gets into the area of what sounds like noise. It is true that, as with Christopher Okigbo, we can enjoy Okai without fully grasping the logic of his verse, and any attempts to work out a consistent logic for it may only destroy our spontaneous joy. Unfortunately, however, he does not always exhibit the necessary control which we find Okigbo exercising over his words, their sounds and the images they suggest. It is not always easy, if at all possible, to identify any meaninful connection between the sounds of his words, and though we may be "impressed" by the clever conjunction of sounds, even our sensory or emotional experience remains unordered. Where images are suggested by the sounds and/or "intrinsic structure" of the words, such images remain blurred.

There is more to Okai's poetry than just sound and a conscious attempt to establish a link with the oral tradition. There are other explanations for the attraction and fascination of his songs. Some of these are his preoccupation with social problems, his imagery, sense of humour and dramatic presentation of ideas and events, as well as the energy which constitutes an undercurrent of his verse.

Okai has been described by some as a love poet. There is much truth in this. Among his works are such easily identifiable love poems as "Flower-fall," "Jonice," "Pastoral Prelude," "Nocturnal Prelude," "Rosimaya," "Fugue for Fireflies," and "Dreamdom Communique to Valerieville." Most of these are in part praise songs to the beauty and perfection of a lover, but they are also explorations of the poet's own emotional state as conditioned by the lover's qualities. The turbulence of his passions is often captured in appropriate imagery and verse movement:

> gigantic and gentle in our homing joy
> we journey
> > towards
> > > the centre
> > > > of our
> tenderness . . .
> and the prairie fires in my skin all hail thee
> and the honey hunters
> > in my lips
> > > all hail thee
> and the night antelopes
> > in my noon-cells
> > > all hail thee
> and the village milk-maids
> > in my marrow
> > > all hail thee
> and the leap-year dancers
> > in my hair
> > > all hail thee

140

and the hoi poloi in my loins all crave thee
holy holy earthy glory;
AVE VALERIE . . . ! AVE VALERIE . . . !
(*Lorgorligi,* pp. 126-8)

Sometimes Okai's imagery is stark naked and shocks with its unchecked eroticism:

> I
> shall cause
> To be sculptured
> I
> shall cause
> To be erected,
>
> A phallus-erect
> Marble-granit
> Totem
> Right into the naked navel
> Of the virgin open—ocean: (*Oath,* pp. 135-6)

This type of imagery is not limited to love poems. Some of the others with much more serious and lifty themes are also marked by this fondness for the erotic. "Rhododomdroms in Donkeydom," the title piece of a forth-coming volume, opens with an account of the creation of the world as given in Yoruba mythology. The great creation myth is presented as a sexual drama which opens with "two hands spreading a woman's thighs part," and the arrival of Oduduwa (the god of creation) is announced in terms suggestive of the climax to a sexual act.

However, love and sex are not Okai's basic preoccupation. He is first and foremost a poet with a definite social call. In a recent symposium on "The African writer and his society" held at Legon, Okai made this point clear when he declared that "in Africa, the poet cannot afford to just play around with words. It is natural that he should handle some of the realities of his society." This is what he seeks to do in most of his poems. The very choice of title poems for his volumes is indicative of his acceptance of this responsibility. In "The Oath of the Fontomfrom" we see the poet's role in the symbolism of the primal drum, the focal point of a society's communal will to live in spite of enemies.

> Yet they shall seek
> after me—
> They shall seek to break
> my neck,

141

> Bury me
> > alive
> > > massacre my children
> > And squeeze me
> > > > into a bottle.

The poet is sought because the enemies of his people know that

> > when you want to starve
> > You paralyse
> > > its source,
> > > > the river,

and because he has "torn down the mask from the faces of our ill-wishers." But like the chief-priest, he accepts his heavy responsibility with goodwill. He will carry the burden of his people, still "proud and even strengthened that they aim at [him]." He is the source of inspiration and "a voice of vision":

> > Let no hand carve
> > > > our tombstone
> > Now . . .
> > > we have already in our time,
> > Out-lived
> > > > the sharpness of the sword,
> > The din of the struggle,
> > > > > the clashes of cutlasses;
> > We shall yet outlive
> > > > the weight
> > > > > > of lead.   (*Oath,* p. 19)

In "Lorgorligi Logarithms" the poet takes us into the complicated realms of what he once called "the arithmetic of life." *Lorgorligi,* we learn, is a Ga picture word for that which is "meandering, labyrinthine, zigzag, something that is not straight." First, the poet calls on several people, friends as well as enemies, to come witness how

> > the quantum physics of existential
> > inequality
> > blows up the dorkordiki bowl of human
> > sanity.   (*Lorgorligi,* p. 13)

142

Several things do not go straight with our world. For twelve years out of seventeen the heart of Seth Solomon Asare Bonsu did not beat smoothly, "due to circumstances beyond our control," and now he has "obeyed the temporal laws of gravity." Three years ago, the poet arrived here in Ghana, "hoping he had come, believing he had landed," but it was in the wrong season. The intelligence service people discovered that he was from a country

> with which our masters in the west
> were not
> on Ayeeko terms (ha! ha! ha!).

So they took his passport, re-stamped it and put him back on the next plane

> to a western port of entry where I would be
> quarantined and where my whole mind would be
> properly disinfected with our master's almighty
> izal and dettol.

Here Okai is re-enacting his own story of how after graduating with an MA (Litt.) from the Gorky Literary Institute in Moscow, he had to be sent to London to take an M.Phil, in Russian Literature in order to properly qualify for a lectureship in the University of Ghana where he now teaches. If the world were not "lorgorligi," this would not have happened to him.

Both Apronti[5] and Dseagu[6] have rightly drawn attention to Okai's constant dwelling on the tragic side of life. The title poems of his two forthcoming volumes confirm this. "Rhododomdroms in Donkeydom" deals with the worries of an artist, the creator, operating within a broken-down social order. As Okai himself explains, it is about "beautiful flowers in a kingdom of fools." The other volume, "The Gong-Gongs of Mount Gontimano," promises to take us back to another version of the poet's social role. Here, he is no longer the communal drum, but a town-crier with an iron bell, shouting himself hoarse from the mountain top. By implication, the message must be urgent and crucial, a further development in the "lorgorligi logarithms" of life. However, although he has a fondness for tragic themes, Okai's point of view is not necessarily "more pessimistic than optimistic," as Dseagu suggests. He is a man with a healthy respect for life and he confronts the problems of the world without sounding apologetic about even his failures. He loves to dramatize the pain being inflicted on him, but he does not bemoan his plight:

> You are stepping upon my raw eggs—[testicles?]
> You are stepping upon my raw eggs
> and Jesus wept . . . but I shall not.   (*Oath*, p. 82)

Okai spares himself the weakness of self-pity:

> You spoil my market,
> You walk on my green grass,
> And of course, I am not complaining
> You ask my name twice
> You muffle my chant
> And of course, I am not complaining.   (*Oath*, p. 95)

He may not complain, but he often warns and threatens, as is seen in these lines from "Afadzato" which at once impress with the forthrightness of the poet and the boldness of his imagery:

> I am a hangman . . .
> I enjoy hanging . . .
> But only with a clear conscience . . . if standing
> on my testicles you see me still quiet, do
> not think me dumb or blind or dead . . . I
>   am merely taking my time to make
>   sure it is my testicles and not my
>   toes you are standing upon . . . I
>   am merely taking my time to make
>   sure exactly who it is standing
>   on my testicles . . . for I hate to hang
>   the innocent . . .   (*Oath*, p. 94)

Even in the most hopeless moments when

> survival is slippery
> the human head
> is weighed down with the pressure
> of tears   (*Lorgorligi*, p. 49)

the poet's indomitable spirit soars above the skies, assuring the world:

> Let no hand carve
>   our tombstone

> Now . . .
>   we shall refuse to die!
> Our dove
>   shall fly
>   across the flames
> Of the big bonfires
>   of time—
> But her feathers
>   shall stay unburnt.   (*Oath*, p. 20)

A mood of resolute defiance runs through Okai even in his most tragic moments. It constitutes a point of equi-balance to what might otherwise have been a negative view of life. "Lorgorligi Logarithms," for all its dwelling on the tragic, ends on a note of triumph. The poet had earlier diagnosed his society's malady:

> motherland's nose, TAFLATSE, is running
> et cetera
> and god where are you, et cetera
> our tap-root TAFLATSE is all rotten
> and all we do is follow TAFLATSE any fool
>   (*Lorgorligi*, p. 24)

One would have thought that with their tap-root all rotten the people must be heading for an inevitable collapse. But the poet soon transforms our lament into shouts of victory:

> woman! woman!
> how often you carry the heaviness
> of your soul . . . only to empty it into songs . . .
>
> though our dialectic has been arrested
> and frozen in mid-season
> yet the algebra of the revolution
> is being worked out . . .
>
> and one of these days I am going
> to make you
> my kingmaker
>
> *le peuple; out!* the masses, yes!   (*Lorgorligi*, p. 51)

145

Closely linked with this spirit of defiance, a keen sense of humour runs through Okai's poems. Sometimes it is enough for him to just sit back and, with good-humoured contempt, reflect upon the foolishness of a world in which "tomatoes are envying potatoes." Such a world must be coming to an end, but the poet is too amused to grieve; he only needs to take note of these things and move on:

> I shall put a pipe to my lips
> And allow the tobacco-coated smoke
>
> To ascent with the redigested memories
> That refuse to fade away . . .   (*Oath*, p. 96)

Okai's sense of humour is often at work even when he is most serious. Where it succeeds, it has the effect of taking the bite off the unpleasant truths placed before us. Thus in the following lines, our attention is quickly shifted from the misery of the hunchback to the hurried flight of a man haunted by his own conscience:

> the hunchback hums a hymn you
> happen to know and suddenly
> you decide you are in a hurry   (*Lorgorligi*, p. 34)

Okai sometimes over-indulges his sense of humour and makes one feel cheated. It is as if a man comes to you with tears in his voice, and when you begin to lament with him, he suddenly breaks into laughter. This is what happens, for instance, in "Adikanfo" when at a particularly solemn moment in our lament for young Bonsu, we are unexpectedly introduced to the image of the rainbow urinating upon us:

> your dew turns its back on our dawn
> are we to look for your smile in the lightning
> the rainbow pees upon our peace.   (*Lorgorligi*, p. 15)

One very interesting aspect of Okai's sense of humour may be seen in his various persentations of the image of God. His god is a very fascinating version of the almighty Creator-God. He is certainly an artist with a gift for perfection (as seen at work in "Flowerfall"), but above all he is very human, alive, and extremely practical, even if quite overwhelmed by his responsibilities. In "Modzawe" (*Oath*, pp. 126–7) we meet God in the flesh. He is a patriarch and has woken up at dawn to have a bath before sunrise. He has a bath towel thrown over his shoulder and is walking briskly "to the rising sun's river-sea." Suddenly he is confronted by one of his great-grandchildren who has a complaint to make. There is something pathetic in both the physical and emotional state of this great-grandchild:

> I shall step into his way, and
> Planting my one one-quarter feet
> Firmly upon the febble earth,
> I shall weep the hell world out
> Of my inside and thereafter shout:
> Someone has stolen away
> My great grandmother's bones!
> Let human beings be human beings again
> Let human beings be human beings again
> Let human beings be human beings again

In "Invocation" (*Oath,* p. 74) God assumes the image of a busy electronics operator at the control tower of a gigantic communications network. He is quite agitated because the switchboard is jammed and there is a breakdown in communication between heaven and earth, and some men on earth are forcing words into God's mouth. In "Dedication" (p. 73) the picture is even bolder. We are warned not to "start hurling blocks towards the heavens,"

> . . . for even God in his
> chambers, squatting in his
> hyena skin pajamas has not
> finished signing all his third
> party insurance papers.

These unusual images of God form part of a major characteristic of Atukwei Okai's craft. In the use of imagery he has a preference for the dramatic. He is not given to painting still-life. His is a universe of great energy and constant motion, often bordering on a clash of wills but never degenerating into chaos. Even Okai's love passion in "Dreamdom Communique To Valerieville" is realized in the images of prairie fires, honey hunters, night antelopes, tornado silences, village milkmaids, leap-year dancers, dawn detonators and Kikuyuyan hyenas. In "Evesong in Soweto" a man stands accused by his own conscience and we see him as a tragic hero in a little dramatic sketch:

> when your conscience takes
> a penalty kick against the
> goal of your deeds and dreams
> you may leave behind
> the same old lord
> and the same old god
> the same old song
> the same old song
>
> only send me
>
> another dream
>
> a different dream   (*Lorgorligi*, p. 58)

Another poem in which we find an unusual dramatic use of imagery is "999 Smiles" (*Oath*, pp. 38–41) which tells the pathetic story of two great friends who have fallen out. One finds himself "perched" on top of the world, but he is not content with just looking down upon those below. Rather he chooses to worsen their misery by throwing stones at them. His one-time friend's misery is intensified by the knowledge that he cannot even react in self-defence, for his brother has taken the precaution of stealing away his only weapon, his hands. But what pains him most is that not so long ago they were such great friends, fully agreed on several truths of life. The extent of their friendship and agreement is presented in an unforgettable metaphor which opens the poem:

> nine hundred and ninety-nine smiles
> plus
> one quarrel ago, our eyes and our
> hearts
> were in agreement full

and the pain is effectively registered by the lines reiterating the betrayer's criminal act of

> hurling . . .
>   stones . . .
>   at us . . .
>
> infernal . . .
>   stones . . .
>   at us . . .

> sinister . . .
> stones . . .
> at us . . .

Contrasting with this type of imagery developed into dramatic sketches are other examples suggestive of the quiet and tender side of things, as in "Adikanfo" where the poet announces his second homecoming "from the doldrums" and tells us:

> I am manuring my memory into
> a fertile remembrance of things recent and past

and in "Kperterkple Serenade" where his tenderness is seen in the image of a sunrise:

> with the politeness of a sunrise I knock
> upon your door
> but you do not want to know
> peace
> unto your ashes

Atukwei Okai's poetry deserves attention. There is great originality in his approach, though as often happens with men who choose to go their own way, there are moments of failure. The successes, where they do come, are of great significance. The man Oshamraku Atukwei, organ-grinder to God and man, has recorded a plea for remembrance which we should take note of:

> And when they ask who the hell I was
> and what the hell on earth
> I did, remind them I cared
> enough to rise at dawn and
> roll my mat, and that I, too, during
> the festival of the soul, sang our
> world.   (*Oath*, p. 119)

REFERENCES

1. John Okai, *Oath of the Fontomfrom and Other Poems* (New York: Simon & Schuster, 1971), p. 75. The other collection of Okai's poetry discussed in this essay is *Lorgorligi Logarithms* (Tema: Ghana Publishing Corporation, 1974).

2. K. K. Dei-Annang, "Discipline in the Making of Poetry," *Universitas*, II, 1 (1972), p. 115.
3. A. Irele, "The Criticism of Modern African Literature," in C. Heywood (ed.), *Perspectives on African Literature* (London: Heinemann, 1972), p. 20.
4. Donatus Nwoga, "Annual Report on West Africa," *Journal of Commonwealth Literature* (December 1974), p. 37.
5. "John Atukwei Okai: the Growth of a Poet," *Universitas*, II, 1 (1972), p. 124.
6. In his Introduction to *Lorgorligi Logarithms*, p. xix.

THREE YOUNG GHANAIAN POETS: VINCENT OKPOTI ODAMTTEN, KOFI ANYIDOHO, AND EUGENE OPOKU AGYEMANG

Kofi Awoonor

In one of the more recent critical works on West African poetry, *Four Modern West African Poets,* Romanus Egudu, a critic and I suspect a poet, throws up a number of final judgements. Here are a couple of examples:

> Lenrie Peters' poetry is indeed universal poetry. There is only little specifically local or African aesthetic element. His fusion of the indigenous with the foreign shows a clear bias for the latter; yet the psychology portrayed cannot be other than that of the African. What makes his poetry a success is in this ability to achieve universal appeal, a quality we find more in him than in any other modern West African poet.

and

> All said and done, the problem of conflict of cultures under- lines most of Awoonor's work . . . Awoonor made clear that both the urban and the rural dwellers have each his own share of the bitter cup of experience resulting from the clash of cultures . . . he looks on the heathen brothers with passion, nostalgia and admiration,—and looks on his educated and Christian brothers who have rejected the indigenous culture with pity and utter contempt.[1]

The sociological judgements contained in these quotes reveal certain fundamental problems which both the critic and the artist have to grapple with. When it is stated that a poet's imagination "is so fettered to the native traditional mode of expression that it rarely exercises its own original power of creation," we are confronted with a verdict that scarcely concerns itself with the creative process *ab initio,* or with the examination of the evidence based on valid critical assumptions that the artist carries and expresses in his work the various historical and cognitive models of his existence.

In a now celebrated article by three young Nigerian critics entitled "Towards the Decolonization of African Literature" that appeared in *Okike* number 6, an amplification of this peculiar problem emerges. Brilliant, iconoclastic, and irreverent, hilarious in parts though the article is, it fails to come to terms with the creative process that is an embodiment of two basic dimensions. To quote Okigbo's lines:

> the only way to go
> through the marble archway
> to the catatonic pingpong
> of the evanescent halo   ("Distances")

and ask the naive question "What does this mean? Is this a joke?" reveals the critics' inability to go beyond what they heard as the music, and what they sensed as "pleasurable." Their verdict: "Nonsense, but pleasurable nonsense" destroys their own socio-cultural prescriptions as to what good traditional African poetry is, particularly when they quote the most nonsensical drivel of a poem, Matei Markwei's "Life in our Village," as an example of simple and vivid poetry that conveys the experience of moonlight play.

What both Egudu, on the one hand, and Chinweizu and Co. on the other hand, failed to do in their critical studies is to examine the various poems they selected at two levels of perception. Poetry is both accessible and esoteric. Its accessibility is contained in the source retrievance of sounds, words, vocables, in the aurality of the music, in what exists as the identifiable fixtures of a communal engagement, in what is common property. Throughout time, this element is ritualized; by ritualized one refers to the commonplace features, the agreed upon gestures, and the vatic elements of our everyday life which cease to amaze and surprise us. The second dimension of a poem is what I will label the esoteric; this is the hidden element; it is magical, enigmatic, existential, individual, secret. It is the element that explores and states the poet's ultimate private vision. It belongs to an intimate magical world, psychic, full of private emotions. It is this aspect of a poem that eludes most critics because they fail the initiatory tests which all good poets impose upon the reader. No naive process of inquiry, as illustrated by our two sets of critics, will achieve any elucidation of any poem. Egudu refuses even to recognize this esoteric dimension as an aspect of the individuating process of the artist. The others, Chinweizu and Co., where they perceive it, believe it is obscurantist and nonsensical. Indeed, much of so-called oral poetry is obscure, esoteric. This is the specific force of the individual poet's personality projected upon the first popular dimension. The two are not mutually exclusive.

In a short piece I collected seven years ago, Dunyo, a traditional poet, states:

> I know not what I did against
> the owner of life
> and he cooked his meal of corn for me.[3]

The words, the sounds, and the music are readily accessible. On the surface, this is a simple dirge, a lament. But somewhere in the poet's private psyche nursed by a particular personal history we must search for the meaning of such phrases as "owner of life," "cooked his meal of corn for me," and more significantly the sensibility, the import of the opening statement

> I know not what I did against
> the owner of life.

Who is the "owner of life"? Is the question rhetorical? The answers do not exist in any socio-cultural inquiry, but in the search and discovery of the private man in the poem, beyond the music, beyond the images, beyond the agreed forms and marketplace models. In another short piece from the same poet:

> Dunyo has become the path
> He has become the waist bead
> From seven, only one is left,

we glimpse yet another feature of the esoteric beyond the accessible words. Our judgement of these lines will go beyond mere language, sociology, and anthropology. It will seek from the ultimate depths of the poet's being, a meaning which does not correspond with information or facts.

In a recent collection of poems, the late Pol Ndu from Nigeria answers some of our inquiries, and reveals yet other sets of difficulties that can emerge in the cramming and overloading of the first aspect of the poem— the accessible. I stated that the accessible is the commonality, the sounds, words, the utterances, the public linguistic gestures and mannerisms of the poem. It seems to me that recent Nigerian poetry in English has begun to suffer from overloading this first dimension. And it is being done in two ways. The first is by continued imitation of the English and American "classical" models; the second, and this is more deadly, by conscious imitation of the earlier Nigerian poets who themselves began as imitators but later mastered the form in order to state the second dimension.

There are major weaknesses in pure language-bound derivation for poetry, which reveal the problems in the accessibly impressive open-ended linguistic experimentation that sacrifices the inner esoteric secret message. For poetry, though written in the language of the market place, ultimately deals in codes that contain its own intimate cypher. This cypher is traceable to the more intimate personal gestures, the personal variations on the public themes, in the initiation into the passions, emotions, and the concretization of the general abstracts of our universe into the personal testimony.

On this score, I believe a good deal of recent Nigerian poetry is manouvering itself into a corner. I believe its earlier impressive marks, scored for it by many western critics, have been responsible for the ossification of the form. Beyond Okigbo, Clark, and Soyinka, there seems to be a cul-de-sac, a verbal arid land where the same half-arsed clever poems are being written.

Beyond the yeoman services of these early poets, it seems some of the new generation of Nigerian poets have seized upon distinct fragments of their failures and are essaying rather pathetically to transform these into regional virtues. Of course, a sensible level of poetic competence emerges in the works of such younger poets as Lfeanyi Mankiti, Jemie, Chinweizu, and a few others.

Within the context of recent West African poetry, it is useful to draw attention to the work of three young Ghanaian poets who seem to be maturing very fast, and are attaining this credible maturing within a short period. Ghanaian poetry had once been burdened by the dull hymnology of very poor political verse, and recently had been subjected to the screaming hysteria of Atukwei Okai's verse. It was difficult to believe that the new poetry was ever going to divest itself from the effervescence of the enthusiastic poetry of well-trained amateurs and political poseurs. But a vein of good poetry seems to be emerging beneath the welter of some of the most appalling dirt.

The first of these young poets whose work I want to discuss is Vincent Okpoti Odamtten. In his yet unpublished collection, *A Deathbed Rebirth*, which was awarded the 1977 Valco Literary Prize for poetry, we are presented a young and exciting talent that has quickly grasped the fundamental impulse of the poetic art.

The opening piece in this collection is divided into five movements.

This poem reveals a closely worked progression in both style and matter, a cumulative linguistic process that explores the individuating scope of public and social experience within the inner muscular energy and nervous tensions of personal anguish and frustrations. The first movement is a recollection of a time past, a childhood spent in England, accentuated by

> pipes cracking with
> frozen water

and the purgatorial winter existence without a bath in four days. Then follows the homecoming where the real hurts of Europe are exchanged for the horror of cultural non-recognition as a kin;

> back home I land in warmer times
> a sweaty night

evokes the paradoxical ecstasy and dreadful confusion of the tropical points of an African return, the promises and the despair of the heat stated in the beautiful phrase "land in warmer times" presented in a juxtaposition achieved in the jostling discomfort of "sweaty night." Already Odamtten understands verbal precision as a poetic base even if he suffers from unfocused collocations as "hiatus of inertia" and poor line structure. The notebook on a return to the native land proceeds however with a variation that is realized in the dramatic dialogue that characterizes the second movement. It seeks to underscore the fundamental despair through the borrowed black American lingo:

> It's cool, brother.

The third movement is the statement of the public concerns within the private manner and pain. In this movement, Odamtten's mastery of the shunted line, and of a sudden and unexpected lyrical verve is strong. From the weak, flabby and near rambling lines such as

> through bureaucracies of words
> . . . .
> one time before I might have said so

the poetry of social conscience emerges with clear and crystal images whose absence the reader had earlier sensed with mild unease.

155

> I know no end
>   except of a rope
> no ground
>   except of a frostysoil

reveal not only superb line structure, but also a wonderful fusion of two images into one precise vision, that of a suicide dangling upon a rope. The death image explodes in Mao Tse Tung's famous revolutionary slogan without the sniggering connotations which usually accompany it. But the slogan brings in the burning of dreams

> for those who scratch it [frostysoil]
>   with their hoes
> is of a barrel
> the end of a gun which
> is the end
> of our bankers and their creditors—
>
> the Free world.

The poet has moved from the personal frustrations of a European childhood through the irritations of a homecoming that promised warmth and fetid nights to the larger issues of social justice, exploitation and poverty and the promises of a revolution. This sudden political impulse that is sprung upon us has the pleasure of being anticipated beyond the personal statements of the first two movements. And this is where the significance and promise of Odamtten's work lies. Movement IV is a summation of the longer political question explored in the posturings of a socially and economically deprived people, who have lost their tongue in the pacificatory embrace of Britain and on the large expansive gestures of the American dream machine. But they are not lost completely because these kingdoms whose knowledge and money enslaved others will soon have their

> torch (is) nearly eclipsed
> by the Rising Sun
> into the grave.

China perhaps? We may ask Chairman Hua Kuo-FENG about this. Political poetry has the tendency of being tedious and wearisome with set and naive assumptions mostly clothed in rather ineffectual language. But here, in the political poetry of Odamtten, there is a tentative subtlety, if not a capacity to achieve clearer and more registered imagery.

Movement V begins rather poorly with lines such as

> Retrospective probings
> into our frenzied redemption

damming the flow of earlier thoughts that engendered expectations of a sharper poetic focus. The social conscience, which should have become the climactic point of intensity, and significant language, serving as vehicle for the ultimate statement, are thrown away in verse that seemed not to belong to the earlier movements of the poem. But this movement, in spite of the near hysteria of

> Oh Lord we shall
> we shall

Simmers down into the personal pathos of the lines

> until the end
> which is only the alternate beginning
> of another stay
> one which must be
> that I might die
> that we might live
> to give . . .

The simplicity of these lines saves this last movement; it imports to the whole poem a unity that is at once elusive and tenuous. For we return to the poetic individual, to the ultimate sublimation of the self and that sacrifice called forth from each one by the all.

In another long poem entitled "And Freedom was a Voice," Odamtten's ironic interpretation of political events achieves a simple grandeur that is effectively sharp. The opening lines

> for we who learn
> the art
> mimickry is easy
> by the time we enter
> the inner sanctum of humanity,
> Storehouse of knowledge

carry an easy conversational tone that does not anticipate the first true burst of outrage

> . . . we blindly
> add the mortar and bricks
> to our prison walls wars rage smashing while
> Southern fascist walls
> Vietnam rings in our ear
> and we are caught in the fever
> of debates, demos, symposia
> talking Black Unity
>   African Unity!
>   Unity
>
> And we passed our resolutions
> attached minority reports
> and had a good time being
>   week-end
> dam builders and cane cutters
> not like the labourers
> Back in the world.

There is a fundamental rawness in the language of this poem, the awkwardness of the third line in the second stanza being the most obvious example. Yet what must be accessible is clear, precise, carrying with it a certain briskness and urgent fury, an anger which is both private, personal, and communal:

> at the noon of our liberty
> our brothers came
> dressed in black suits to dig
> our democratic graves
> and while we slept
> sweltering in the afternoon heat
> our brothers from Sandhurst and St Cyr
> thinking they were new leaders
> reborn to guide our faltering steps
> into the whole of their digging
> playing games with words
> for we are the sparks
> to burn their uniforms
>   . .   . .
>
> after their end
> we shall make
> our entrance
> after the
>   Revolution

This is poetry marked by a direct appeal, if perhaps at times marred by poor lines and weak weaving of predictable sequence.

Odamtten has a few fundamental weaknesses which time and practice will eliminate. The first of these is a kind of casual and tedious prosaicness which is due to an absence of any rigorous technical sense. Lines are at times slack, as revealed in portions of the last poem. Secondly, he seems to work out his thoughts without any referents whatsoever. The impulse of poetry is essentially an imagistic one, the dependence on a series of cognitive references, the creation of significant metaphors which have long become the riding horses of all languages. Without these, poetry is denuded of that primary allusiveness, that deep and penetrable enigma which teases the mind, and finally captivates it with the mental and hypnotic magic of its own. It is what imposes variety and complexity, which are the essential features of language, and therefore presents us the individual poetic imagination in the nature of that esoteric and existential quality I spoke of. And this desire to use images and even existent symbols that are culture derived, indicates a fine quality of mind which bases itself in associations, and in sensations of sound and ideas. It carries poetry beyond mere rhetoric and sententious speech. Life, culture, and experience impose a primary complexity; the poet's function is not to avoid this, but to restate it according to the grouping consciousness of his own intellect and the counterbalancing force of his various emotions and social experiences. One hopes that Odamtten will move swiftly away from the sounds and the vocables, which he has already grasped, into the exploration of the magic of ideas in concrete terms, into the point when he will recognize the world as the large inescapable image store house from which he can steal each recognized gem with gleeful and witty impunity. But his work has a ringing bardic quality, the raging voice of the prophet of the market place, a linguistic naivete which can at best be described as simple and amply original. He already has begun to recognize objects for what they signify or represent. Soon he will learn to weave them into the clearer fabric that he calls his "kente of words" with greater certitude.

The other young Ghanaian poet whose work seems to me to also hold great promise is Kofi Anyidoho whose first book *Elegy for the Revolution* has just been released by Greenfield Review Press in the U.S. Anyidoho has already been introduced to readers of African poetry through such journals as *African Arts, Okike, Nimrod, Chindaba,* and others. *Elegy,* the work of a young man, though uneven in parts, reveals two fundamental facts about this young poet: an individual and original style largely learned from a continuing tradition and fed through his sharp grasp of language, and a deep sense of the impulse of the public statement as contained in the Ewe traditional poem of which Anyidoho has been a keen student and translator. In a brief overture, the poet evokes the tremendous beauty of these original gifts with such power as to reveal the whole book as a careful and at times painfully worked field of precious items.

> The dreams we placed among the thorns
> are still unhatched
> these debts we owe our orphan clan
> > are yet unpaid
> > and you—you
>
> Whatever befalls the leopard in his ambush
> the panther could not betray the spirit of the hunt.

The first two lines are evocative, built around the image of the bush fowl, that, seeking protection for its future young lays its eggs among thorns. "Dreams," "thorns," and "unhatched" state disparate ideas and concepts in one unified sensibility of pathos and helplessness subsumed by a great promise. The desolation of that condition is repeated in the line

> These debts we owe our orphan clan
> are yet unpaid

The idea of debtors to an orphan clan is a reemphasis of the primary concept of that state of abject helplessness. The last two lines, a tremendous tour de force, proclaim the relentlessness of the struggle in the image of those two noble beasts, the hunted and the hunter, leopard and panther, who must continue the struggle. This is part of one of the most successful poems in the collection. The opening lines state the major theme which is echoed throughout the poem. They constitute an invocation and a salutation to a dead man,

> Adonu-Adokli
> Dancer-Extra-Ordinary
> who threw dust into Master-Drummer's eyes
> So you've gone the way of flesh

His departure to the land of death is stated in two pithy lines which reveal the traditional sources of the whole poem's inspiration. The dead one

> danced on heels in a backwards
> loop into the narrow termite home.

Here, the idea of the reversal of the living world's various attributes in the spirit world is affirmed in the powerful image of the dancer who wheels backwards on agile heels and swings into a loop. The pulsing lively and

160

energetic nature of this action is sharply dimmed by the fantastic image of the grave,

> the narrow termite home.

This image expresses both the malevolence of death's decay and the paradoxical notion of the grave as home—destination and haven existing within the same context, expressive of man's mortality and the comfort of death.

The last part of the poem is a pithy statement containing both a salutation and the lyrical agony of the dirge as a personal testament of loss. The salute is direct:

> Katako Gako
> Old Mad—one says
> he captured King Cobra's neck with naked hands
> Yah Kumasi the Fearless Ghost
> Wrestles a soul from jaws of Death

The next section of the poem represents one of the best examples of Anyidoho's work.

> Come, blood of spirits
> Daze my eyes to fear
> I toss these rising doubts to thunder
> and stagger back into my soul, still
> holding firm onto this growing confidence
> this piece of our broken covenant
> whatever befalls the panther in the desert
> The leopard would not forget the jungle war.

There are some minor linear weaknesses, however. The ending of line 4 is unsure, and line 5 is flabby with a rather poor phrasing in "holding firm onto" and "growing confidence," cliches all. But they were preceeded by the powerful energy of line 3 where the impact of the state of daze becomes an echo of the earliest lines that evoke the dance in the words "stagger back into my soul" which constitute a variation on

> Danced on heels in a backwards
> loop . . .

The last two lines restate the defiance and bravado embodied in the image of the panther and the leopard, fearsome predators whose personalities

161

are assumed by both the dead and the mourner. The last line reaffirms the memory of the eternal struggle of life, against death, against annihilation.

Anyidoho's strongest poetic art lies in his capacity to explore the landscape of the dirge, and to discover within the existing tradition which he has learnt so well a clarity of language and depth of sensibility that reveal a maturity that borders on the precocious. I said he has learnt well the Ewe dirge, for he once worked out translations of these dirges in a series of brilliant short papers. From here he learnt the power of the lyrical statement as the element of poetic composition, and the exploration of significant folkloric imagery in which traditional concepts have long been clothed.

The achievement of "Dance of the Hunchback" specifically reveals these qualities. The poem is perhaps his best. The opening lines

> mine is the dance of the hunchback
> Along these quiet drains of town
> I crawl my way with strain and shame.
>
> I leave paved streets to the owners of the earth,

ego's self constitute the general statement, though here based in knowledge and self pity. The hunchback "crawls" in the byways but his is a dance of pathos. The next line

> He died. My mother's only son. He died

expands its lyrical brevity into the scope of the personal lament, in the repetition of "he died" and in the phrase "my mother's only son" which is a direct translation from the Ewe "danyevi deka." The poem moves into the narration of the coming of elders with expensive funerary items— velvet robes, diamond rings, glass coffin with rims of gold, cases of schnapps, barrels of gunpowder; the impact of this lies in the ironic power of an earlier line that revealed that the dead man died of "innate poverty" the eternal situation typical of the African condition.

> Going down on knees
> I whisper my brother's spirit-name
> I whisper it thrice and offer all
> I have: a tear and a song.

The pathos of these lines echoes through the repeated images of the poor hunchback who drags his shame in public squares and bylanes in the company of the hedge-hog and the crab, nature's primal cripples who also carry a "tedious destiny." The last fragment expands upon the idea of the hunchback's dance derived from a proverb that he too claims that he is doing the dance, but onlookers cannot tell because of his hunch.

> I do my best to fall in step
> with rhythms of grace and pomp
> But the eyes of the world
> see only a moving bundle of fun
> and upon my chest they heap
> a growing burden of scorn.

Kofi Anyidoho is a young poet whose work so far reveals a depth of lyricism and a fundamental grasp of imagery as an element of general and particular statement. His clear understanding of Ewe dirge form has widened his own primary appreciation of the substance of the lyrical form of lament as both a personal and a public statement. However, like his contemporaries, his work suffers from a slackness of language, syntactic looseness, poor line endings. He will gain more from a technical control of lines, which will go far to support his already finely developed sense of imagery. These images are drawn within the structure of contradictions that reveal a precocious grasp of both social truth and general philosophy of all our existence. His other great strength is a lyrical cadence, felicitously well-ordered single lines that compensate for the technical slackness that marks a good deal of his writing at this point. It is this technical competence one hopes he will develop, forging it as the main body and spirit of his poetry with a greater degree of technical certitude.

If our two young poets have ventured into the domain of the public statement through the means of the private and personal attestation, our third poet, Eugene Opoku Agyemang, again a contemporary of these two, remains a poet of the inner energy, of the private sensations and personal testimony. Though the least loud of the three, his poetry works through a series of personal affirmations, possessing a tender quietude and a voice that hovers between a whisper and total silence. Though gifted with a superb ear, Opoku-Agyemang tends to overwrite the sentiments that at times cloy in that saccharine sweetness in which most youthful poetry tends to indulge. The triteness of

> I love I adore
> Need I say more

in "Ecstasy" is mercifully not the main feature of his work. For in "A Dreamer Come Home" he is capable of these lines that leap with such life and meaning:

> once in the middle of this gloom
> you gently picked the harmattan's peeling skin
> And wove a sound off my pleading arms.

In his yet unpublished manuscript entitled *A Flow Like Discord* a casual reader will be struck by the musical quality of Opoku Agyemang's work. This attests of course to his possession of a very finely tuned ear for sounds. But this is a superficial judgement per se, because the deceptively musical style more often than not masks a strong sense of word, and a seriously worked out semanticism which could be overlooked in a cursory reading. It is in the realization of this other quality that one revises the opinion, to some extent, that he is merely a poet of the private psyche. In a "Taste of Desire," a deceptively simple and lyrical verse develops into a strongly felt poem which has lines such as

> And in the lonely streets
> Ribs primly stand out
> to be counted
> In lonely steets
> In the terse gaze of desire
> The profile of our dear dying estate
> Rise to pass the passage of life's fire

which were preceded by unrealized portions as

> And everything
> That goes on
> Goes to leave us
>   Behind
> And the night goes on
>   Forever . . .

To appreciate Opoku Agyemang's talent as a poet of great promise, it may be useful to do a close analysis of one of his long poems, "And So What." The poem opens with a fragment from the Spanish poet Garcia Lorca

> I am thirsty for odors and laughs
> I am thirsty for new poems
> poems with no lilies or moons
> and no love affairs about to fail

The fundamental impulse of this fragment seems to be irrelevant to Opoku Agyemang's poem. But this is not a moot point. His is a poem of

164

repudiations and self-denials, whilst Lorca, the revolutionary optimist, seeks the magic of new and concrete sensations.

The poem is divided into what one may call two movements. This division is both structural and stylistic. The first part is made up of 16 lines of direct statements and repudiation.

> And so what
> If by so many words
> I howl the hyaenas hymn
> By silly repetition

Hyaena's hymns, signifying impotent howls of the social paraiah closely relates to the series of statements that proclaim the poet's condition. The repudiations are not necessarily statements in absolute negatives, for the last line recognizes the "call of stars." What is this call? Could it be a recognition of that affinity with the distant force of creation, what most poets affirm as the creative energy itself, the eschatological referent point where man's being emanates? What is fascinating here is the relationship between this "call of stars" and "roots that stretch earthbound," emphasizing an umbilical relationship that links earth to the heaven. In the second movement, uneven in parts, the poet attains a greater lyrical strength, and a sharper focus in imagery. The simplicity of

> . . . I have lost count
> of my loss
> On landscapes lost to lies

conceals a depth of pathos in the anger of the alliterative. But in the next lines

> There is storm in the eye of glee
> Perfidy in the redeemer's chaste grunt
> and a story in every kernel that escaped
> the cracker's greed.

we receive both the gifts of clear lyrical verve and powerful images. "Storm in the eye of glee" not only expresses a precise and acute image, but also constitutes a well-worked rythmic piece that is later echoed in the "cracker's greed." But there is a kind of awkwardness in

> and a story in every kernel that escaped

Another poet would break it into

165

> and a story in every kernel
> that escaped the cracker's greed.

to achieve a more balanced rhythmic flow.
In the last fragment, the poem becomes both an echo and a variation on
the borrowed fragment from Lorca.

> If I thirst secretly for the odour of laughter.

Here affirmations replace the self deprecations of earlier lines. There is an
element of defiance and hope despite the persistent mood of despair

> . . . I hold my head
> Over the entrails of rising incense
> Through joys rituals nipped in the mud
> and in the passage of smoke
> There is a meat of peace
> In the teeth of every howl.

The image of "entrails of rising incense" is cryptic and powerful. But it is
the idea that the poet holds his head over these entrails that carries the
image beyond a significant if commonplace observation. Do we conclude
now that "hyaena's hymn" is the "every howl" of the last line? We can.
The association is obvious.

If I said Opoku Agyemang's work is more ego-based than that of the
two other poets under discussion, it is not to suggest that he lacks any
significant exterioration, or tangible public concerns. These are, however,
adroitly worked into the series of personal affirmations and self-laments,
as reflective of the general human condition. He is more the poet of the
self. His greatest strength is music, a lyricism that is lightfooted, tender if
at times tedious. He too will grow.

Recent Ghanaian poetry, as represented by the work of these three
young poets seems to have come a long way. There is an energy that gives
both private and public account more competently than one has witnessed
in the poetry of other parts of West Africa. The learning process for these
poets is less clogged, less rigid; they imitate no one; their sincerity is
direct. They have a few technical problems, but these are not insoluble
given a closely organized and arduous apprenticeship which they are so
humbly serving.

But all said and done, the poet is he who explores sensibilities beyond
culture and sociology. At the primary level, he is engaged in the business
of language as it is available to him. The sounds, music, and words of a

language are his commonly held part of this public dimension. This may be defined for him within the construct of time, history and geography. It states that public domain of experience, it explores the heard sounds of the village lane and the market place. But beneath and beyond the public gestures and the mannerisms are the details of the flicker of the left eye, the gurgling sounds of death and the secret laughter heard and known to only one. But the poet initiates. He leads the hearer through the open fields, the market places, the bylanes into a little shrine. And there the first man of earth is met, raw, energetic, subtle, serious, tragic in the full and complete splendour of his primal nakedness. To this shrine there are no secret lanes and private roads. All avenues are open. But it is the poet who leads. The details of language, culture, history may define the variations. But they are all variations upon the same theme—man.

Somewhere in the true poem, the two dimensions of public and private attributes are unified. There occurs a deep relationship between the publicly owned linguistic landscape, and the private esoteric magic land of the intimate poetic self. It is this relationship which most critics of recent African writing fail to examine. There is a frenzied eagerness to resort to anthropology, sociology, and history for answers to the simplest demands of a poem. Whatever constitutes regional variations may be traced in the first unit of the poem, in the open-place linguistic peculiarities. These make up the larger manners and gestures. But the real essence of the poem lies in its second dimension, in the peculiar details of each word either alone or in collocation with others, in the nature of the very poetic statement, in the mental condition of the poem, and finally in the personality of the poet, perceived in the poem within the context of his life, his people, his human condition.

167

DRAMA

DRAMA IN GHANA

Charles Angmor

Modern dramatic expression in Ghana has two distinct forms, namely, operatic drama and literary drama. Both forms satisfy the basic element of drama as the representation of life through an enacted theme, but differ from each other in their mode of enactment; and further, they both owe their development to the same sources, that is, indigenous Ghanaian verbal art and Western dramatic art.

Operatic drama has developed in three directions: the cantata of Christian societies, the comic play of itinerant musical bands known as concert parties, and the folk opera which is a recent development in imitation of the European opera. A feature common to these modes that makes them operatic is the element of music that constitutes an essential part of the representation. The cantata and the folk opera employ music and gesture as their media. Their affinity with traditional Ghanaian drama lies in what Professor J.H. Nketia defines as "dance drama," that is, that form of drama "expressed through music, poetry, mime, and movements of the dance."[1] The cantata has had a long tradition with the Christian churches in Ghana and was a contriburtory factor in the development of the other operatic dramas. In the case of the folk opera, the other factor is the European opera which is well known in learned Ghanaian theatre. Its pioneers are G. Adali-Mortty and Saka Acquaye who between them composed the first Ghanaian opera *Obadzen*—the text by the former and the music by the latter. The second opera, Saka Acquaye's *The Lost Fishermen,* was originally composed in Ga and later translated by the composer into English.

The comic play combines spontaneous dialogue with music and action to dramatize simple themes drawn from everyday social experiences, and its characteristic vein is comic even in presenting sad or pathetic experiences. Its beginnings can be traced back to the first three decades of this century and its origins found in the school play, the cantata and the cinema.[2] These three inspired theatrical spirit in the youth of the time, and coupled with the indigenous tradition of story-telling, gave birth to the comic play. Efua Sutherland identifies the following persons as among the pioneers of the comic play in south-western Ghana: Teacher Yallay, who started the tradition as a one-man cast; and Ishmael Johnson (alias Bob Johnson), Charles B. Hutton and J. B. Ansah[3] whose association together led to the formation of one of the earliest bands of comedians by the name of the Two Bobs in 1930. Connecting the influences which contributed to the making of the pioneer comedian Bob Johnson, Efua Sutherland says:

> From these experiences (i.e., the cantata, the school, and the cinema showing such stars, as Charlie Chaplin) came the memories with which he (Bob Johnson) started to work on his own plays. But he did not compose anansesem (folktales), neither did he compose cantatas. . . . He took ordinary life stories and with them composed plays by the method of "Kasa-ndwom. Kasandwom." (Speech and song. Speech and song.)[4]

This style of acting real life stories in speech and song embellished with the art of character disguise through facial make-up and also female impersonation was the tradition of the comic play that has been preserved to this day by Ghanaian comedians.

All the three modes of operatic drama operate as popular theatre, but whereas the folk opera is written, and the cantata is based on biblical literature, the comic play is unwritten. These qualities coupled with the musical frame distinguish these theatrical arts from literary drama, which will be the focus of this paper.

Ghanaian literary drama is at present in its seminal stage. Its identity will depend on form: whether it should be a pseudo-Ghanaian drama, a mere imitation of other cultures, or whether it should be fully Ghanaian will depend to a large extent on the theatricals it exploits.

The second issue considered here is the literary value of this drama, for the writer's aim is two-fold to create both theatre and literature. Therefore, the objective in this discussion is to examine both the dramatic and the literary merits of the plays.

Of first consideration are the origins of this type of drama. These are indigenous as well as western. And, as in the case of the other genres, this drama is composed by persons of Western learning who by their education had gained knowledge of European and American literature and acquired the resultant acquaintance with Western literary aesthetics. Thus, the Western influence on these people goes beyond the cantata, the school play, and the cinema. It is the total impact of Western civilization upon the educated Ghanaian with such strands as the arts, the sciences, diverse systems of philosophy, and theatrics, that is operative here. In our literary drama, therefore, one identifies significant features that are the direct influences of the West as well as evidence of the playwrights' efforts to create an African theatre. So that one might better appreciate what the writers are doing and the direction in which this drama is developing, it is useful to see it in relation to its parental bodies; that is, its indigenous and Western roots.

Drama as usually defined is theatre; it is the abstraction of life; it is simulated life. But in certain respects Western drama is different from Ghanaian indigenous drama, for though the latter always has a theme, it does not relate a story in all its manifestations, nor is it the product of conscious art because it is generally a series of established customary or spontaneous acts: it does not operate as a rule on conflict and its resolution but generally on consensus and consummation; that is to say, its spirit and all its components are geared towards a common end, as evident, for example, in the rites of initiating a priest of a diety, or female puberty rites.

Two types of indigenous drama can be distinguished: that which is real life, and that which simulates life. This classification embraces the three types into which Professor J. H. Nketia categorizes African traditional drama: the former covers the two types he describes as "ceremonial" and "dance" dramas, and the latter, what he terms "narrative" drama.[5]

This brief background sketch is intended to point out the ares in which the Western tradition of theatrical drama and the Ghanaian indigenous traditon have contributed toward the evolution of our literary drama. The educated Ghanaian has known drama as a conscious art and as theatre from his contact with Western literature and theatre; the very format of Ghanaian plays (for example, the division into acts and scenes, and characterization) follows the styles of their Western progenitor. From the same source came the concept of dramatic conflict which has hitherto led to the practice of constructing plays of two tempers, tragic and comic. These two factors, the format and dramatic conflict, are the fundamentals of Ghanaian literary drama as it has evolved so far. It is upon these that the playwrights have woven dramatic elements drawn from their indigenous resources to create the Ghanaian brand of literary drama.

J. B. Danquah and F. K. Fiawoo

The seeds of literary drama can be traced to about the same period as those of the two well-known operatic dramas (the cantata and the comic play); that is, during the first two decades of this century. One finds evidence of this in a play that has lately come to light, *The Blinkards*,[6] published posthumously in 1974 under the authorship of Kobina Sekyi and reputed to have been written in 1915. It was not until the 1940s,

173

however, that we see the first flowering of literary drama in the publication of *The Third Woman* and *The Fifth Landing Stage*[7] written by J. B. Danquah and F. K. Fiawoo respectively. Up to that time there was no professional theatre in Ghana, and this factor needs to be borne in mind when assessing these early plays.

Obviously, these plays were prompted by the writers' knowledge of Western literary drama and its performance by schools, as well as their desire to cultivate a Ghanaian literature. Fiawoo's play alone gives enough evidence for this assertion which is borne out firstly, by his remark in the preface that his play does not conform to the Greek rule of drama (that is, the three unities, which is a direct reference to Aristotle's *Poetics*) and secondly, by the fact that he wrote his play first in the Ewe language before translating it into English which demonstrates his yearning for a native literature. The absence of professional theatre at the time these plays were written affected their creation as will be demonstrated presently, and one might say that both plays were conceived more out of the yearning for a literature than out of a concern for genuine theatre.

It was with Efua T. Sutherland that play writing with equal attention to both literature and theatre began. In 1957 she began working toward the creation of what has become the Ghana Drama Studio with the express aim of providing a studio for practicing playwrights. It has had a tremendous effect on play writing, for persons engaged in writing have also had some contact with the theatrical side of drama through the Studio. Sutherland has been engaged in both the writing and the productin of plays. Other writers like J. C. de Graft and Kwesi Kay are actors; Ama Ata Aidoo had also worked with Sutherland at the Studio. Thus, since 1957, Ghanaian play writing has become theatrically oriented.

Consequently there is a marked difference in dramatic quality between the plays of the 1940s and those written after Independence. Because the early playwrights' aim was strongly literary, their attention was mostly on the content of their works rather than the possibilities of presentation on the stage. Danquah derives his themes from various sources one of which is Akan cosmogony into which he incorporates the legend of the dispersion of the Akan tribes. Accordingly, the play covers two worlds—that of the gods, named Nyankonse (or Heaven), and that of men named Tekyiman which is the legendary home of the Akans. There are two sets of characters as well—spirits and men.

In the play the last act of creation has just been completed—that of the Third Woman who is to be instumental in refining man's depraved nature through her union with him, so he is destined to be married to Kwadjo Piesie, the young man who is in fact more enlightened than the others and is to save his country from the evil of Kwesi Sasahooden, the gnome, in the sub-plot.

Besides the cosmogony in the subject, there is the analysis of Oni, the Third Woman, and the Christian conception of her role. Ontologically, she is a composite of three elements: the physical; the Okra or Soul, who guards and directs her life; and the Sunsum who is her evolving (in Danquah's words, the expanding) attribute of her soul. This idea is expressed between Sunsum and Oni thus:

> Sunsum: Okra's dominion, as thy soul's guardian,
> I acknowledge. And my own expansion
> Should not trespass bounds of your personality
> Where lies my function to safeguard its growth.
> Oni: It is my fortune, then to have such good friends;
> Companions and partners in adventure
> The culmination will be our union,
> With such concordance in each companion.
> So for all life, or life in part, I will assume
> With me is Okra and with me Sunsum. (Act II, Sc. 2)

Oni is thus created according to the law of the triangle: matter is imbued with Soul essence and the result is a conscious man; but the consciousness, or personality, is a growng, evolving, entity which explains the purpose of Okra's incarnation.

As hinted above, there are Christian overtones surrounding Oni's role. She is a perfect product of Odomankoma's work. She crushes the serpent's head; and at her entry into Tekyiman Kweku Ananse, the demiurge, kneels to her addressing her with:

> Peace on earth, the positive joy of peace
> Peace! Perfect product of the perfect will. (Act V, Sc. 5)

She is destined to improve the nature of man by establishing peace on earth. This is symbolized at her coming in two miraculous phenomena: firstly, the state swords, symbol of war, falls from its place in the shrine of the goodess of war; secondly, the statue of war changes into a palm tree as it crashes. Finally, the man to marry her, Kwadjo Piesie, has to prove his worthiness of her by overcoming Kwesi Sasahooden, symbol of the devil, and thus eliminate the plague of death from Tekyiman. Oni's coming, therefore, brings peace to Tekyiman. Thus, in her one discerns the image of the Christian Virgin Mary—"Blessed among women"—and surrounding her role is the doctrine of the salvation of the world.

The Third Woman is essentially a drama of ideas, drawing its themes from three main sources: legend, folklore, and Christian doctrine. Its preoccupation with ideas, and the blank verse through which these are conveyed all give the play an elevated, literary tone. But the play is so overloaded with such a flux of ideas that Danquah's point of view is blurred; of all the ideas displayed, it is difficult to pinpoint Danquah's central theme. It would seem that he uses the dramatic medium only as a means for an intellectual array of ideas.

Compared with drama after 1957, *The Third Woman* is quite distinct in certain respects: it is diffuse in ideas and leisurely in tempo. With these characteristics and the ponderous versified language, it is very different from present-day plays which are slanted towards the modern, fast, and short-spaced theatre.

Fiawoo's play stands in a similar light to Danquah's. Its subject-matter is anthropological, reflecting certain modes of Anlo traditional life towards the end of the nineteenth century.

I do not intend to discuss Fiawoo's play in detail, for both plays have common peculiarities that can be attributed to the literary situation of their time, and therefore, the above discussion on Danquah's stands, *pari passu,* for the two as the first products in the development of Ghanaian literary drama.

The next phase in the development of our literary drama comes after Independence. Three playwrights stand out in this period. They are Efua T. Sutherland, Ama Ata Aidoo and J. C. de Graft. They are outstanding in this phase because they are the first group of writers to have so far published two plays each which are generally regarded both as literature and theatre. In the case of Efua Sutherland, the very new type of theatre that is witnessed in this period is owed to her creation of the Ghana Drama Studio.

Efua T. Sutherland, Ama Ata Aidoo and J. C. de Graft

Efua Sutherland's first play, *Foriwa*[8] dramatizes a community's awakening from an old-fashioned, into a modern, conception of human society. It is, therefore, at once a juxtaposition of traditional inaction and tribalism on the one hand and modern progressiveness and national consciousness on the other. Her second play, *Edufa,*[9] exploits the folk theme of witchcraft to examine a modern Ghanaian's values in life. Edufa is a prosperous society man who sacrifices the life of his wife though witchcraft so that he might live longer than his normal life-span. Only when his wife is about to die does he wake up to the profundity of his loss and the baseness of his action.

In both plays one notices the explicit dramatization of the development in man's consciousness. This is a feature common to the six plays by the three authors and will be elaborated upon presently. In *Foriwa* this quality is expressed in symbolism. The play opens at dawn when the street is faintly visible. Only in Labaran's camp is there any light—a lantern is burning on his table. He is awake at his table studying some papers. Then come his first words. "Kyerefaso has long been asleep."

This opening is significant for it introduces at once two forces in the plot—the drab, decrepit village of Kyerefaso, and Labaran, the live current that is to help in igniting it into a new life. The time of day, equally significant, thus symbolizes the dawn of consciousness in Kyerefaso. Further, at the end of the play, Labaran who has all along been slighted by the village community as *Otani* (stranger from the north) is seen holding hands with the princess of the village on the symbolic, old brick foundation, and even Sintim, the arch reactionary, looks on this union with undisguised approval. In this play, therefore, the dawning of a new consciousness is manifested in Kyerefaso's acceptance of Labaran not only as the ideal of self-help, but also as a member of the community— even as husband of their princess. In terms of present-day Ghanaian society, this is symbolic of the elimination of tribal discrimination. This step and the settlement of peace between the village and the Queen Mother with the resolution that Kyerefaso is "tired of parading in the ashes of their grandfathers' glorious deeds" complete the ideal society envisaged for the independent Ghana. Thus, Sutherland's vision in this play is communal.

In her next play, however, her vision is individualistic for here her focus is on the modern Ghanaian's personal philosophy of life. The ideal by which Edufa's life is matched is expressed in two stages, first through his father, Kankam:

> What do I want, you say? . . . I want the courage that makes
> responsible men. I want truthfulness. Decency. Feeling for
> your fellow men. These are the things I've always wanted.
> Have you got them to give? (Act I, Sc. 4)

and again more concisely by the Chorus: "One man's death is the death of all mankind" (Act II, Sc. 1).

Edufa is morally hollow: he lives only by the selfish motive of enjoyment and social prestige. Hence, he has no scruples in sacrificing his wife for his advantage—an act which in motive and process bespeaks spiritual blindness. On awakening he cries:

> . . . let me not be charged for any will to kill, but for my failure
> to create a faith . . . If only I hadn't been so cynical. (Act I, Sc.
> 4)

One might say that Edufa's life has come to this low ebb because, deracinated from his native traditions, he fails to respect their higher values (demonstrated in his lack of respect for his father), while at the same time he has not evolved any sane principle out of his Western education to be able to resist such a practice as witchcraft. The central point of view that seems to emerge in this play is that it behooves the modern Ghanaian to evolve out of both his native culture and Western education, (or contact with Western civilization) appropriate values for purposeful living.

Clearly, then, both *Foriwa* and *Edufa* offer us a dichotomy of themes, each play being poised on traditionalism and modernism. This is a feature Sutherland's dramas have in common with those of Ama Ata Aidoo, namely, *The Dilemma of a Ghost* and *Anowa*.[10]

The Dilemma of a Ghost is a domestic comedy dramatizing the well-known literary theme of the cultural complex of the African been-to, that is, the African who has been overseas. Ato Yawson, the hero, a young Ghanaian man, returns home from America after his education with an Afro-American wife, and the problem that arises is that of reconciling his acquired Western way of life with that of his native home. By his education and marriage, Ato's life and that of his relations have become diametrical, and it becomes his responsibility to harmonize the two.

The two outstanding areas where conflict arises are the rites of stool veneration and the child-bearing ideal of marriage perpetuated by Ato's relations. He can no longer regard these ideals in the same light as his relations, but even when he wants to pay lip-service to them, his wife pulls him to the opposite stand. Moreover, he lacks enough tact to handle the situation, showing himself utterly unequal to the challenge. At the end of the play it is his mother who leads Eulalie, his wife, into the old section of the house while he remains dazed and unreconciled.

The physical setting reflects the opposing poles of the drama. It is an old family house with a new annex. The illiterate, traditionalist members of the family live in the old section while the annex is reserved for Ato, the new man. This device is not a mere dramatic fancy, but a true reflection of similar situations that arise in Ghanaian life. The ambivalance of the plot is dramatically clinched at the end of the play when Ato, in his bewilderment, is torn between going to the annex and going to the old section. This is symbolic of his inability to resolve his dilemma. Another device to dramatize the theme is the underlying dream-story of the ghost, derived from Fanti folklore, which parodies the story of Ato; for Ato has become a ghost, his true native personality having been negated by his westernization.

In her second play, *Anowa,* Aidoo uses another device to represent the conflict of ideals. She creates a heroine at variance with her environment because she is in advance of her time. The play is set in the latter part of the nineteenth century. It is the era in the Gold Coast when it was the practice to buy slaves for use in farming and domestic work. It was also the day when girls rarely had the audacity to determine their own marriage in flagrant disregard of their parents and relations. It is in these two respects that the heroine, Anowa, refuses to conform to the conventions of her time firstly, by deciding her own marriage, and secondly, by rejecting the practice of slavery upheld by the husband. The result is a breakdown of relations between Anowa and her relatives because of her marriage, and later between her and her husband due to his indulgence in slavery.

Another factor underlying the breakdown of Anowa's marriage is Kofi Ako's practice of witchcraft through which he sacrifices his sexuality for material riches. As a result, there is no issue from the marriage. The very idea of witchcraft is obnoxious to Anowa's moral sense, and this together with Kofi Ako's loss of sexuality shatters their union. Thus here also, in respect of witchcraft, Anowa stands at variance with a belief and practice of her time. Her outlook on life is seen as being modern in terms of present-day westernized Ghana. It is interesting to compare how the conflict of ideals is generated in Aidoo's two plays. Whereas in the earlier play the conflict stems from cultural polarization of the hero through formal education, in the latter play it is the result of the heroine's natural insight bringing about a higher idealism.

The third playwright, J. C. de Graft, stands apart from the other two in the type of material he utilizes for his drama. His two plays, *Sons and Daughters* and *Through a Film Darkly*[11] both limit their purview to present-day Ghanaian life. The former concerns children's choice of career, and depicts the conflict that arises from a father's possessive eagerness to launch his children into what he considers respectable, money-earning professions and the children's relentless determination to pursue different careers of their own choice. In the play, the father, James Ofosu, wants his son, Aaron, to be an engineer, while the latter wants to be an artist; and the daughter, Maanan, wants to be a professional dancer while her father wants her to be a lawyer. This conflict is in fact a modern variant of what Aidoo presents in a traditional context in *Anowa*. It is an issue as old as man which social anthropologists identify as the conflict of adjacent generations.

De Graft's second play dramatizes what may be described as plagues from the past. It represents how the romances of a young man's earlier life, apparently forgotten, plague and ruin his future. John's past romances were with Rebecca, a Ghanaian, and Molly, a British girl. Out of the Molly affair, de Graft weaves a sub-theme of race prejudice. So he dramaitzes the plagues of John's past in two stages; firstly, the sub-theme of John's albinophobia exhibited when he meets Janet, and secondly, the main tragic theme that emerges with the return of Rebecca.

It was noted earlier that a feature of these plays is their dramatization of the development of human consciousness. This, at first, might seem a needless remark because all drama has at least as its ultimate aim the enlightenment of man. Yet, though all drama may have this concern, the procedure of presenting it is not the same in all cases, and further, the method a dramatist adopts to highlight this ideal might suggest his literary vision.

The dramas of Sutherland, Aidoo, and de Graft follow the pattern of representing the emergence of the human consciousness from darkness to light. This is quite explicit in their comedies. In their tragedies, though Anowa and John commit suicide, they do so, not in a scandalous rejection of a life in which they have failed to play a creative part, but in the spirit of stoics playing their parts in the midst of odds involved in the very act of living.

What emerges from this enquiry as the literary outlook of Sutherland, Aidoo, and de Graft is that they are at once optimistic and pragmatic. This point is important because a writer's vision is one of the fundamental interests in literary appreciation.

A characteristic of the plays that comes to light is that they are poised on conflict, a feature which has been acquired from Western literary drama. *Foriwa* exhibits a conflict between the traditional reaction of Kyerefaso and the modernism emboided in its leader, the Queen Mother, while *Edufa* illustrates man's desire to hold onto a pleasurable life against the natural law of death. Both of Aidoo's plays and de Graft's are based on the conflict of values.

De Graft's *Through a Film Darkly* is, from the point of view of theme, the most stimulating of the three Ghanaian tragedies, and this is chiefly because its interest lies not so much in telling a tragic story as in exploring emotional experiences through the ethical law of causation. On reading or seeing the experiences involving the leading characters of these tragedies (John, Anowa, and Edufa), one can tell where in each case the weight of the experiences lies: the experiences of Edufa are not only physical but superficial; those of Anowa are balanced between the physical and the emotional; and in the case of John's, the physical serves, as it were, only to manifest the emotional. In John's story, especially, those experiences that are basic to the tragedy have become part of his psyche—his affairs with Rebecca and Molly—and are objectively forgotten and therefore seem out of place in his present life; yet, they are eventually recalled as having potent effects in the present. In the case of Anowa, there is an overt progress of the change from childhood to death in adulthood. The difference between the two is effected through the style of presentation; but of course this is what demonstrates the artist's emphasis.

The subject matter of *Edufa* is quite specious, considering its witchcraft theme. But we have to turn to mythology to find parallels of the self-sacrifice symbolized in Ampoma. A Ghanaian example is the Ashanti legend of Tweneboa Kodu who offered his life to save his king and his people; another is the Greek story of Alcestis who also offered herself to die in place of her husband, Admetus, when even his parents would not do so. However, the story of Edufa has quite a different purport from these parallels, for whereas the legends are designed to illustrate the inspiring spirit of courage and patriotism in the case of Tweneboa Kodua, and love in the case of Alcestis, Edufa's is designed to denounce the practice of witchcraft and magic. Thus if Edufa's story was brought down to a real life situation, Ampoma would not make her sacrifice in full knowledge of her husband's motives.

As a work of art, the tragedy of Edufa is not convincing, and this is because the combined theme of witchcraft and self-sacrifice is not sufficiently conceptualized with the result that the play is wanting in logic (and hence, consistency) and effective language just when these are needed to heighten the drama. The lapse in logic is evident in a monologue of Edufa regretting his crime. He cries:

> . . . a man needs to feel secure . . . !
> If I must be condemned, let me not be charged for any will to kill, but for my failure to create a faith.
> Who thought the charm made any sense? Not I. A mystic symbol by which to calm my fears—that was all I could concede it . . .
> If only I hadn't been so cynical. I bent my knee where I have no creed and I'm constrained for my mockery. (Act I, Sc. 4, p. 20)

If Edufa had confessed that he believed in the charm but had intended to neutralize its deadly effect on the victim after he had secured its desired effect on his life, his inability to offset the price would have created a more sympathetic disaster. He is not simple-minded: to live as an educated, sophisticated business man and at the same time be so naive as to go after a vain "mystic symbol" merely "to calm fears" for which human life should be risked, is a contradiction that belongs to the portraiture rather than to the portrait. Edufa cannot claim to have committed his deed out of cynicism, otherwise he would not have risked human life, much less his own wife's. And yet, from the trend of his argument, his expression "cynical" does not denote philosophical cynicism, but a sarcastic, sneering attitude. Even if the expression is considered in the former denotation of the word, it is still wide of the mark for Edufa to claim to be a cynic. It must be remembered that this argument is a free-will confession of Edufa to himself; it is the working of his conscience, and as such, a reflection of his true feelings. This then is the fallacy underlying the story of Edufa. And as it involves the very foundation of the drama, it renders it superficial and thus weakens its impact.

The linguistic failure in *Edufa* results from the author's overeagerness to demonstrate intense emotion, because while her expression is generally apt in ordinary situations, in the case of intense moods, her language becomes exaggerated and theatrical. The following extract in which Edufa expresses his moody distress illustrates this point:

> He knows it all. I can swear he is too true a man to play me false. But I could not risk confirming it. I dread the power by which he knows, and it shall not gain admission here to energise that which all is set this day to exorcise. (Act I, Sc. 4, p. 20)

In the final clause of this speech the language suddenly becomes scholarly owing to such words as "admission," "energise" and "exorcise" making it sound rather artificial after the simple, heart-felt cry:

> Father!
> Call him back that I may weep on his shoulder. Why am I afraid of him? He would stand with me even though he rages so? (p. 19)

The author seems to think that to give vent to intense emotion she needs an uncommon language which in fact defeats her aim, as for example in Kankam's last speech to Edufa: "I am not proud that my life water animated you." The image of the close bond of blood-relationship between parent and child is suddenly spoiled by the one neutral word "animated."

This linguistic failure might be explained by the fact that men in agony or under stress do not in general think of learned expressions. Similarly, under such circumstances, far-fetched ideas need judicious application if they are not to sound stilted and ridiculous as happens in the first extract quoted above, in which the failure is not really due to inadequate language but to a misuse of ideas. Thus, the representation of Edufa's agony here fails, sounding artificial because he overstates it and the effect is melodramatic which is quite incongruous with the original temper of the drama.

Two things stand out in *Foriwa* and *Edufa* about Sutherland's art: one is her great interest in story dramatization, and the other is her effort to localize her drama. The result is that first, she externalizes her themes (unlike de Graft whose art is prone to abstraction) and second, she does this by exploiting forms of Ghanaian traditional drama and objective imagery. Thus in *Foriwa*, though it is not the aim to dramatize a community festival, it is made the background for the themes. And in *Edufa* the subject of witchcraft is developed with its related rituals of herbal bathing, fumigation, and dirging. The use of objective imagery is evident, for example, in the white lamb, the old foundation, and the handshake in *Foriwa*, and in *Edufa*, in the charms and the owl. But Sutherland's emphasis on spectacle slips into two weaknesses noticeable in *Foriwa*: the tritenss of subject which is due to the author's failure to intellectualize the themes of self-help and national unity and to raise them above the level of the popular slogans that were used in the First Ghana Republic; and the other is the inclusion of the scene of Mr. Anipare and Auntie Docia for the mere sake of its traditional spectacle without any corresponding relevance to the arguments of the drama. In effect, *Foriwa* does not rise beyond a polished popular play.

Ama Ata Aidoo's art displays the same technique of localized drama. But whereas Sutherland's gaze rests on the spectacular, Aidoo's is further directed to the intricacies of personal character; and thus, in drama she reveals the same interest in men as individuals that she demonstrates in her short stories. Hence, in addition to using traditional dramatic media, such as the ancestor cult in *The Dilemma of a Ghost*, libation, the procession of Kofi Ako in palanquin, drumming and horn-blowing in *Anowa*, she also exploits human characteristics like insinuation, gesture, and gossip not only to portray personal idiosyncrasies but also for dramatic effect. In *The Dilemma of a Ghost* while the gossip between the two women neighbours reflects their individual characters, it also contributes towards audience appreciation of the main action of the drama.

An example of Aidoo's dramatic use of gesture and insinuation in *Anowa* is seen when Badu remarks: "I am in disgrace, so suck your teeth at me." This is a reply to Anowa's unspoken thought, but it is gestured by sucking her teeth. At the end of the drama, in his musing, Old Man says to himself:

> Perhaps, perhaps, perhaps. And yet no one goes made in
> emptiness, unless he has the disease already in his head from

the womb. It is men who make men mad. Who knows if
Anowa would have been a better woman, a better person if we
had not been what we are? (Phase Three, p. 64)

And this musing is followed by the stage direction: "Old Woman glares at
him, spits, and wobbles out coughing harder than ever before."

In *The Dilemma of a Ghost* there is the following direction: "The old
woman spits significantly" which, coming after Esi Kom's question,

But how is it, my child, that she comes from America and she
has this strange name?

suggest the old woman's contempt for both Ato and Eulalie. In Act IV
there is also this sardonic statement from Esi: "I'm very quiet." These
examples illustrate the fact that besides the traditional dramatic forms,
the exposition of certain attributes of character peculiar to the world of
the drama constitutes yet another direction in which Aidoo seeks to
localize her drama. Another device serving the same end is her use of
transliteral English for her non-literate characters. For Aidoo, therefore,
drama is more than just dramatizing a theme; it is a medium for the
exposition of the peculiarities of individual human beings.

Thus in her drama she displays a sensitivity to language which gives her
plays greater depth than those of Sutherland and de Graft. Notice, for
example, evidence of creative imagination behind the following extract
revealed through the perceptive choice of language and thought:

Nana: My spirit Mother ought to have come for me earlier.
Now what shall I tell them who are gone? The daughter
of slaves who come from the white man's land.
Some one should advise me on how to tell my story.
My children, I am dreading my arrival there
Where they will ask me news of home.
Shall I tell them or shall I not?
Someone should lend me a tongue
Light enough with which to tell
My Royal Dead
That one of their stock
Has gone away and brought to their sacred precincts
The wayfarer! (Act I, p. 14)

If one compares this passage with dialogue from *Sons and Daughters*, it
may be observed that both writers intend to elevate some thought by

exploiting linguistic resources, and that whereas de Graft resorts to trite images and undue repetitions which defeat his attempt to rise, the very phrasing and wording of Aidoo's gives it an easy and smooth take-off. The difference lies in the writers' sensitivity to language. Though in terms of theme Aidoo's plays are not exceptionally striking compared with those of de Graft and Sutherland, they have the advantage of her use of language.

The arguments put forth in this discussion point to the conclusion that in Ghanaian literary writing, the development of drama is as yet minimal. One cannot overlook the fact that a play might be theatrical and yet not be literature. This is the direction in which our literary drama has moved thus far. Although the plays highlighted in the discussion can stand as theatre, not all of them can be considered literature; in general they are limited in the imaginative and linguistic tension, all of which contribute to the literary interest of drama. Thus, the two early plays of the 1940s and four post-independence ones; namely, *The Dilemma of a Ghost, Anowa, Edufa,* and *Through a Film Darkly* may be liberally admitted as having some measure of these basic requirements which seems to suggest that the direction in the development of our literary drama is towards theatricality.

Another conclusion from this discussion relates to the form of Ghanaian literary drama. The term "Form," as stated earlier at the beginning of the chapter, is used here to designate the totality of characteristics that make theatre; it includes both the literary and the theatrical features that are the result of the artistic techniques of the playwrights.

The format of the majority of the plays is modelled after the conventional western practice of arranging the plot into "acts" and "scenes." In *Through a Film Darkly* and *Anowa,* however, there is what might be regarded as some departure from this order. The former is quite a short play and straightforward so it requires no elaborate sub-divisions; the latter is arranged in three parts each labelled after the setting of its action—Phase One, "In Yebi"; Phase Two, "On the Highway"; and, Phase Three: "The Big House at Oguaa."

Four of the plays (those of Sutherland and Aidoo) begin with a prologue either in the form of a monologue or a dialogue. One is familiar with this style in western literature. An example of a different form of prologue is the musical one used by the Concert Parties.

In the presentation of character, only in Aidoo's plays is there any significant exploration of human character through the dramatization of personal idiosyncrasy, and this, together with her use of language to distinguish between characters, makes her drama more innovative than those of the other two playwrights.

185

Another feature of the Ghanaian literary theatre is its emphasis on dialogue with action as opposed to the music, speech and action of the Concert Party theatre which is due to its aim to appeal to a literary audience.

Thus, these characteristics together with the principle of conflict noted earlier give the Ghanian literary drama a strong western outlook. Yet, one recognizes the efforts of all the playwrights, except de Graft, to blend elements from their indigenous tradition with elements of western drama in order to evolve a type of theatre that might be Ghanaian. Albert Gérard's comment on African literature is therefore apt—"the literature of present-day Africa emerged from the cross-fertilization of conservative and innovating trends, and the precolonial tradition has influenced the orientation of modern writing."[12]

NOTES

1. J. H. Nketia, *Ghana-Music, Dance and Drama*, The Ghana Information Services, Accra, 1965, p. 29.
2. Efua T. Sutherland sketches the theatrical development of one of the pioneers of the Concert Party in a booklet, *Bob Johnson*, and in doing so, unearths the origins of the comic play. (Anowuo Educational Publications, Accra, 1970).
3. Ibid., pp. 6–8.
4. Ibid., p. 12.
5. J. H. Nketia, op. cit., p. 29.
6. Kobina Sekyi, *The Blinkards*, Heinemann (AWS), 1974.
7. J. B. Danquah, *The Third Woman;* F. K. Fiawoo, *The Fifth Landing Stage.*
8. Efua T. Sutherland, *Foriwa*, State Publishing Corporation, Accra-Tema, 1967.
9. Efua T. Sutherland, Edufa, Longmans, London, 1967.
10. Ama Ata Aidoo, *The Dilemma of a Ghost*, Longmans, Accra, 1965, p. 12; idem., *Anowa*, Longman, London, 1970.
11. J. C. de Graft, *Sons and Daughters*, O.U.P., London, 1964; idem., *Through a Film Darkly*, O.U.P., London, 1970.
12. Albert Gérard, "The Preservation of Tradition in African Creative Writing," in *Research in African Literatures*, Vol. 1, No. 1, p. 35.

LANGUAGE AND DRAMA: AMA ATA AIDOO

Dapo Adelugba

The Ghanaian writer, Ama Ata Aidoo, born in 1942, is perhaps best known for her collection of short stories, *No Sweetness Here,* but she has also written two plays, *The Dilemma of a Ghost,*[1] written and staged in 1964 and published in 1965, and *Anowa,*[2] published in 1970. I intend in this paper to examine her two plays, with special emphasis on her deft use of language.

Speech, in Aidoo's plays, is an index of social class, age, and background; it is also a vehicle for characterization. John Millington Synge, the Irish dramatist, said in his Preface to *The Playboy of the Western World,* "Every speech should be as fully flavoured as a nut or an apple." Miss Aidoo's speeches certainly have this quality. Her success in creating levels of language, in matching literary grace with veracity of characterization, in suiting, for the most part, the action to the word, the word to the action, is commendable in such a young dramatist.

Looking closely at *The Dilemma of a Ghost,* one can identify six levels of language: the American English of Eulalie Yawson, the educated African English of Ato Yawson, the stylized poetry and prose of the Prelude, the childlike talk of Boy and Girl, the chit-chat in verse of the 1st Woman and the 2nd Woman, and the language of Nana, Akyere, Petu, Mansa, Akroma, and Monka. Within this spectrum there is a wide variety of linguistic usage. For Eulalie, English is a first language: thus her language falls (or should fall) within the linguistic category, E_1. Ato's English, a second language acquired through education, is E_2. The poetry and prose of the Prelude also fall within the E_2 bracket, being the creation of a dramatist for whom English is a second language. As for the Boy and Girl, there is no evidence to suggest that they are not speaking English: so their language falls with the E_2 category.

The fifth and sixth levels are of especial interest. Although "transcribed" into English by a dexterous dramatist, there is every reason to believe that these speeches are made by characters who speak a Ghanaian language, probably Fante, and Aidoo (like Synge *vis-à-vis* the Gaelic-speaking characters—as opposed to his English-speaking characters—in his Anglo-Irish plays) wants us to believe so. I would suggest that we put

187

these transcriptions ("translations" would be an inappropriate word!) in a special category which we shall describe as E_3. Aidoo's most memorable passages are in this E_3 category, a significant fact which we shall re-examine a little later, after we have examined each of the six levels of language in *The Dilemma*.

Aidoo's attempt at E_1 proves abortive, not so much because she is herself an E_2 speaker (many E_2 writers have succeeded in recapturing in their writing the essence of E_1) but probably because of her mere passing acquaintanceship with the American—and indeed Afro-American—variety of E_1. Ato's impatience with Eulalie's "running-tap drawl"[3] is doubly ironic because neither the drawl nor the "running-tap" quality comes across in the writing. The playwright's reliance on gimmicks is all too transparent. For example:

> I must *sort of* confess that I am finding all this *rather cute* (p. 19)

or

> Sugar, don't *sort of* curse me and your Pa every morning you look your face in the mirror and see yourself Black . . . (pp. 19-20)

or

> . . . you *cannna do nothing* about it (p. 20)

or

> My people! *Add it,* Moses. I shall say anything I like. I am *right tired* (p. 45)

or

> *Aren't they gotten* any meaning on this rotten island? (p. 45)

The following are just not American:

> Or are you too British you canna hear me Yankee lingo? (p. 28)

and

And give them the opportunity to accuse me of unadaptability.
(p. 28)

And the following are samples rather of West African incorrect sentences
than of Afro-American speech:

> I wish you were right here, not even in the States. (p. 20)
> Now you dare not confess it before them, can you? (p. 42)

Quite often Aidoo gives Eulalie the academic West African language
one is more likely to hear along the dormitory corridors of the University
of Ghana and it might well be Ato speaking in such instances as:

> What a blasted mess! (p. 37)

or

> That shows you that after a year of marriage I am still in love
> with my husband which, incidentally, is a wonderful achieve-
> ment. (p. 37)

In the following short extract it is difficult to tell which voice is Eulalie's
and which Ato's:

> Have you been drinking Coke?
> Mm . . . yes.
> Excellent of you. I can't bear it warm.
> And of course you carried a refrigerator down here.
> I am sorry.
> Christ, what are you apologizing for? After all, I was only
> feeling a bit homesick and I drank if for sentimental reasons. I
> could have had a much cooler, sweeter, and more nourishing
> substitute in coconuts, couldn't I? (p. 21)

We should also note how stilted and artificial it sounds, especially the last
speech quoted, which is not Ato's, who has acquired English through a
laborious process, but Eulalie's, for whom English is a first language. One
has to differentiate between this kind of artificality, which is a fault in
playwright, and the other kind, used of characterization, which is best
illustrated by Eulalie's first long speech (as Voice) in Act II.

Ato, perhaps, much more than Eulalie, is emotionally callow and out of touch with reality, traits which he shares with Achebe's Odili in *A Man of the People* and a good number of E. M. Forster's young heroes and heroines. This quality of callowness is well depicted by Aidoo, partly through his actions and partly through his words. He says to his wife in Act II:

> Those were only funeral drums. But I think you must have a siesta. If you don't you'll have a nervous breakdown before you've learnt enough to graduate in primitive cultures. (p. 21)

In addressing the illiterate elders of his family in Act I, Ato adopts a lecturing tone most unsuitable for the occasion:

> Please, I beg you all, listen. Eulalie's ancestors were of our ancestors. But *(warming up)* as you all know, the white people came and took some away in ships to be slaves . . . (p. 12)

Instead of adjusting to his family's horror at his marriage to "the offspring of slaves" (p. 13)—the words are Nana's—he proceeds to deliver an academic disquisition:

> ATO: *(Moving to the front of the stage)* Heavens! Is there any reason why you should make so much fuss? All because I have married an American Negro? If you only know how sweet Eulalie is! *(He looks at the women and whistles)* Now all this racket you are putting on will bring the whole town here. (pp. 13–14)

Both Eulalie and Ato start out at the beginning of the play as immature, idealistic, and callow. While Eulalie seems to be on the path to better self-knowledge and understanding at the end of the play, significantly the "voices of the children" are still the "echo" of Ato's "own mind" (p. 50) which indicates that maturity and resolution are yet to come.

The Prelude, a kind of introduction or prologue, is given to the Bird of the Wayside who speaks very much in the educated accents of the playwright-narrator, except for the transcription of the Hornblower's message which is not a particularly elevated piece of verse:

> We came from left
> We came from right
> We came from left
> We came from right

> The twig shall not pierce our eyes
> Nor the rivers prevail o'er us.
> We are of the vanguard
> We are running forward, forward, forward . . . (p. 2)

All through *The Dilemma of a Ghost* there are uneven attempts at poetic diction: some sections are very successful, others border on the banal. But these are faults that can be excused in a writer who was only twenty-two when the play was written.

The Prelude's loaded statement prepares us for the surprises we are to meet in the play:

> . . . the day of Planning is different from the day of Battle. (p. 2)

The Prelude is racy and vivid and falls in the main within the E_2 category. In addition to the Hornblower's message there are a few phrases which are redolent of E_3 but it is difficult to tell whether these are direct transcriptions from an original Ghanaian language or, as Karen Chapman suggests in her Introduction to the 1971 Collier Books edition4 of the play, biblical allusions:

> Look around you,
> For the mouth must not tell everything.
> Sometimes the eye can see
> And the ear should hear.[5]

The Boy and Girl appear in one brief scene at the beginning of Act III. Their accents are authentically childlike as they play their children's game, and their song serves as ironic commentary on Ato's plight and the play. Aidoo's verse is not elevated but it serves the intended purpose admirably:

> BOY: What shall we do now?
> GIRL: Kwaakwaa.
> BOY: All right, I will hid, you will find me.
> GIRL: No, I will not find you, I will hide.
> BOY: I say, I will hide.
> GIRL: No, I will.
> BOY: I will not allow you.
> GIRL: Then I will not play.
> BOY: If you do not, I will beat you. *(Hits her)*
> GIRL: *(Crying)* Beast!

191

BOY: Oh, I did not mean to hurt you. But you too! I have told you I want to hide . . . Let us play another game then. What shall we do?
GIRL: Let us sing "The Ghost."
BOY: Ghost . . . Ghost . . . ah, yes! *(They hold hands and skip about in circles as they sing)*
> One early morning
> When the moon was up
> Shining as the sun,
> I went to Elmina Junction
> And there and there,
> I saw a wretched ghost
> Going up and down
> Singing to himself,
> > "Shall I go
> > To Cape Coast,
> > Or to Elmina
> > I don't know,
> > I can't tell.
> > I don't know,
> > I can't tell." (pp. 23–4)

The children repeat the song but *"halfway through the lights go out. When the lights come up a few seconds later, the children have vanished"* (p. 24). Adioo thus ensures that the audience's minds will keep turning over the words of the song and their possible meanings. She ends the play with the children's voices singing the same song. The children themselves do not appear, however, for the voices serve as an "echo" (p. 50) of Ato's mind.

The simplicity of the language here not only aids truthful characterization but also makes it easy for the audience to remember the theme song: a more complex pattern of words might be less memorable. The appearance of children in a play which deals with adults is also sure to add to the interest of the audience.

Almost as interesting to an audience as children is the appearance of comic characters, especially at moments in a play when tension has been built up to high point. Now, the 1st and 2nd Woman are not totally comic: there is a serious side to their portrayal. But they help to break the tension and serve as contrast to and commentary on the serious happenings within Ato's family clan. Aidoo has individuated these two characters: one has children and the other is barren—a fact which affects their attitudes to life and to the affairs of Ato's family. Their two different perspectives are again the playwright's way of ensuring audience interest and involvement. The 1st Woman is by and large the rational and individualistic voice, the 2nd Woman (the fertile one) emerges as more sentimental, and she is a mouthpiece of the traditional views of the community, even when these are not based on reason. For example, in Act II:

> 2nd W.: Have you forgotten the daughter of this same
>   Esi Kom? Have you not heard it whispered?
>   Have you not heard it sung
>   From the end of the East road
>   To the beginning of the West
>   That Monka never marries well?
> 1st W.: But if Esi Kom bears a daughter
>   And the daughter finds no good man
>   Shall we say
>   It is Esi Kom's fate in childbirth,
>   Or shall we say it is her daughter's trouble?
>   Is not Monka the sauciest girl
>   Born here for many years?
>   Has she not the hardest mouth in the town?
> 2nd W.: That is as it may
>   But Esi Kom suffers for it.
> 1st W.: My sister, even from bad marriages
>   Are born good sons and daughters. (pp. 16–17)

Aidoo has given the two Women a conversational kind of verse. This sets them apart from the protagonists of the drama, and it is a verse flexible enough to serve comic purposes. The Women's speeches have the flavour of gossipy excitement. The fecundity of translation and the graphic images, especially in Act IV, remind one very much of the Neighbours in John Pepper Clark's *Song of a Goat*.[6] One short extract will illustrate these features of the writing:

> 2nd W.: . . . my sister, roll your tobacco and stuff your pipe.
>   It has been good going,
>   The roof leaks more than ever before.
> 1st W.: But how can it be?
> 2nd W.: If Nakedness promises you clothes,
>   Ask his name.
> 1st W.: But I ask, how can it be?
> 2nd W.: You ask me?

> 1st W.: But you know, my sister,
>   That my name is Lonesome.
>   I have no one to go and listen
>   To come back and tell me.
> 2nd W.: Then scoop your ears of all their wax
>   And bring them here.
>   Esi Kom is not better than she was.
> 1st W.: Why?
> 2nd W.: They never ask "Why?"
>   Is it not the young man's wife?
> 1st W.: What has she done now?
> 2nd W.: Listen, I hear she swallows money
>   As a hen does corn.
> 1st W.: Oh, Esi Kom!
> 2nd W.: One must sit down
>   If one wants to talk of her affairs.[7]

Clearly this admirable piece of dialogue is not mere translation. It is a kind of invention that comes out of a sensitive synthesis of the literary felicities of two different languages—English and a Ghanaian language, probably Fanti. It is especially to be noted that Aidoo does not strike one false not in her creation of E_3: her success could only have come out of a strictly disciplined artistic mind which keeps a steady eye on integrity and objectivity.

When we more to the sixth group we find that the prose of the illiterate protagonists of the drama is not only vigorous but austere and economical. The degree of ease in the use of traditional saws, proverbs, and imagery is determined by the ages of the users. Nana, the oldest of the group, evinces the most felicitous use of this kind of language; next to her in competence and assured ease are Ato's Elder Uncle, Petu, and his Elder Aunt, Akyere; then comes Esi Kom, Ato's mother; then Akroma and Mansa, Ato's Younger Uncle and Aunt, and finally, the novitiate in E3, Monka. This hierarchical arrangement might be partly a matter of instinct on Aidoo's part, but one cannot but think that, for the most part, it is a matter of careful craftsmanship.

Although Nana speaks in prose most of the time, she moves into the realm of verse at moments of intense passion, but even at such moments Aidoo has seen to it that the integrity of E3 is not violated. We may note, among other things, the trinal union of the dead, the living and the unborn in traditional African cosmogony which makes a speech like the following possible:

NANA: My spirit Mother ought to have come for me earlier
　　Now what shall I tell them who are gone? The daughter of slave
　　who came from the white man's land. Someone should advise me on
　　how to tell my story.
　　My children, I am dreading my arrival there
　　Where they will ask me news of home.
　　Shall I tell them or shall I not?
　　Someone should lend me a tongue
　　Light enough with which to tell
　　My Royal Dead
　　That one of their stock
　　Has gone away and brought to their sacred precincts
　　The wayfarer! . . .
　　They will ask me where I was
　　When such things were happening,
　　O mighty God!
　　Even when the Unmentionable
　　Came and carried off the children of the house
　　In shoals like fish,
　　Nana Kum kept his feet steadfast on the ground
　　And refused to let any of his nephews
　　Take a wife from a doubtful stock . . .
　　If it is true that the last gets the best of everything
　　Then what is this
　　Which my soul has drawn out of me? (pp. 14–15)

In reproving Ato In act I, Nana says cryptically:

　　Ato, do not talk with the foolishness of your generation. (p. 13)

In Act III Petu answers Ato's question, 'You went to the farm?', with the
dry wit E₃ facilitates:

　　My master, where else have I to go? . . . Since the morning has
　　found us, we must eat. And as you know, some of us are not
　　lucky enough to be paid only to sit in an office doing nothing.
　　And that is why I have to relieve the wayside herbs of their
　　dew every morning. (pp. 24–5)

Esi's speech towards the end of Act III has the graphic image:

195

> The vulture, right from the beginning, wallows in the soup he
> will eat. (p. 31)

She speaks 'English' only once in the play in her attempt to make Eulalie
feel welcome:

> 'My lady', I am saying goodbye. (p. 27)

By putting 'My Lady' in inverted commas, Aidoo has indicated that the
speaker at this point breaks into 'English' temporarily. 'I am saying
goodbye' is probably said in the customary language.

Monka is given the saucy lines in the play and this is in tune with her
age and character. She, like the older generation, sometimes carries off E_3
in telling imagery such as:

> If nothing scratched at the palm fibre, it certainly could not
> have creaked. (p. 29)

But sometimes her speech betrays the inadequacies of the apprentice:

> There are two kinds of offers. One which comes right from the
> *bowels,* the other which falls from the lips only. (p. 30)

In the context 'bowels',[8] which here sounds crass, is certainly not the
word the Elders would have used.

All told, Aidoo is more successful with E_3 than with E_2 and E_1, but one
hopes that as she develops as a playwright she will listen even more
carefully to the speech of her educated compatriots so as to achieve
greater success in her creation of dialogue. The six levels here identified
certainly recommend themselves for future efforts in dramatic writing,
not only in Ghana but indeed in all other African countries which share
the same kind of heritage.

Karen Chapman, in her Introduction to the Collier Books edition of *The
Dilemma of a Ghost* to which we referred earlier, points out some of the
technical faults in the play. One might add the occasional clumsiness in
stage directions, for example, in Act I:

> *Everyone repeats her words to create confusion*[9]

and the occasional lapse in action:

Eulalie's eyes follow (Ato) as he goes back to the room and she is still looking in his direction when he returns some minutes later. (p. 21)

Karen Chapman has also pinpointed the most commendable aspects of Aidoo's artistry:

> . . . control of language is her forte . . . The dignity of her characters is defined, to a degree, by their idiom. (Christina) Ama Ata Aidoo's gifts are evident, particularly in her evocation of local colour and manners, her controlled lyricism, and her skill in tracing the curve of delicate human emotions.[10]

While one cannot totally endorse the last item in Chapman's list, one feels that Aidoo's delineation of delicate emotions, which is adequate in this early work, will improve with time.

Anowa, Aidoo's second play, was published in 1970. *Anowa* is a dramatization of an old Ghanaian legend. It centres on two protagonists, Kofi and Anowa. Although this play is not as rich in the individuation of charcters as *The Dilemma,* it uses some of the techniques of characterization and presentation in the earlier play. Indeed, some characters seem to reappear, albeit in slightly different guises. The Old Man and the Old Woman remind one of the 1st Woman and the 2nd Woman in *The Dilemma.* They take two different attitudes (as in *The Dilemma*): the Old Man being by and large the voice of reason and individual choice while the Old Woman represents the voice of emotion, prejudice, and communal compulsions. Instead of the Prelude (the Bird of the Wayside in *The Dilemma*), Aidoo gives the Old Man the prologue, a long opening speech which sets the scene.

Aidoo's description of her characters establishes them as the two-dimensional characters of fable, with the exception of Anowa. 'a young woman who grows up' and Kofi Ako, 'her man who expands.'[11] In the list of dramatis personae, she describes the other characters thus:

OLD MAN
OLD WOMAN } Being The-Mouth-That-Eats-Salt-and-Pepper
A MAN And A WOMAN: who don't say a word
OSAM: her (Anowa's) father who smokes a pipe
BADUA: her (Anowa's) mother who complains at the
   beginning and cries in the end
BOY: a young slave, about twenty years old

GIRL: a young slave girl
PANYIN-NA-KAKRA: a pair of boy-twins, whose duty it is
   to fan an empty chair.
HORNBLOWER
OTHER MEN and WOMEN: slaves, carriers, waiting
   women, drummers, messengers, townspeople.[12]

In introducing into the drama the elements of crowd, procession, music, movement, and mime, Aidoo seems to wish to create a theatre of rich texture which would compensate for the simplicity of the fable. These elements are not, unfortunately, utilized to full advantage.

Why, we may ask, does Aidoo include among her dramatis personae 'A Man and a Woman who don't say a word?' With the benefit of hindsight it would be easy to see, once one has read the entire play, how their brief mime at the beginning of Phase I is a metaphor of Kofi and Anowa's plight:

> . . . A Woman comes in frm the lower left, carrying a wooden
> tray which is filled with farm produce . . . Close behind her is a
> Man, presumably her husband, also in work-clothes, with a
> gun on his shoulder and a machet under his arm . . . Finally,
> the Woman misses a step or kicks against the block of wood.
> She falls, her tray crashing down. (p. 9)

Indeed, *Anowa* is laden with symbols at every turn. For example, the Boy and Girl (older versions of their prototypes in *The Dilemma*) who prattle in a wise childlikeness, like Shakespeare's children, not only make ironic comments on the play but also mirror the Kofi-Anowa relationship in miniature. And as in the Old Man/Old Woman scenes, the Boy tends to be the rational element, while the Girl seems more emotional and commu-nity-psyche-oriented.

The chair which the pair of boy-twins fan with ostrich feather fans in Phase 3 is 'empty' (p. 51) (barren, like Anowa?). It becomes a focus of attention partly because of its position of dominance on the stage and also by virtue of Anowa's obsession with it:

> Stop fanning that chair . . . stop fanning the chair. (p. 52)

When Kofi, on entry, occupies the chair, a funeral march is played. So the chair becomes, in a sense, a symbol of impending doom. When the lights fade out on the Kofi-Anowa scene and are brought up on the Yebi setting, we again see 'a gilded chair' (p. 62) in the centre. A group of women sit around the chair 'as though it is the funeral bed . . . All are in deep red mourning' (pp. 62–3).

Through such well-chosen, economical techniques Aidoo connects the two scenes of action and gives us a unified design. The use of the *Atentenben* (intended as a symbol for Anowa)[13] at the end of Phase I and again at the end of Phase 3 also helps in achieving unity of design.

The levels of language in *Anowa* do not parallel those six levels discussed with regard to *The Dilemma of a Ghost*. The society in the later play has had a uniform pattern of exposure. There is no evidence that any member of the community has had a Western education: the nearest one comes to this possibility is Anowa's carping remark to Kofi in Phase 3, suggesting that he has 'learned the ways of white people' (p. 54). There is no concrete evidence of 'schooling' in the Western tradition. it would seem, then, that ideally all the characters in the play would speak E_3, but in fact this is not totally the case.

The Boy and the Girl, as well as the pair of twins in their brief appearance, speak E_2. One might say in extenuation that this might well be an immature form of E_3. But with Kofi and Anowa, who also speak E_2 part of the time, their language would be more difficult to defend, unless it can be proved that they have been exposed to some kind of education, the discussion of which does not fall within the province of the play. What seems the most likely explanation, however, is that the playwright is dealing with a situation different from that she was confronted with in *The Dilemma of a Ghost:* here she is dramatizing an old Ghanaian legend for the benefit of present-day audiences and readers, and since the society is homogeneous, a laborious creation of levels of language might not have recommended itself to her. This is not to say that there is no individuation in the speeches of the different characters.

Osam and Badua conform to the level of language we have described as E_3 in our discussion of *The Dilemma*, and Anowa seems to be undergoing a successful education in E_3 in Phase I. Her comments,

> Please, Mother, remove your witch's mouth from our marriage. (p. 18)

and

> Mother, I shall walk so well that I will not find my feet back here again. (p. 19)

almost match Badua's in acidity and appropriateness. She keeps this quality in Phases 2 and 3, where, admittedly, both she and her husband oscillate between E_2 and E_3. There are obvious similarities between the newly-weds in both *Anowa* and *The Dilemma of a Ghost,* except for the shift of the 'ghost' role from husband in *The Dilemma* to wife in Anowa: 'I wander around like a ghost,' (p. 54) Anowa says of herself in Phase 3, and earlier in that Phase the young girl says of her: 'Now she flits about like a ghost, talking to herself' (p. 48). Of course, the ghost symbolism is less multi-layered in implications here than in *The Dilemma.*

While Kofi and Anowa can harangue each other in the educated accents of their prototypes, Ato and Eulalie, they can also fence in proverbs with deft accuracy, as in Phase 2:

> KOFI AKO: Anowa, the farmer goes home from the
> farm . . .
> ANOWA: *(Gets up and starts walking before Kofi Ako)* And
> the fisherman brings his boats and nets to the shore . . .
> KOFI AKO: And if you know this already, then why?
> ANOWA: They return in the morning.
> KOFI AKO: But we have finished doing all that needs to be
> done by us.
> ANOWA: Kofi, one stops wearing a hat only when the head
> has fallen off.
> KOFI AKO: *(Irritably)* Anowa, can one not rest a tired neck?
> (p. 35)

The Old Man and the Old Woman speak in a poetic version of E_3 and in a heightened prose version at the end of the play. The Hornblower's verse form of E_3 is adequate, if not particularly elevated.

In these two plays, then, Ama Ata Aidoo has shown how dexterously language can be manipulated to serve dramatic ends. She has a gift both for the sparse economical language of sadness and despair and for the gaiety, rollicking boisterousness, and acid wit of comedy, satire, irony, and parody. Aidoo's use of language is an indication of how educated dramatists can portray with veracity and accuracy the different generations and levels of education in present-day Africa.

NOTES

1. *The Dilemma of a Ghost* was first presented on stage by the Students' Theatre, Legon, on 12, 13, and 14 March 1964 at the Open-Air Theatre, Commonwealth Hall, University of Ghana, Legon. It was directed by a Nigerian, Mr Olu Nye Ogunsanwo. The play was published in London by Longman in 1965. A Collier Books edition appeared in 1971 in their African/American Library series.
2. *Anowa* was published in London by Longman in 1970.

3. Christina Ama Ata Aidoo, *The Dilemma of a Ghost* (London, Longman; Accra, Ikeja, 1965), p. 3.
4. Christina Ama Ata Aidoo, *The Dilemma of a Ghost* (London, Macmillan, Collier Books, edn., 1971), p. 22.
5. Aidoo, *The Dilemma of a Ghost* (London, Longman, 1965), p. I.
6. John Pepper Clark, *Three Plays* (London and New York, O.U.P., 1964). *Song of a Goat* is the first play in this volume which includes *The Masquerade* and *The Raft*. The original publication of *Song of a Goat* (Ibadan, Mbari, 1962) seems to be out of print.
7. Aidoo, *The Dilemma of a Ghost* (London, Longman, 1965), pp. 33–4.
8. We may compare with this the felicitous use of 'bowel' in *Anowa* (London, Longman, 1970), p. 30, when, Badua says:
   You have always feared her? And is that a good thing to say about your own bowel-begotten child?
9. Aidoo, *The Dilemma of a Ghost*. (London, Longman, 1965), p. 10.
10. Aidoo, *The Dilemma of a Ghost*. (London, Macmillan, 1971), pp. 23, 25.
11. Ama Ata Aidoo, *Anowa* (London, Longman, 1970), unnumbered page before p. I.
12. Ibid., loc. cit.
13. Ibid., p. 2 (Production Notes).

FICTION

AMA ATA AIDOO: THE ART OF THE SHORT STORY

Lloyd W. Brown

As students of African literature we usually deal with the African woman as a topic in that literature, but very seldom as a contributor. The neglect of the African woman as writer results, in part, from the invisibility, or near invisibility, of women writers in general; but that universal problem has been compounded, in this instance, by the relatively short supply of women writers in Africa. Ama Ata Aidoo of Ghana has managed to survive this double handicap, if one may judge, not by the number of studies of her work (for these are rare), but by her continuing popularity in the accepted arenas of public attention—anthologies, reprints, and mass circulation interviews. She has attracted some attention as a dramatist, but it has been as a short-story writer that she has been most prolific. And it has been in the short-story medium that she has been most successful in developing narrative techniques that are integrated with those thematic perspectives which she derives from the traditional situation and the contemporary experience of the African woman. In other words, Aidoo's art as a short-story writer combines her narrative materials and structures with narrative points of view which, in turn, reflect a variety of insights into the situation of Aidoo's women. Briefly, there is a general tendency to use traditional story-telling techniques (from the African oral tradition) as the media for traditional viewpoints in a rural society. And, in turn, a more self-consciously Western style or structure is the medium for the Westernized female consciousness, or at the very least, for the insights of a Western education, into the ambiguities of female roles in both traditional African and contemporary Western societies.

"In the Cutting of a Drink" exemplifies the first category in that the oral framework of the story's narrative structure complements the rural tradition of the male narrator's background. The title itself establishes the communal ritual which envelops the story-teller's art within the oral tradition. The "cutting" (i.e., pouring) of a drink is the narrator's reward-and-incentive in the telling of the story. And the story-teller's occasional break from his narrative to call for his drink ("Cut me a drink, for my throat is very dry, my uncle . . .") serves a multiple purpose. Artistically, it heightens the dramatic suspense of the narrative, since this thirsty self-interruption usually occurs at crucial points of the story. And in this regard the call for a drink emphasizes the orality of the narrator's art, both in a literal sense and in the implied reference to the physicality of the oral form ("my throat is dry"). At the same time the call for a drink affirms the traditionally communal orientation of the story-teller's art by claiming the story-teller's due reward for a communal service. And the total effect of this communal emphasis is the heightening of our awareness of moral as well as auditory relationships between the story-teller's techniques and the traditional values of his audience. He is a young man in a rural village describing to his older relatives the strange life-style of the modern, Westernized city which he has recently visited in a search for his sister Mansa who had left home twelve years before. The story-teller's audience therefore represents those family values and sexual mores which are alien to the ways of the city:

> . . . uncle, we had gone to a place where they had given a dance, but I did not know.
>
> Some people were sitting on iron chairs around iron tables. Duayaw [his host] told some people to bring us a table and chairs and they did. As soon as we sat down, Duayaw asked us what we would drink. As for me, I told him *lamlale* but his woman asked for "Beer" . . .
>
> Yes I remember very well, she asked for beer . . . I sat with my mouth open and watched the daughter of a woman cut beer like a man. The band had stopped playing for some time and soon they started again. Duayaw and his woman went to dance. I sat there and drank my *lamlale*. I cannot describe how they danced.[1]

But he does eventuallly describe not only how they danced but also how he himself danced with the "bad" women of the city in that night club. And he also describes the long straightened hair (like that of a white woman), red, painted lips ("like a fresh wound") and skin-tight dress ("There was no space between her skin and her dress") of these "bad women." Indeed, the story-teller's gradual relaxation throughout the narrative not only enables him to speak of the (hitherto) unspeakable, but also parallels, even symptomizes, the gradual evolution of his moral viewpoint away from a total identification with the traditional mores and towards an ambivalent awareness of the city and its "bad women." One of these prostitutes turns out to be his sister who rejects his family solicitude and his rural morality. But, significantly, his resigned declaration at the end of his narrative echoes the anti-conventional ethic of the modern city:

> What is there to weep about? I was sent to find a lost child. I found her a woman.
>
> Cut me a drink . . .
>
> Any kind of work is work . . . That is what Mansa told me with a mouth that looked like clotted blood. Any kind of work is work . . . so do not weep. She will come home this Christmas.
>
> My brother, cut me another drink. Any form of work is work . . . is work . . . is work!

The verbal echo of Mansa's defiance is significant in that the once naive story-teller now seems to have comprehended something of her world. His quest for Mansa has turned out to be a broadening of his own worldly wisdom and the discovery of his own sexuality in the sexually liberated atmosphere of Accra. And in this context the maturation of Mansa, of which he is so acutely aware, is an externalization of his own experience. To paraphrase his own words, a boy was sent to find a child, and a man found her a woman. Hence the narrator's own maturation is implied by the shift of narrative judgement and style from the tentative, even reticent, naiveté at the story's beginning to the boldly stated observations at the end. This maturation, this acquired ability to perceive the sexual ways, and roles, of the modern urban world is celebrated in that repeated "cutting" of drinks ;the alcoholic bravado effects a kind of Dionysian conclusion.

However, this acquired perception, or understanding, does not involve a total acceptance. The celebration of that knowledge about the world and about his own maleness, which he derives from his contact with the adult urban woman, does not mean that he has broken away from the rural traditions of his village. After all, that final demand for the cutting of a drink re-affirms all those moral and communal relationships, which the call implies, between story-teller and audience. The verbal echoes of Mansa's value system does suggest a perception of her world as it is, and of his own sexuality as it has been jolted into life by that world. But, simultaneously, the final cutting of drinks is as much a (re-affirmative) celebration of the village life-style as it is a celebration of his new knowledge. Of course, that new knowledge tempers his inherited conservatism: hence the repeated echoes of Mansa's liberated work ethic is neither exclusively condemnatory nor sympathetic; it is both pitying and self-pitying, gently mocking and at the same time tinged with sexual regret. The empirical consciousness of the narrator and his audience has been exposed to the new order that seems, incomprehensively, to flourish beyond the well-defined boundaries of village and custom. But, notwithstanding the disturbingly ambiguous shock of that exposure, and notwithstanding the imminent arrival of that new order in their midst (in the form of Mansa's Christmas visit), the old order of clearly defined sexual roles and familiar conventions lives on—for the time being at any rate. And the "cutting of a drink," both as social event and narrative art, celebrates that continuing, though precarious, order of things in which the woman is still her mother's daughter rather than her own bad woman, in which mother and daughter function within the cohesive structure of a homogenous family unit and extended communal family, and in which the artist and his art are still organic parts of the communal experience.

The focal point of all this is, of course, the woman's role. The urban woman's relatively unrestricted sexuality arouses the male narrator's possessive puritanism; but, simultaneously, it stirs the erotic self-consciousness which challenges that masculine puritanism. Moreover, the archetypally "liberated" woman of the city represents a broader cultural challenge to the older Africa order, from a brash alien life-style. For if the coherent family structure (which is emphasized by the narrator's asides to uncles, brothers, and his mother) represents a stable, conventional tradition, the "bad" women of the city are symbols of a new uprootedness that is both exhilirating and destructive. But above all, the woman of the city bears a radically subversive image precisely because she can no longer be perceived or described within a conventional, familial context: she is no longer a woman of the family, and quite apart from the morality of her sexual choices, this uprooted condition is "bad" (i.e., disturbing, menacing), from the settled communal viewpoint of the old order.

In "A Gift from Somewhere" the oral background of the Aidoo short story once again represents that older African order. And, in turn, the traditional society is conscious of an alien world on its periphery, particularly as this strange world is perceived by the woman herself—in this case, the *rural* woman. Mami Fanti's situation is familiar enough in the context of rural family life: she has already lost two children to sudden, mysterious illnesses; and now her third child is dying. These background facts are quickly outlined in the opening section of the story through a combination of omniscient commentary and Mami Fanti's dialogue with the holy man (the Mallam) whom she has summoned to save the child. But significantly, as soon as the story shifts to a detailed analysis of Mami's situation, there is a corresponding shift from the conventional

English of the omniscient commentator to those distinctive cadences through which the so-called "Afro-Engish" of writers like Aidoo suggests or reproduces the rhythms and metaphoric structures of their characters' *spoken* (African) languages. In this instance Mami's consciousness and language are vehicles through which the short story examines the implications of Mami's roles as mother and wife. After the Mallam's visit she reflects on those roles as she prepares for the worst:

> . . . I am behaving like one who has not lost a baby before, like
> a fresh bride who sees her first baby dying. Now all I must do
> is to try and prepare myself for another pregnancy, for it seems
> this is the reason I was created . . . to be pregnant for nine of
> the twelve months of every year . . . Or is there a way out of it
> all? And where does this road lie? I shall have to get used to
> it . . . It is the pattern set for my life.

Mami's stoical reserve towards child-bearing is in marked contrast with the popular mystique of motherhood, especially in the kind of society in which the role of mother is the *sine qua non* of one's womanhood. As one of Flora Nwapa's Ibo women exclaims in the novel *Idu,* "What we are all praying for is children. What else do we want if we have children?"[2] Mami's rather *un*quiet desperation really implies a rebellion, however covert, against conventional expectations of her as a woman. And notwithstanding the note of fatalistic acceptance at the end, that rebellious tone controls the reader's (or rather, her audience's) response to the succeeding monologue which constitutes the remainder of the story. That monologue opens several years later with the celebration of her child's recovery, and is couched in the highly formal, lavishly effusive, style of traditional "praise" oratory:

> But you know this child did not die. It is wonderful but this
> child did not die. Mmm . . . This strange world always has
> something to surprise us with . . . Kweku Nyamekye. Some-
> how, he did not die. To his day name Kweku, I have added
> Nyamekye. For, was he not a gift from God [Nyame] through
> the Mallam of the Bound Mouth . . . Nyamekye, hmm, and
> after him I have not lost any more children. Let me touch
> wood. In this world, it is true, there is always something
> somewhere, covered with leaves. Nyamekye lived.

This enthusiastic celebration of the gift of her son's life confirms her sense of womanly fulfilment as a mother. And in this regard her triumph counter-balances the earlier rebelliousness. But in a subtler, more subversive, sense Mami's joyous celebration of Kweku's "gift" of life is also linked with that earlier impatience at the "set," traditionally defined, pattern of her role as a woman. For, in a manner of speaking, Kweku *is* her "way out" from her traditional pattern. His future offers her a vicarious means of breaking out by way of the Western education that will remove him from a traditional rural life-style. Thus, as she explains to her enraged husband, she has specific reasons for excusing Kweku from the customary farm chores: he is growing up to become "a scholar and not a farm-goer." The father's anger arises from a two-fold recognition. First, Kweku has become an alter ego for Mami Fanti, one which reduces the significance of the father's world (she never identifies *him* by name) by vicariously projecting her into that other world with which Kweku's Westernized future is associated. Secondly, Mami Fanti's total absorption with Kweku is not simply the self-justifying, self-fulfilling mystique of motherhood, but also a means of compensating for what Mami sees as the limitations—the set patterns—of her situation. Mami herself makes this compensatory motive quite clear when she reflects on her husband's puzzling (or so she claims) resentment of Kweku: "But I do not even care. I have my little ones. And I am sure someone is wishing she were me. I have Nyamekye." Hence when she looks at a reminder of her husband's resentment (a scar on her arm), she automatically erases this memory with a dual image of Kweku: her son's miraculous survival assures her of her womanliness in the traditional, maternal sense, but he is also the focal point of her muted, but continuing, impatience at the limited patterns of her life: "And as for this scar, I am glad it is not on Nyamekye. Any time I see it I only recall one afternoon when I sat with my chin in my breast before a Mallam came in, and after a Mallam went out." The old roles continue, but in a state of tension with Mami's other, less accepting, identity. And it is on this note of ambiguous tension that Mami concludes her monologue.

Mami Fanti's monologue is an appropriate narrative form for the individual's highly introspective awareness of the relationship between her identity and her environment. But Aidoo reverses the process in "Something to Talk About on the Way to the Funeral" where it is the individual woman herself who is the object of scrutiny by the community. And, appropriately enough, this scrutiny is presented in a continuous dialogue between two village gossips on their way to the funeral of their subject, Auntie Araba. Of course, given the circumstances the central character never appears in the narrative. Neither does the omniscient narrator, for the dialogue is unprefaced and uninterrupted by any third person or by anonymous commentary. And apart from the obvious fact that they are from Auntie Araba's village the speakers' identities remain undiscovered, apart from the kind of self-revelations that are intrinsic to their roles and styles as narrators. Altogether, Aidoo conceives of her narrative form as an auditory experience. Thus there is a clear emphasis on the reader's role as an uninvited *outsider* from a literate, and literary background: the reader is an invisible eavesdropper who is almost literally listening in on the community's collective views bout an individual woman, her close ties with this traditional community, and her links (as well as the community's) with that other society which is represented by the reader's literate mode of perception. In this regard Auntie Araba is archetypal. Her story demonstrates the vulnerability as well as the strengths of women in both Westernized and traditional African societies. To be more precise, this is really a summary of Aunti Araba's life: as the young servant of "some lady relative" she becomes pregnant by her employer's husband, and is sent home "quietly" in order to save the relative's marriage; her son Ato grows up to be a "big scholar" who, in turn, fathers a child by Mansa, a young woman in the village; Auntie Araba takes Mansa and the child after the latter had been expelled by Mansa's parents; both women live together as mother and daughter with a thriving bakery business while Ato leaves for a university abroad on the understanding that he will marry Mansa on his return; Ato subsequently breaks his promise in order to marry into a powerful and wealthy family whose daughter he "had got . . . into trouble." Mansa leaves to live and and work in the city, but Ato's treachery and the loss of Mansa prove too much for the aging Aunti Araba who dies shortly afterwards.

The narrators clearly perceive Auntie Araba's life in representative terms. Their recollection of Araba's young beauty provokes a wry comment on modern sexual attitudes: "If she was a young woman at this time when they are selling beauty to our big men in the towns, she would have made something for herself," but "it is a crying shame that young girls should be doing that. As for our big men! Hmm, let me shut my trouble-seeking mouth up. . . . You know, indeed, these educated big men have never been up to much good." The vulnerability of women like Araba and Mansa is traced to the privileged selfishness of "big" educated (Westernized) men like Ato and to big men in the traditional mold (such as Araba's first lover). "Oh women," exclaims one of the narrators *apropos* of Ato's infidelity. "We are to be pitied!" But if these women think that their situation is pitiable, they refuse, nonetheless, to be self-pitying. For they emphasize the strength of will and purpose which allowed Auntie Araba to survive, even transcend, disasters throughout most of her life—a quality that has been inherited by the level-headed and persevering Mansa. So that in the final analysis, the funeral both mourns the sexual inequities that beset women like Auntie Araba, in town and country, and celebrates the resiliency with which these women of rural backgrounds cope with their vulnerable situation. And, appropriately, this celebration of strength-in-weakness draws upon a traditional ceremony like the Ghanaian funeral which is analogous—as far as tradition is concerned—to the oral, auditory, form through which Aidoo's narrators describe their rural experience. Finally this ambiguous image of the rural woman is comparable with her own self-image in "A Gift from Somewhere"—and with her situation in "No Sweetness Here."

In "No Sweetness Here" the perspective on the rural woman shifts from the largely rural viewpoints, or self-images, of the village to the insights of a Western-educated young woman. The narrator is a school teacher through whose eyes we view Maami Ama, one of the village women. Maami is very attached to her son Kwesi who is also one of the narrator's pupils, but loses him, first to her estranged husband in a divorce hearing, and shortly after, to a fatal snake bite. The decidedly non-rural sources of the narrator's Western bearing and style are readily apparent in a mockingly scandalous candour about sex which evokes the notorious image of the sexual "liberated" Western, or Westernized, woman: "He was beautiful, but that was not important. Beauty does not play such a vital role in a man's life as it does in a woman's, or so people think. If a man's beauty is so ill-mannered as to be noticeable, people discreetly ignore its existence. Only an immodest girl like me would dare comment on a boy's beauty. 'Kwesi is so handsome,' I was always telling his mother. . . . His eyes were of the kind that always remind one of a long dream on a hot afternoon. It is indecent to dwell on a boy's physical appearance, but then Kwesi's beauty was indecent."

On the surface, Aidoo seems to offer a fairly straightforward contrast between a narrator whose education and occupation effect the image of the self-sufficient outsider, and an older woman of traditional background. And this apparent contrast is the more marked when we consider the emphasis on Maami's vulnerability: her intense attachment to her son is as ambiguous as Mami Fanti's maternalism in "A Gift from Somewhere" in that this attachment both assures her claim to womanliness-through-motherhood and compensates for the limitations of her role ("a lonely mother and a lonely son") in a society of male prerogatives; and the male's prerogatives are underlined by the fact that the divorce proceedings which are modelled on tribal custom allow her no recourse against her husband's exclusive claims on *his* son. But looked at more closely this contrast is less clear-cut. If Maami Ama's intense attachment to Kwesi compensates for her sense of isolation and vulnerability, so does the narrator's. For Kwesi's future education, career, and even sexual exploits

have become a vicarious means of fulfilment for a woman whose education and occupation—albeit Western—have brought her a smaller degree
of choice or mobility than her liberated rhetoric implies. Significantly,
too, this vicarious self-fulfilment excludes the domineering male figure in
the story, Kwesi's father, Kodjo Fi: "In my daydreams . . . [Kwesi]
would be famous, that was certain. Devastatingly handsome, he would be
the idol of women and the envy of every man. He would visit Britain,
America and all those countries we have heard so much about. . . . In all
these reveries his father never had a place." On the whole, the narrator's
insights into the ambiguous position of the rural woman reflect the
ambiguities of her own situation. She too has a sense of personal vulnerability and limitations which she attempts to transcend through Kwesi's
male future. Indeed, it is a major, and recurring, irony in Aidoo's work
that the "progressive," "liberated," and "sophisticated" images of the
Westernized woman are really masks: underneath there are the familiar
vulnerability and new, self-destructive insecurity in a time of conflicting
cultural values. This is clear enough in the "bad" city women of "In the
Cutting of a Drink" and in the narrator's uneasy sense of kinship with the
isolated and victimized mother of "No Sweetness Here." Hence the title
of the latter work establishes a contextual irony for the narrative as a
whole: on the one hand, it does imply a rebuttal of the notion that the
situtation of the rural woman is all sweetness, a notion that is fostered in
the works of a writer like Nigeria's Cyprian Ekwensi whose "bad" city
women (especially Jagua Nana) usually retreat to unspoilt rural roots to
re-discover a lost innocence; but, on the other hand, the title offers an
even more personal reference, to the narrator's own individuality and to
the lack of real "sweetness" (fulfilment behind her liberated Western
image. Similarly, in "Everything Counts" the young university teacher
who upholds her racial and sexual integrity by disdaining the national
craze for European wigs still suffers from a sense of isolation—particularly since the Ghanaian "brothers" who have encouraged her in her
militant African womanliness are still comfortably, and indefinitely, settled in Europe as perpetual students, with European girlfriends.

At the very least, however, the narrators of "No Sweetness Here" and
"Everything Counts" command respect because they are acutely aware
of the irony of their situation as supposedly "liberated" and "independent" Western women. The doubledealing of her "brothers" overseas
and its implication for her own isolation are not lost on the protagonist of
"Everything Counts." And the narrator's conscious identification with
Maami and Kwesi in "No Sweetness Here" attests to her awareness that
her own situation is no less vulnerable than Maami's, and that conversely,
her advantages as an "educated" woman are not necessarily superior to

that resiliency of spirit which Aidoo invariably attributes to her rural women. There is no such awareness in the more intensely satiric "Two Sisters" where Aidoo ironically dons the style of the woman's magazine format in order to take a close survey of the urban middle-class woman. Her findings are not re-assuring. On the one hand, there is Connie, unhappily married to a compulsive philanderer, and on the other hand, there is her sister Mercy whose notions of "liberated" womanhood take the form of successive affairs with married politicans possessing large cars and healthy bank accounts. Aidoo's plot is pointedly hackneyed, for the ultimate irony of the sisters' lives is the essentially *déjà vu* quality of their borrowed middle-class aspirations. As Aidoo's personified Gulf of Guinea muses, people are "worms" whose lives are both contradictory things and "repetitions of old patterns." Their tragedy as women, and the tragedy of their social milieu as a whole, consists of the fact that they are all living stereotypes whose experiences are a succession of second-hand clichés—Mercy's neo-Hollywood obsession with "sexy" clothes, uniformed chauffers, and vulgarly large American cars; Connie's desperate determination to be respectably, even happily, married, and her hackneyed conviction that the new baby will, somehow, restore the marriage.

With her usual fastidious attention to the thematic function of her short-story techniques, Aidoo embellishes this description of a Westernized middleclass with all the popular banalities of Western women's magazines. Unlike the acutely self-conscious narrators of "No Sweetness Here" and "Everything Counts," the vapidly Westernized Mercy thinks in unconscious clichés:

> As she shakes out the typewriter cloak and covers the machine with it, the thought of the bus she has to hurry to catch goes through her like pain. It is her luck, she thinks. Everything is just her luck. Why, if she had one of those graduates for a boyfriend wouldn't he come and take her home every evening? And she knows that a girl does not herself have to be a graduate to get one of those boys. Certainly, Joe is dying to do exactly that—with his taxi. And he is as handsome as anything, and a good man, but you know. . . .

Aidoo offers no easy solutions. Connie's baby effects a "magical" restoration of her failing marriage, a reconciliation that is suspect precisely because it is so sudden, so unfounded, and so obviously a mocking confirmation of Connie's wish-fulfilment. As for Mercy, having barely survived one "heart-breaking" liaison she is all set to embark on another at the story's end—and her prospects are no more favorable than before.

Like the ironic techniques of the narrative itself, their lives have settled into a "repetition of old patterns." Once again, Aidoo has fused her narrative art with the perspectives and roles of her African women.

NOTES

1. References to all stories cited in this study are based on Aidoo's short-story collection, *No Sweetness Here* (London: Longman, 1970).
2. Flora Nwapa, *Idu,* African Writers Series (London: Heinemann, 1970), p. 150.

THREE GHANAIAN NOVELS: *THE CATECHIST, THE NARROW PATH,* and *A WOMAN IN HER PRIME*

Robert McDowell

Potential readers of African novels in English (and particularly Americans), while watching for some political calm to descend over the vast African continent, have been largely oblivious to the literary maturity of Africa's young writers, in spite of the fact that African literary growth has far outstripped most other developments in modern African life. Thanks largely to British (and some African) publishers, western readers have come to know a few of the more important black writers from several countries: Chinua Achebe, Cyprian Ekwensi, and Amos Tutuola from Nigeria; James Ngugi from Kenya; Peter Abrahams, and Alex La Guma from South Africa.

And now, equally provocative as books by these writers are three recent novels out of Ghana: J. W. Abruquah's *The Catechist* (George Allen & Unwin, 1965), Francis Selormey's *The Narrow Path* (Heinemann, 1966), and S.A. Konadu's *A Woman in Her Prime* (Heinemann, 1967). They illustrate not only "the slow, placid prose of West Africa" (to borrow a phrase from Lewis Nkosi) but also some of the primary themes of West African writing. These are by no means the majority of Ghanaian fiction writers, but they are of great importance as novel writers.[1]

The first two of these novels, like South African fiction, have been written close to the authors' own experiences. Abruquah certifies in his "Preface" that

> This book is based on a framework of reality—my father's life. Much of the detail, but not all of it, is fiction. Where real names are indispensable, they are used. But the family represented here is all mixed up and renamed, with fresh characters assigned to different members.

Candid in its revelation, *The Catechist* is almost embarrassingly intimate at times because of its first-person narration. Essentially, it is the late nineteenth and early twentieth century annal of Afram, who should by

rights have been a Christian preacher, but who remained a lowly catechist, shuffled around mercilessly to many run-down churches in remote
communities, always moving, and while rearing his sons as educated
men, failing himself to gain a dignified position in life:

> I went. Always on the move. I was only a few months at
> Bobikuma; a year at the next Station, and so on until I was
> transferred farther and farther from home again. At most
> Stations I replaced inefficient Ministers who had ruined the
> mission house, estranged their congregations, and neglected
> their duty . . .

Thus the author narrates through the simple rhythms of the father, "the
chief actor himself." It is indeed a fitting narration, for it is people of this
catechist's era who felt most powerfully the bewildering rush of European
ways, and it is to him and his contemporaries that history bequeathed the
difficult task of spanning two cultures—the life of the rural African village
and that of Europe-oriented Christianity. Clearly Afram exists between
the two worlds:

> I was a Christian who still held tenaciously to the ancestral
> beliefs of my people.

Always the catechist feels the new system of which he is an active part
pushing him, and more especially his sons, away from tradition:

> My own son now tells me my ideas are utter rubbish.

The congregations to which he ministers are no less a trial:

> On Sundays I conducted service in a little Wesleyan Chapel
> and preached to a congregation just emerging from paganism,
> myself a near pagan. I don't think Christianity meant more to
> those people or to me than a mere substitute for the witch-
> doctor.

When finally, aged and broken, Afram goes into retirement, he is understandably bitter about his career:

> I went quietly into obscurity with no laurels and no respect; no
> last-minute farewells or godspeeds; no visible means of sup-
> port save that which my own sons were hopefully expected to

give. For Catechists are the scum of the earth and command no respect and expect none. They are entitled to no gratuities or pension and when they are strong enough to outlive their usefulness . . . "God will provide."

Beyond doubt, the core of this novel has to do with estrangement: with Afram's constant dwelling among strange people with strange ways; with his separation from those close to him. Brought up as a boy in a wholly African environment, Afram seems much of the time to be unconscious of the potential for change in the alien Christian beliefs which he disperses to his fellows. But, of course, how can he *in medias res* know the new ways that must necessarily open up after the European invasion of African minds. It is ironic that Afram's greatest pride is in the education of his sons:

My own personal failures were as nothing compared with the achievements of my sons.

The rapid move away from the spirit presences of the Fante, the swift turn toward the technological twentieth century life—inshort, the move from all that Afram felt most comfortable in, is manifest in these educated young Ghanaian men.

Francis Selormey's novel is strikingly similar to Abruquah's. Once more the story is biographical and is in large part the story of the father, Nani. Like Afram, Nani is a Christian, a Catholic who translates for the white priests, directs the church choir, and performs as headmaster of a primary school. In this novel the son, Kofi, narrates. He describes himself (born in the 1920s) as caught between traditional African modes and Christian ones: he is born in a French hospital at Lome, but cured of his first illness by a witch doctor. A little later his sister Ami has both the traditional and a Catholic baptism:

A strong drink called "Akpeteshi"—was poured out, that the unfriendly spirits might drink it and become drunk and so forget any evil designs they might have had on the child.

. . . . .

In the afternoon, Ami was baptized in the Catholic Church and given a Christian name.

This family, like Afram's, is constantly forced by the church to move. With each new school Nani takes over, Kofi feels that he is treated as an example for the rest of the pupils. The father is indeed often overly severe. Once, for instance, he hangs Kofi up by bound wrists, beats him as he hangs on a wall, takes him to the classroom and gives him twenty-five more strokes with a cane, then kicks him in the side. Not surprisingly, the child is unable to rise from his bed for a week.

But not all is horrible in *The Narrow Path*. There are pleasant episodes such as Kofi's relationship with a kindly teacher and scout leader, and his fruitful years with the family of his "master." Yet throughout the story, family difficulties build up until events seem to scream out at us. Nani is transferred by the church again and again, always to more primitive areas with poor schools and few Christians. In one community there is a murder by witchcraft. With the expense of the children's schooling and the necessity over and again of constructing new housing, the family breaks apart. The mother goes to her people and Nani stubbornly keeps the children and goes to live with his family near his new school. As with Afram's sons, Kofi, at the end, is going off for a higher education:

> The college was 200 miles away, and it seemed to my mother that I was going to the end of the earth. We all rose at dawn on the day of my leaving. My mother filled a calabash with water and sprinkled corn-dough into it. She raised it to the east and to the west, and she invoked all the family gods, and asked that they would protect me on my journey, guard and guide me. . . .

Clearly, Selormey's is a story of disintegration, experienced not just once, but many times. Every move was a nightmare to the family:

> Ho was an inland town, eighty-six miles away. None of us, except my father, had ever travelled so far. We were to leave our family and friends, to leave the sea and the shore, the lagoon and the coconut trees, and the fresh fish that formed the most valuable part of our diet. We felt lost and bewildered. People said that the customs of the Ho people were different from our own. . . .

The change of worlds over a short span of time has been made to appear vast. Kofi's grandfather had had eight wives; his son had gone into a strange religion called Catholicism; the grandson, Kofi, becomes a college graduate, and much less conservative than his father. In the end, the larger family relationship is in shambles for Nani. He and his wife have experienced a terrible breach; there grows an ever greater rift between him and his son Kofi; and Kofi's cousins all label him as conceited because of his book learning. Without knowing, Nani has, like

Afram, participated in a bewildering cultural transition; he has been very much part of a European-instigated revolution.

The closeness of Abruquah's and Selormey's works to many Nigerian novels is often great, as one would expect from writers whose nations have shared similar colonial experiences. Perhaps most evident here is the sort of thing one reads about in Chinua Achebe's novels—the breakdown of the communal code in African life, and the subsequent vulnerability of Africans to European individualism. There is here the feeling of a whole civilization having been slowly dissolved. When colonial administrators and churchmen force drastic changes in the patterns of an essentially rural African life, all social loyalties are necessarily shaken at their roots.

Quite different from these two novels, but equally involved in telling the story of Ghanaians, is Konadu's short novel, *A Woman in Her Prime*. It is a lyrical description of a simple people, untouched by Europe, villagers caught up completely in animist ritual, a group very much at the mercy of the elements, people still called together by the crier pounding a gong. *A Woman in Her Prime* is an interesting foil for the other two books: while they are powerfully disintegrative, this annal shows essentially the coherence of traditional village life. And though the heroine undergoes many trials throughout the story, her life seems to come to a natural and satisfactory full circle in the end.

The woman in her prime, Pokuwaa, has tragically failed to conceive. This attractive woman and successful farmer has divorced her first two husbands, believing them to be incapable of giving her a child. With the third marriage there is again reason to believe that her partner is at fault. Perhaps because he has another wife, Kwadwo spends most of his time sleeping when he is around Pokuwaa. From the community, however, Pokuwaa has plenty of encouragement to bear a child. Her mother, as indeed the entire village, seems to inject prayers for fertility into most of their chants:

> Let all who are barren bear children.
> Let all who are impotent find remedy.

But such supplications appear more and more futile to Pokuwaa, and so she finally declares to Kwadwo:

> I will not go on with the sacrifices.

. . . . .

> "I am a woman," said Pokuwaa. "And a woman does want a child; that is her nature. But if a child will not come, what can I do? I can't spend my whole life bathing in herbs."

Pokuwaa's old mother expresses the dismay of the whole village over her daughter's plight:

> What is the fate of a state destined to be if its women refuse to give birth? Where are the sons who will defend the land going to come from?

When at last Pokuwaa does conceive, there is nearly delirious joy in her family, and a celebration of sorts in the village:

> Under the village silk cotton tree, many calabashes of palm wine passed round amidst male jokes aimed at the man who was expecting a child with such unrivalled pride. If the heavy rains had not let themselves down, and broken up the daily party, the men would have been pleased to continue using Kwadwo to justify long drinking bouts.

As for Pokuwaa,

> The rain could not dampen her spirits. Her mother, Koramoa and Kwadwo were around her; her child inside her, kicking.

Whether or not the conception proves that supplications to the Great God Tano have been noticed, everyone in the community besides Pokuwaa believe it. At any rate, Pokuwaa, now at a fairly advanced age for child bearing, achieves fulfillment at the end of the story. Here are problems which work themselves out in the ordinary course of events in the milieu of the traditional Ghanaian village. The heroine, often at odds with herself as well as with her immediate family, is nevertheless a character who despite a time of great despair, never flagrantly abandons time-honored modes. She is never seen as an outsider; she remains essentially an integral part of her village.

The history of the revision of Ghanaian life as seen through the characters of Abruquah and Selormey is provocative. But this sort of movement and change is not, as Konadu shows us through his work, the only possibility for the Ghanaian novel. *A Woman in Her Prime* exhibits the sort of existence which preceded the dissolution recorded in Abruquah's and Selormey's works. It is a fascinating picture of people absolutely free from European inhibitions. Certainly it proves once more what a rich mine of material West African writers have at hand. Konadu's novelette suggests something of the natural joy we feel in Nwankwo's *Danda*, while at the same time something of the compelling fascination of animism so powerfully rendered in the several short books of Amos Tutuola. Whatever else these recent novels from Ghana tell us, they prove once again the ability of African novelists to directly confront the diversity and complexity of African experiences and intelligently interpret them for the world.

NOTES

1. One can always make a fairly quantitative case for the novel, simply because of its ability to tell "the whole story" in a way the short story cannot. This, naturally, does not dismiss the significance of Ghana's better short story artists: Christiana A. Aidoo, Kwabena Annan, Ellis Komey, Peter Kwame Buahin, and others.

STRUCTURE AND IMAGE IN KWEI ARMAH'S *THE BEAUTYFUL ONES ARE NOT YET BORN*

Gareth Griffiths

Kwei Armah's first novel has made a strong impression on the growing audience for African novels. Its central themes are familiar, perhaps inevitably so, but its treatment shows a striking originality especially in the use of image and metaphor. They are employed as the main structuring device, and through an examination of their development and interrelationship the reader can come to terms with the intentions and achievements of this very complex novel and with the vision of Ghana which it sets out. The story traces the progress of a man through the corruption and political chicanery which envelops the society of a newly-emerged nation. It presents a startling picture of the scramble for place and preferment, and the nauseous fear, suspicion, and uncertainty which this creates in public and private life.

The novel is different from earlier studies of this theme in a number of interesting ways. It provides a totally inside view of the corrupting process. The detached stance of earlier commentators, e.g., Peter Abrahams in *A Wreath for Udomo*,[1] is replaced by a picture whose reference points are all internal. No character in the novel is allowed to rise above the confusion and impenetrability of the action. Even the narrator, although allowed the freedom to comment from time to time, has been strictly limited, indicating that the interest of the book is firmly on the existential rather than the political plane. What Kwei Armah sets out to show is the experience of living in a corrupt universe. The limitations and confusions of such distancing are overcome through the guide which metaphor and image offer the reader.

The hero, unnamed, and referred to throughout simply as "the man" is an office-worker employed by the State Railway. The novel centres on the daily round of routine, boring and meaningless activity which is the "work" of the new, urban, clerical class. The messages which the man sends and receives along the telegraph wire are communications in a void . . . "On the Morse machine there was a long roll that could only raise thoughts of people going irretrievably crazy at the long end of the telegraph. Maybe also the famous rattle of men preparing to die. In a while, when it was no longer possible to ignore the rattle, the man rapped back once for silence, then tapped out the message, 'Shut up!'

The roll came again, defiantly insistent. The maniac at the other end of the line had grown indignant. Another rap. Short silence. Then the man asked in half-conciliation, 'Who be you?' A roll now, very long and very senseless. But at the very end it carries a signature, 'Obuasi.'

That at least was something, and should deserve a reply. The man held the Morse knob again, lightly. 'Hello.'

With amazing speed, an answer comes back, this time entirely coherent, decipherable at the last. 'Why do we agree to go on like this?' Then again the rattle" (p. 30). The new bush-telegraph raps out its message of frustration. Like communications between lost planets the messages flash across the void of Ghana, from one pointless and distressed life to another. In the offices around him men devise elaborate systems for manufacturing unnecessary work. They file multiple copies of meaningless documents. They devise elaborate rituals for the purchase of inedible food. In the centre of this void stands the hero. Gradually, however, corners of the veil are drawn back from his anonymity, and we catch glimpses of his home and his family; but he is never allowed to merge completely from the impersonality which guarantees his representativeness, and the automatic and objective tragedy of the world in which he lives. But here, in the opening sequences, the man is a mere object, not even the centre of attention at first. We meet him through the eyes of the bus-conductor whom he "observes" furtively smelling the money he has collected. But the "watcher" is really a "sleeper" as the conductor quickly discovers, and in an instant he has moved from abject submission to violent attack. The sleeper awakens to a stream of violent abuse, the spittle of his helplessness trickling down his face. In this world to sleep is a crime. Men must be awake all the time, awake to a world that watches, ready to punish. Only in the cosy and secure relationship of briber and bribed can "brotherhood" exist; at all other times man is either destroyer or destroyed.

The world outside the individual reflects the world within. The novel operates through a series of remarkable metaphorical links which institute a set of correspondences between the body of man, his society and his landscape; between, too, the inner processes of feeding and reproduction and their social equivalents, inheritance and consumption; and, finally, between the personal rot of conscience and ideals and the physical decay and putresence of the world in which this rot occurs. Central to the exchange is the question: where does the rot begin? What is the relationship between the processes of corruption and decay in the individual and in the society around him? What, if any, are the casual relations between one and the other?

Here is the narrator's reflections on the uselessness of any effort to stop the rot in the bannisters of the railway offices by applying thick, disguising coats of polish: "The wood underneath would win and win till the end of time. Of that there was no doubt possible, only the pain of hope perennially doomed to disappointment. It was so clear. Of course it was in the nature of the wood to rot with age. The polish, it was supposed, would catch the rot. But of course in the end it was the rot which imprisoned everything in its effortless embrace. It did not really have to fight. Being was enough. In the natural course of things it would always take the newness of the different kinds of polish and the vaunted cleaning power of the chemicals in them, and it would convert all to victorious filth, awaiting yet more polish again and again and again" (pp. 14–15).

But, in dreadful harmony with this natural rot and decay is the conscious activity of men: "And the wood was not alone. Apart from the wood itself there were, of course, people themselves, just so many hands and fingers bringing help to the wood in its course towards putrefaction. Left-hand fingers in their careless journey from a hasty anus sliding all the way up the bannister as their owners made the return trip from the lavatory downstairs to the offices above. Right-hand fingers still dripping with the after-piss and the stale sweat from fat crotches. The callused palms of messengers after they had blown their clogged noses reaching for a convenient place to leave the well-rubbed moisture. Afternoon hands not entirely licked clean of palm soup and remnants of *kenkey*. The wood would always win" (p. 15). There is no simple relationship between the activities of man and the natural processes he aids, thwarts or corrupts. In a real sense the physical corruption which the book details *is* the result of man's conscious neglect or aid. The inadequacy of the plumbing facilities, the discrepancy between the promises of the anti-litter campaign and the implementation of it, these things are not separable from the corruption and inadequacy of the governing class which they expose and attack. But beyond this there lies a level of pre-condition, a level only available to symbolic exposure. Filth is, after all, also a natural and necessary condition of life. Ordure is the end-product of life, and the source from which fresh life grows. It is at the level of metaphor that this truth is exposed and contemplated.

The predominant metaphor is that of eating, or rather of eating, digestion, and excretion. This metaphor is linked, as is common in African writing through oral usage, to the theme of corruption and bribery. Money is food. The metaphoric link is a graphic illustration of the primitive economic nature of even the wealthiest of the West African states.[2] In this world the "consumer" society is a literal reality.

> '. . . I won something in the lottery,' he said.
> 'Lucky you,' the man said, 'How much?'
> The messenger hesitated before replying, 'One hundred cedis.'
> 'That's not very much,' the man laughed.
> 'I know,' said the messenger. But so many people would jump on me to help me eat it.' (p. 21)

The novel dwells obsessively on the process by which the body converts food into excreta, reflecting the obsession with which society "consumes" goods, the "shining" things which it covets. But just as food must issue in excreta, so such consumption must issue in bribery and corruption, the excrement of an aggressive drive for the new life. Each man's bodily processes become a metaphor for the corruption in which he lives, his own body a paradigm for the landscape he inhabits.[3] This metaphor helps to structure the book since it is instrumental in relating the hero's discovery of the relationship between the bloom of life and the dung and filth which feeds it.

But before we examine the metaphors further, we ought to look at the way in which the narrative is structured. Basically the story is of a railway-clerk who is under pressure from his society and his family to conform to the ethics of the rat-race. His refusal to do so leads to his increasing alienation from life. The ultimate end of such a stance is that of his friend, the Teacher, who has withdrawn from life, from family and work, and who advocates passivity and negation, "the mystic path," as the alternative to the inevitable corruption which, by osmosis, must affect all those who remain in contact with life as it is. The anonymous hero rejects this solution, or rather, has no alternative but to reject it, since, as he tells Teacher, ". . . you know it is impossible for me to watch the things that go on and say nothing. I have my family. I am in the middle" (p. 109). Gradually, despite his attempt to remain as negative as possible in the transaction, he is drawn into a scheme which his wife and mother initiate, to aid a corrupt minister, Koomson, to avoid Government ownership laws. His wife agrees to act as the nominal purchaser of a fishing-boat from which Koomson hopes to make a substantial profit. In the event she gets little from the affair, except some free fish which the man refuses to eat. Despite his recognition that Teacher's doctrine of withdrawal is unworkable, he continues to pretend that he can be "in the world but not of it." The crisis comes when the regime is overthrown in a coup and Koomson arrives at the man's home seeking help. The man helps to smuggle him from the house through the latrine hole. After getting him safely away on the fishing-boat, he swims ashore and returns home to a country where, with the new government safely installed, the round of corruption has already started up again.

There is almost no examination of motive, and we are given little direct help towards understanding the significance of the action of the novel, except in the sixth chapter which is pivotal to the structure and which I shall examine. But a careful reading of this difficult novel reveals that Armah has brought into play a pattern of images which define the issues, and complement the limited viewpoints of characters and narrators.

The novel falls into three distinct sections. The first, which we have begun to examine, introduces us to the daily round of the man's life, and to the pressure of family and friends which he feels to join in the struggle for the "good things" of life. We are introduced towards the end of this section (Chapter 4) to the figure of Koomson, the black-whiteman who is pre-eminently one of the "heroes of the gleam," the possessors of the Mercedes and the new suits. ". . . Outside the seller sweetens her tones. 'My own lord, my master, oh my white man, come. Come and take my bread. It is all yours, my white man, all yours.' The car door opens, and the suited man emerges and strides slowly towards the praise-singing seller. The sharp voice inside the car makes one more sound of impatience, then subsides, waiting. The suit stops in front of the seller . . ." (p. 43). Armah dwells on Koomson's suit, which replaces the man entirely. He is the white man because he is a white shirt, gleaming through a darkness into which his body merges. He is literally the gleaming clothes he stands up in. "The suited man looks around him. Even in the faint light his smile is easy to see. It forms a strange pattern of pale light with the material of his shirt, which in the space between the darknesses of his suit seems designed to point down somewhere between the invisible thighs." The black-whiteman is invisible because he is merely a caricature. He has no sical or economic reality, no personal identity. His reality is defined solely by the objects with which he surrounds himself, and from which he builds a "personality."

After the meeting the man returns home to his wife, and tells her of the meeting. She attacks him for his inability to succeed in the same way, and fails to understand when he tells her that he cannot because the price of such "cleanness" is "the slime at the bottom of a garbage dump" (p. 52). She responds by telling him that he is like the chichidodo, the proverbial bird who "hates excrement with all its soul." But who feeds on maggots which "grow best inside the lavatory" (p. 52). This image is one of those which will recur, and help to define the tension the novel explores.

In the following chapter we meet the complex figure of Teacher, for the first, time, a juxtapositon which is significant since he represents the opposite extreme from Koomson as I shall show. It is necessary to be very precise here. The figure we meet originally is *not* Teacher, but an extension of the role he plays in the symbolic patterning in which the book operates. When the man leaves his home to escape the nagging pressure of his wife, he begins to muse on a figure he had once known called Rama Krishna. This man, a Ghanaian who "had taken that far-off name in the reincarnation of his soul after long and tortured flight from everything close and everything known, since all around him showed the horrible threat of decay" (p. 55), is clearly related to the actual Teacher whom the man then proceeds to visit. The confusion of persona, the multiple characterization, shifting time-sequences and rapidly alternating narrative viewpoint which this episode establishes is continued through-out the crucial chapter six. The effect of introducing this Doppelganger for Teacher is to prepare us for the realization that Teacher's stance, although directly opposed to that of Koomson's, is equally dangerous. "Rama Krishna's" flight, we learn, has been a failure. His attempt to live outside the corrupt cycle of eat and be eaten, to supplant the killing of living things for food by a diet of honey and of vinegar, to ". . . live on the fragrance of the earth,/and like an air plant be sustained by light" (p. 56) has resulted not in serenity but in decay. His ultimate solution, "the one way" to salvation that he discovers "Near the end" is a rejection of life. He rejects women, and through yoga attempts to convert the life-giving seminal fluid to the purpose of rejuvenation. But he is rotting inside, and when he dies his heart is seen to be "only a living lot of worms gathered together tightly in the shape of a heart." As the man reflects, "and so what did the dead rot inside his friend not have to do with his fear of what was decaying outside of himself? And what would such an unnatural flight be worth at all in the end? And the man wondered what kind of sound the cry of the chichidodo bird could be, the bird longing for its maggots but fleeing the faeces which gave them birth (p. 56). The image is clearly associated now with the man's awareness that "there was too much of the unnatural in any man who imagined he could escape the inevitable decay of life . . ." (p. 55). Thus, when Teacher is finally introduced he is naked, for it Koomson's life has reduced him to a mere suit of clothes, then Teacher's life has had a reductive effect too. Without the guidance of the imagery we might assume Teacher's nakedness a pure symbol of inno-cence. But in the context Armah so carefully establishes, we are able to see the extremism of his stance, to see how it too depends on a selected notion of life, a refusal to accept the inevitable relationship between maggots and excrement, between the dung and the blossom. Teacher, the naked man, is as far removed from reality as Koomson, the suit. They both represent extremes which fail to meet the requirements of reality, that the ideal and the sordid should be seen to coexist in the same universe, and in the same compass of experience. The Africa to which Teacher is attuned is an idealized Africa, the Africa of self-conscious 'purity,' not the teeming cess-pit of Accra from which he seeks refuge within the castle of his skin. The music he plays is "at once very far away and very African" (p. 58). It is not the music of the here and now. When the Radio Ghana programme begins "a very ordinary 'high life' " he is about to switch it off when it is replaced with the "sweet sadness of congo music," which makes him desist (pp. 58–59).

Teacher, then, is both a figure from the past and character existing in the novel's "present." He is Rama Krishna, the lost friend, and Teacher, the present comforter. To try and fit him into a realistic category is to fail to see the novel's intention. Teacher is a symbol of a kind of African experience, a symbol of the timeless, non-technological, romantic, and anthropological African experience. He is juxtaposed to Koomson, the black-whiteman, the modern elitist, the hatchet man of the consumer revolution. But Teacher's stance is as dangerous as Koomson's, for his withdrawal is ultimately no answer to the challenge posed to the hero by the "blinding gleam of beautiful new houses and the shine of powerful new Mercedes cars." Because of this, he has become a figure without hope: "When you can see the end of things even in their beginnings, there's no more hope, unless you want to pretend, or forget, or get drunk or something. No, I also am one of the dead people, the walking dead. A ghost. I died long ago. So long ago that not even the old libations of living blood will make me live again" (p. 71). Now Teacher is clearly identified with the old sources of African culture, the non-European, the non-technological sources, the world of the dead gods where spirit and matter are interfused. But in him they are separate. He is dead. His only answer now is withdrawal and death. In a gesture of resignation he turns on the radio, and the voice of his opponent is heard, loudly and clearly: "The naked man turned on his bed. He turned the left knob on the radio till it would go no farther, and then gave the tuning knob an inward pull that slid the red line smoothly across the glass face. When it stopped a male voice, huge like a eunuch amplified, burst the air with a hollered sound that kept its echo long afterwards, a vibrating '. . . ericaaaaa!'. . ." (p. 71). We are irresistably reminded of Sartre's comment that "The European elite undertook to manufacture a native elite. They picked out promising adolescents; they branded them, as with a red-hot iron, with the principles of western culture; they stuffed their mouths full with high-sounding phrases, grand glutinous words that stuck to the teeth. After a short stay in the mother country they were sent home white-washed. These walking lies had nothing left to say to their brothers; they only echoed. From Paris, from London, from Amsterdam we would utter the words 'Parthenon! Brotherhood!' and somewhere in Africa or Asia lips would open '. . . thenon! . . . therhood!' It was the golden age.''[4] What Teacher has not learned, in the style of the above critique, is that "No one has clean hands; there are no innocents and no onlookers. We all have dirty hands; we are soiling them in the swamps of our country and in the terrifying emptiness of our brains. Every onlooker is either a coward or a traitor.''[5]

Chapter six which follows, and which I have said is pivotal, explores this issue in depth. We are presented with a symbolic history of the childhood and youth of a man which embodies the history of the liberation movement itself. As Eldred D. Jones said, reviewing the novel, "sometimes it is difficult to tell whose mind we are being shown.''[6] The narrative viewpoint moves between Teacher and the hero. The confusion of the two is deliberate since later, in the final chapter, we note that the hero inherits memories (the figure of Maanan) which belong to the portions of chapter six narrated by Teacher. This confusion merely stresses once again that we have to frame demands other than those satisfied by conventional novel structure. The figures and events are not merely aspects of an autobiography, but aspects of an historical process and a general cultural experience. Each section of the chapter is introduced by the printed device of a flower, recalling our attention to the central metaphor of the entanglement of growth and decay in the organic world, reminding us that "out of the decay and the dung there is always a new flowering" (p. 100). The chapter begins with an image of birth, but a strangely ambiguous one. "Why do we waste so much time with sorrow and pity for ourselves? It is true that we are men, but not so long ago we were helpless messes of soft flesh and unformed bone squeezing through bursting motherholes, trailing dung, and exhausted blood" (p. 72). It is a birth which is described in terms of an ending. We come into the world like dung. Our birth is like the end of the chain of life, the excretion that follows the eating of food. The end of sexual love is this squalid and undignified entrance into the world, an entrance which reminds us forcibly that in our end is our beginning, and that in dung and blood we must go out again. To be born is to commit oneself to a process over which one has no control. Our adult pretensions to direction and choice are illusions. Our dreams of withdrawal and security, of the ability to remain still above the flux are illusions. "We could not ask then why it was necessary for us also to grow. So why now should we be shaking our heads and wondering bitterly why there are children together with the old, why time should not stop when we ourselves have come to stations where we would like to rest" (p. 72)? This inevitable aging and decay is the fate of movements and ideals was well as individuals. The birth and the youth of the liberation movement seemed to offer a new beginning, but that too was subject to decay. The story of a life and the story of a nation are fused in the imagery. The man struggling in the squalor of compromise and disillusion is a vision of Ghana itself, and its whole people. The reminiscences and memories of chapter six are not merely flashbacks in the story of a life, they are also images of the pilgrimage of the colonized through oppression to liberation and independce and on into disillusion and decay.

Ayi Kwei Armah's debt to the acute analysis of Fanon is clear to any reader of this section of the novel. Armah reflects the same interest and concern for the effect of the colonizing process on the psychic life of the African. But he reflects too, with more precision, the striking images of Fanon's prose. Here is Fanon's definiton of the 'progress' of the nation under the leadership of the new elites. "In the colonial countries, the spirit of indulgence is dominant at the core of the bourgeoisie; and this is because the national bourgeoisie identifies itself with the Western bourgeoisie, from whom it has learned its lessons. It follows the Western bourgeoisie along the path of negation and decadence without ever having emulated it in its first stages of exploration and invention . . . it is infact beginning at the end. It is already senile before it has come to know the petulance, the fearlessness or the will to succeed of youth."[7] In a striking way Armah's image of the "man-child" parallels this analysis, reducing Fanon's rational insight to a vivid symbol. "The manchild looked more irretrievably old, far more thoroughly decayed, than any ordinary old man could ever have looked. But, of course, it, too, had a nature of its own, so that only those who have found some solid ground will feel free to call it unnatural" (p. 73). Fanon's analysis is objective, detached. It operates with an intense concern, but from above the disillusion, probing the roots and causes. Armah as novelist has dramatized the experience of the people themselves, their own tangled and confused hopes and their feeling that, perhaps, such decline and such premature destruction of their dreams is natural and inevitable. Throughout chapter six Armah dramatises by image and scene Fanon's analysis of bourgeois corruption and psychic disturbance. This is the view from beneath the corruption, on the receiving end of the ordure and filth which the leadership pour down on the shoulders of those who lifted them up (pp. 95–96).

The novel pictures vividly the process by which in the colonial period the envy and aggression of the colonized people finds expression in a self-destructive process in which each turns upon his fellow. The war acted as a catylist, revealing to the African that the white men were not always and everywhere the tin gods of the colonial landscape, and that he too was a potential source of power and force, that he too could move mountains and change the conditions of his life. Upon their return the soldiers find no outlet in the colonial situation for their new confidence and aggressiveness, and find it impossible to live happily under the old dispensations. The aggression released by war is in a heightened form the continual aggression bred by colonialism in the subject people, an aggression founded in envy, and in the desire to appropriate for themselves the status of the white settler, to win back the enchanted garden guarded by force and cruelty which they now see as their lost inheritance.

Here is Fanon on the suppressed aggression of the colonized: "The colonized man will first manifest this aggressiveness which has been deposited in his bones against his own people. This is the period when the niggers beat each other up, and the police and magistrates do not know which way to turn when faced with the astonishing waves of crime . . ."[8]

And here Armah: "Their anger came out in the blood of those closest to themselves, those men who had gone without anger to fight enemies they did not even know; they found anger and murder waiting for them, lying in the bosoms of the women they had left behind . . . the time of the jackknife and the chuke, the rapid unthinking movement of short, ugly iron points that fed wandering living ghosts with what they wanted, blood that would never put an end to their inner suffering" (p. 76). Again, as Fanon had noted, this world is dual, it has two sides. It is not only "ponderous and aggressive because it fends off the colonized masses with all the harshness it is capable of, not merely a hell from which the swiftest flight possible is desirable, but also a paradise close at hand which is guarded by terrible watchdogs."[9] It literally depends on which side of the fence you are born. Thus, the growing child of Chapter 6 is aware not only of the violence and hostility of the world he shares, but also of another world which coexists with this from which he is debarred, an Eden from which he has been driven out. "Fences and hedges. Fences white and tall with wooden boards pointed and glinting in the sun, hedges thick and very high, their beautiful greenness not even covering their thorns. Looking for almonds, the white man's peanuts. Almonds big as mangoes, and some so ripe they had grown all red. Mangoes hanging big and gold, and outside eyes looking and longing. The third boy finds a hold down on the ground, underneath the hedge. Small hole, three boys, three khaki uniforms ruined with thorns and dirt. It seems it may be true that the white men are living ghosts themselves. For a place where people live, there is no sound at all. But it is impossible to see inside, beyond netting at all the windows. Nothing like a long pole lying around. Never throw stones round a white man's bungalow. So three little boys turn their back to the white man's bungalow and bring down ripe mangoes with unripe ones fallen on the ground before. Keeping quiet. The white man, in case he exists, must not be waked up. Then sudden noise of footsteps within, moving out. Such a lot of mangoes and such big mangoes to have to leave behind, and the hole is far too small and the thorns are cruelly sharp, coming through the khaki all the painful way into the flesh. The backward glance gives terror in the shape of two dogs . . ." (p. 78).

Against this background of images which communicate the fears and repressions of the colonized, Armah traces the historical process of dream and betrayal. These scenes appear to be recollections of Teacher rather than of the man, and they centre on his realization that the struggle of the black leadership has not been for 'liberation' but to get into the big castle that the white man has been forced to vacate. Even the young man who has been at one with the people (Nkrumah), and who has inspired Maanan, the bringer of dreams, to believe in reality again,[10] eventually declines into the decay and the falsity. Through this examination of the past in the sixth chapter, this history of disillusion and lost hopes, we are shown the source of the hero's morbid sensitivity to corruption and filth which has dominated the first section of the book. Any notion of gratuitous obsession is no longer tenable. Armah has demonstrably integrated his images to the most important topics of his time and place. He is investigating the most serious question at issue in his society: "How could this have grown rotten with such obscene haste" (p. 103)? Where does this process begin? How then is one to act? If corruption is so general, so natural a condition of life, what use is struggle. It is the air we breathe. "The nostrils, incredibly, are joined in a way that is most horrifyingly direct to the throat itself and to the entrails right through to the end. Across the aisle on the seat opposite, an old man is sleeping and his mouth is open to the air rushing in the night with how many particles of what? So why should he play the fool and hold his breath?" (p. 48) For the man, ascending from the filth of the office latrine, corruption is now part of his own flesh. "On the climb up the man feels his nostrils assailed by something he is carrying within himself, the smell of the latrine" (p. 125). Action taken against the process of corruption and bribery is meaningless. To refuse a bribe is not to foil corruption; there is always another waiting eager to take it. Despite such reflections the man cannot take the leap towards the gleam. But he is increasingly aware that in not doing so he is behaving unnaturally, that he is out of joint with his time. As he reflects, "It is so normal all this, that the point of holding out against it escapes the unsettled mind;" (p. 127). However, in the transactions between his wife, her mother and Koomson he remains passive. But he is aware of the complicity which this action implies. We are aware of the limitations and sources of his indecision and disillusion. We have lived through their history. Now, as he walks through the world the landscape reflects with precise symbolism the society in which he lives. "A dead fish floated in the water at the edge, the silvery flesh of its belly dancing violently up and down with the little waves. When he looked closer he saw a whole lot of little fishes eating the torn white body, Breaking the water's surface at a dozen points" (p. 146). Like the fish, the black-whitemen feed off the decayed carcass of white colonialism. "This was what it had come to: not that the whole thing might be overturned and ended, but that a few black men might be pushed closer to their masters, to eat some of the fat into their bellies too" (pp. 147–48). There is no longer the possibility of dreaming. Wee has lost its potency. To sit and dream under a palm tree, to listen to the music of the Congo, all are irrelevant in a world in which corruption is the condition of life, to imbibe which is coincidental with the act of living and breathing. To have believed otherwise was always an illusion. When, lulled into security by Maanan's dreams, they had sucked greedily at contentment, they had not shut out the rot they had been forced unknowingly to swallow. Below the wee-smokers is the breakwater "used by everybody else as a lavatory . . ." (p. 83).

When the new regime comes there is no false optimism. "New people, new style, old dance" (p. 185). The net of reform will once again be "made in the special Ghanaian way that allowed the really big corrupt people to pass through it" (p. 180). The cloak of anonymity has been allowed to drop to a marked degree. This is Ghana, this is Nkrumah, this is the actual and the here and now. The wheel has turned full circle. From the anonymous corrupt universe of the man's private life, of his body and his immediate surroundings, the metaphors have circled out like stones dropped into a pond, extending the pattern of images until now the body of Ghana and that of the man are continuous, his landscape the landscape of the nation, his sufferings and sufferings of the Ghanaian people. In a corrupt universe the only reality is one's own consciousness. Nkrumah is only a name. He represents nothing. To name him is merely to reinforce the sense of namelessness, the falsity which such particularisation reinforces in a world where overthrower and overthrown are engaged only in a formal reversal of role.

> 'Look, contrey, if you don't want trouble, get out.'
> 'If two trains collide while I'm demonstrating, will you take the responsibility?'
> 'Oh,' said the organizer, 'if it is the job, fine. but we won't tolerate any Nkrumaists now.'
> 'You know,' said the man slowly, 'you know who the real Nkrumaists are.' (p. 186)

This increasing sense of the universality and the inevitability of the corrupting process culminates in the third section of the book in the visit of Koomson, now deposed and fleeing arrest. Koomson, terrified and broken, is a literal body of corruption: ". . . Koomson's insides gave a growl longer than usual, an inner fart of personal, corrupt thunder which in its fullness sounded as if it had rolled down all the way from the eating throat thundering through the belly and guts to end in further silent pollution of the air already thick with flatulent fear" (p. 192). The military arrive to arrest him, but the man decides to help him. The only way of escape with the soldiers already knocking on the front door is through the latrine hole and so into the maze of back-alleys through which the latrine-men carry away the filth of Accra. This escape provides a return to the initial birth image of chapter six. The two men must force their way through the latrine hole, "trailing dung and exhausted blood" to reenter the world. This second birth ironically mocks the first, when it was still possible to believe that 'growth' from youth to age, from purity to decay, might be arrested by choice. This second birth is a deliberate acknowl-edgement that all life is caught in the tension between vigour and decay, between the symbolic blossom which has appeared time and again in the narrative and the hidden dung which sustains it and to which it must ultimately return. The agonizing paradox of the chichidodo bird is the condition of existence. This has been the fearful realization towards which the man has groped earlier, that his own feelings of envy and his sense of a potential fruitfulness in the greed and aggression of his world are signs of the necessity of such things. "Having the whiteness of stolen bungalows and the shine of stolen cars flowing past him, he could think of reasons, of the probability that without the belittling power of things like these we would all continue to sit underneath old trees and weave palm wine dreams of beauty and happiness in our amazed heads" (p. 111). In the first instance disillusion had followed immediately, when he realized that work was not the currency of his time, and that only through corruption could the cars and bungalows be obtained, by "one bold corrupt leap that gives the leaper the power to laugh with contempt at those of use who still plod the daily round, stupid, honest, dull, poor, despised, afraid" (p. 113). But now he realizes that for Koomson too, even for the "successful," the end of the cycle is destruction, disillusion and the inevitable acknowledgement of the relationship between gleem and filth. The shock and horror of Koomson's decline opens even his wife's eyes to the full truth of the relationship between maggots and ordure which she has so glibly assumed. "He went back into the hall and stood quietly beside Oyo. She held his hand in a tight grasp. Then in a voice that sounded as if she were stifling, she whispered, 'I am glad you never became like him' " (p. 194). The birth struggle and the excretory

237

struggle are only foci for a universal action, a mastering peristalsis by which the world digests the human aspirations which each birth renews and each old age destroys. Questions of individual motive are again irrelevant in such a context. The issue of why the man saves Koomson is not answerable, except perhaps in terms of a recognized kinship of all those who experience rebirth. The latrine episode draws together the metaphorical skeins of the book, and insists vividly on the structural identify of birth, excretion, copulation, and death. Metaphorical theme has become the immediate tool of insight and compassion.

Following their escape, Koomson and the man bribe their way to the fishing boat and make their way out to sea. Koomson will now be able to rejoin his family in a neighboring country. But the man has decided to return, and swims ashore. The sea is described as a purifying bath, washing away stench and corruption. But the purification is ultimately unsuccessful. The only escape of that sort would be through death, and this the man rejects. "He held his breath so long that he began to enjoy the almost exploding inward feeling that he was perhaps no longer alive. But then it became impossible to hold on any longer and involuntarily he gasped and let in a gulp of water that tasted unbelievably salty. The surface seemed so far up that he thought it would never come, but suddenly the pressure around his neck and in his ears was no more and he opened his eyes again" (p. 210). When, later, he awakens on the beach he sees the lonely figure of a woman approaching across the sands, and as she draws nearer he recognizes her as the Maanan of his past life, mad now with disappointment and disillusionment. Like the confusion of identify between Rama Krishna and Teacher, Maanan's role is also deliberately obscure. She is and she is not a figure from memory. "The woman laughed at the name, with a recognition so remote that in the same cold moment the man was certain he had only deceived himself about it. Then she walked away towards the distant town, away from the sun with her shadow out in front of her coloring the sand, leaving the man wondering why but knowing already that he would find no answers from her, from Teacher, or from anyone else" (p. 212). The past which the man has searched to discover reasons for the present has failed him. He knows with certainty that corruption will always renew itself, indeed that this is a condition of the renewal of all things, and inseparable from it, the paradoxical "promise of rot" (p. 146). When he returns to the highroad the new state has already begun the old process of bribery. "The policeman who had spoken raised his right hand and in a slow gesture pointed to his teeth . . . The driver understood. Without waiting to be asked for it, he took out his license folder from his shirt-pocket, brought out a cedi note from the same place, and stuck it in the folder . . ." (p.

214). The cycle has turned fully. The old waste expelled, the "eating" process must begin again. As the bus drives slowly away it reveals on its back "an inscription carefully lettered to form an oval shape:

THE BEAUTYFUL ONES ARE NOT YET BORN

In the centre of the oval was a single flower, solitary, unexplainable, and very beautiful" (p. 214). The flower is unexplainable as far as the man is concerned. From his viewpoint, the events of the book are still confused and arbitrary. Armah does not allow us any neat extension of viewpoint, any convenient and sentimental notion of an 'educative process' at work. But the issues of the book are explainable, or at least are more coherent and interrelated than the man knows, and through image and metaphor the reader has been exposed to these connections. The mystic and apocalyptic message of the mammy-wagon reminds us forcibly that there is a muted hope even in this world of the unbeautiful ones, and that the unity of dung and blossom is a radical and healthy reality. But for the man, walking away, there is truthfully limited insight. He has learned enough to survive on the mimimum of hope and confidence; that is all. But it is enough, for he will plant a fresh seed. The beautiful ones may yet be born, one day. In the meantime, "Over the school latrine at the bottom of the hill a bird with a song that was strangely happy dived low and settled on the roof. The man wondered what kind of bird it could be, and what its name was" (p. 215). Unknown to him, his question has been answered, the question he has asked so much earlier, when he "wondered what kind of sound the cry of the chichidodo bird could be . . ." (p. 56). The cry of the chichidodo is not agonized or distraught but "strangely happy," recognizing, if not entirely resigned to, the fact that its tantalizing paradox is rooted in the nature of living itself.

NOTES

All inset page references are to the following edition:
Ayi Kwei Armah, *The Beautyful Ones are Not Yet Born*, (African Writers Series; William Heinemann; London, 1969). The novel was first issued in both America and Britain in 1968.

1. Peter Abrahams. *A Wreath for Udomo*, (Faber; London, 1956).
2. "Wage employment in West Africa is characterized by three marked features—the smaller number of persons involved in it; the dominance of employment in construction, transport and commerce at the expense of manufacturing; and the high porportion of employees in the public sector . . . (in Ghana) less than 25 percent of the adult men are in wage employment." P.C. Lloyd, *Africa in Social Change*, (Penguin African Library; London, 1967), pp. 119–120.

239

3. The paradigmatic relationship between body and landscape, and vice versa is a widespread feature of African and West-Indian writing. See, for example, Aime Cesaire's *Return to my Native Land,* Wilson Harris' *Palace of the Peacock,* etc. For an interesting discussion of this see Gerald Moore, "The Negro Poet and His Landscape" from *Black Orpheus,* reprinted in *Introduction to African Literature: An Anthology of Critical Writing from 'Black Orpheus',* ed. Ulli Beier (Longmans; London, 1967), pp. 151–164.
4. Sartre's introduction to Frantz Fanon's *The Wretched of the Earth,* (Penguin Books; London, 1969).
5. Fanon, p. 161.
6. *African Literature Today,* ed. Eldred D. Jones, no. 3, p. 56.
7. Fanon, p. 123.
8. Fanon, p. 40.
9. Fanon, p. 41.
10. Maanan is another of those complex figures, like Teacher, the permanence and objectivity of whose character is called in doubt as the book unfolds. Maanan is the bearer of dreams and visions, the wee-peddlar who can open up the sordid landscape into a clarity of anger and perception; but she is also a complex symbol of loss and betrayal, especially for Teacher, for whom she is a lost lover.

AYI KWEI ARMAH AND THE "I" OF THE BEHOLDER

D. S. Izevbaye

> How often the unconnected eye finds beauty in death—the
> women looked at . . . whiteness, saw famine where the men
> saw beauty, and grew frightened for our people.
>
> *Two Thousand Seasons*

The theme of beauty and the "I" of the beholder is central to Armah's
fiction.[1] It is the starting point for his social ideas about old Africa and
contemporary Africa. In his treatment of the theme he makes a distinction
between two kinds of beauty—an active, external beauty whose power
makes the beholder's eye a mere receiver of impressions, and a passive
ideal beauty hidden in nature and thus challenging the beholder to test his
ability to penetrate the object to the beauty beyond. The eye of the
beholder thus becomes a moral organ and an index to his moral integrity,
since "the perception of beauty is so dependent on the soul's seeing."[2]
This view of beauty has strongly affected the conception of plot and
incident in Armah's fiction. Just as the strong moral tone in his writing
gives his plot and incident a ritual movement, so is the text flooded with
images of seeing and hearing. Even the characters are generally not whole
persons but active and passive senses, like the watchers and listeners, the
seers and hearers listed in the paragraphs which introduce the characters
in *Two Thousand Seasons*.

This preoccupation does not, however, limit Armah to a philosophical
interest in the question of beauty and the subjective character of seeing. It
is his contribution to the debate on black aesthetics. It therefore has a
political relevance for the celebration of black civilizations which has now
become a major twentieth-century theme. Both the philosophical statement and its political relevance for contemporary Africa are embodied in
"An African Fable,"[3] a story constructed after the theme of a knight's
quest for an ideal which later appears to him in the form of grail or lady. In
this complex little tale an inexperienced warrior mistakes the uncontrolled throb of his own heart for a woman's cry of distress and, because
of an imperfection in his vision, becomes a betrayer where he should have

241

been a liberator. This tale contains the philosophical kernel of themes to bloom later in Armah's fiction: post-independence disillusionment in Africa, the sense of the beautiful as a shibboleth for leaders and liberators, and the theme of Pan-Africanism.

In the warrior's rape of the woman we have the theme of the strong taking advantage of the weak, as a conqueror exploits a people he claims to have saved from oppression. This retold tale of disillusionment has been preceded by various versions presented in a more explicit form, from Peter Abrahams's *A Wreath for Udomo* through *Kongi's Harvest* and *A Man of the People,* until we arrive at its contemporary, *Bound to Violence.* In the new philosophical context in which Armah places it, the story of the new African ruler betraying the people he should help is given its specific political meaning through the use of a symbolic but nevertheless identifiable landscape which the warrior traverses as he wanders south through desert, scrub, and forest, to arrive at the sea-shore goal where he displaces an older warrior whom he finds raping the woman. The comparable sexual licence of the conquerors and kings in *Two Thousand Seasons* becomes a figure for the rulers' exploitation of land and people, and the way they perceive beauty becomes a kind of moral test, as it is also in *The Beautyful Ones Are Not Yet Born* and *Fragments.*

The two types of beauty which Armah distinguishes in "An African Fable" gives us an insight into the psychological impotence of the hero of *The Beautyful Ones.* While "the man's" awareness of true beauty stimulates a powerful revulsion against the corrupt path to wealth taken by the new middle class, his power of perception is, nevertheless, too inactive to resist the impressions of beauty which it receives from the shiny trinkets from Europe:

> There were things here . . . with a beauty of their own that forced the admiration of even the unwilling . . . He could have asked if anything was supposed to have changed after all, from the days of chiefs selling their people for the trinkets of Europe. But he thought again of the power of the new trinkets and of their usefulness, and of the irresistible desire they brought . . . the thought ran round and round inside his head that it would never be possible to look at such comfortable things and feel a real contempt for them.[4]

What poses the social problem in *The Beautyful Ones* is, however, not the inability to purchase foreign trinkets but the ordinary question of daily bread. The economic gap between Koomson, the minister, and "the man"—between ruler and ruled, that is—prepares the way for the class conflict prescribed by Marxists as a solution to social inequality. But the language in which the plight of the poor is described suggests their capacity for endurance and hope rather than their readiness for confrontation. It is still a few days to the end of the month when the novel opens, and the author sees it through the eyes of his characters as Passion Week when life is "not as satisfactory as in the swollen days after pay day." In spite of the figure of religious suffering used here, the image of pregnancy suggests a capacity for hope on the part of the author and his characters. The beauty of the flower in the last chapter has an indirect link with the Passion Week of the first chapter, and the flower is also presented enclosed in an oval shape—an egg or ovary—awaiting the birth of beauty as the workers' Passion Week preceded the birth of the day of comfort. Armah's art is thus too ambiguous for us to see a simplified Marxist solution in it, and his critique of socialism in "African Socialism: Utopian or Scientific?"[5] is a criticism of theories built on simple Marxist oppositions. The importance of African family connections in the plot of his first two novels is an acknowledgement that there are ways in which African family interests can act against African socialism. The artless dishonesty of Koomson, the minister, and the passivity of "the man" in *The Beautyful Ones* can both be traced to family demands on the individual. Because of his loyalty to family, "the man" identifies too closely with Koomson's motives, if not with the means he adopts, for him to have been intended as a class representative in an impending struggle. Perhaps it is this sympathy for Koomson's motives which moves "the man" to help Koomson out of a tight spot during the coup.

Fragments is essentially a representation of the themes of *The Beautyful Ones,* using the benefit of the author's personal experience of the extended family. It contains basically the same cast of characters and roles that we find in *The Beautyful Ones,* using the benefit of the author's personal experience of the extended family. It contains basically the same cast of characters and roles that we find in *The Beautyful Ones.* "The man" is now named Baako Onipa ("Onipa" is Akan for "man"), and Brempong (i.e., "an important person") is mainly Koomson re-christened, although he now trails a larger retinue of relatives and hangers-on, and is a "been-to." His initials, "H.R.H.," foreshadow Armah's denunciation of all forms of African royalty in *Two Thousand Seasons.* Although the first two novels are similar in plot and characterization, the opposition of characters takes place at a higher social level in *Fragments.* In *The Beautyful Ones* Koomson was once an uncouth dockhand now risen to be minister, while "the man" is a secondary school leaver denied university education by lack of opportunity. In *Fragments,* on the other hand, the two protagonists are equipped by their education to join the new middle class, and are equal, at least theoretically. Baako is denied entry into this class because of his refusal even to begin to accept their behaviour patterns. He discovers for himself what it is to be socially isolated when the asylum walls rise around him. And his mother's confession now comes like a belated lesson:

> "We come to walls in life, all the time. If we try to break them down we destroy ourselves. I was wanting you to break down and see the world here, before I saw you yourself were a wall."[6]

Refused entry by his own professional kind and denied emotional support by his kin, he is only let through the gates of madness.

The situations developed by Armah in his novels appear to close some of the main social options for Africa. We might summarize these situations into a statement of this kind: on the one hand the alliance between the privileged class and the poor is arranged by the extended family who ensure the flow of material benefits from rich to poor relations; this reduces the chances of a class confrontation. But then family demands for a share in the rewards of individual ability and training discourage maximum fulfilment for the average gifted individual. This is a very crude summary of what happens to Brempong and Baako in *Fragments*. We may ignore two bits of evidence in order to develop this theme: first, there are hints within the novel that Baako had neurotic tendencies before his return to Ghana, and second, there is the important fact that to give a character in a ritual-oriented society a first name like Baako or "lonely one" is to encourage us to see his malady as a congenital one rather than a means desired by the author to make a social comment. Whatever the case, Baako's progress to full madness is intensified by the family's general lack of real regard for individual feeling. Brempong is sturdy and crafty enough to bear the weight of family demands. But an individual as sensitive and intelligent as Baako can see in these demands only his own death and the sacrifice of his personal talents. Although Juana, his Puerto Rican friend, cannot understand what Baako's grandmother means when she tells her that the family "tried to kill" Baako, the essay draft in which Baako uses the Melanesian Cargo Cult as a model for interpreting the Ghanaian extended family institution clarifies for Baako and for the reader the ritual meaning of family expectations. The ritual death of travelling out to return with cargo for the community is successfully enacted by Brempong and Araba's child (who, unlike Brempong, suffers actual death). The plot also provides instances when the ritual proves abortive, in the stories of Skido, the driver who brings cargo but dies in spite of fulfilling the symbolic death of travelling out, and Baako, who dies symbolically by travelling out but is rejected because he brings no cargo.

This rejection by society is also ritually performed in *The Beautyful Ones*. Koomson the corrupt minister ritually repeats the public crimes he has committed by eating and vomiting what he has eaten. His subsequent escape through the latrine hole and by sea is the national penalty for his failure to distribute cargo to a wider group than his immediate relations. In other words, he is punished for an anti-social act rather than the sin itself. The ritual movement of the last three chapters defines the area of social taint. Before Koomson's expulsion the necessity for social purification is made evident by excremental symbolism. The symbolism works with a logic that is Freudian: eating is impure, excretion a form of purification. The result of this attitude to food and latrines is the hero's recoil from all forms of sensuality, which gives the novel its impression of a horrifying passivity:

> The thought of food now brought with it a picture of its eating and its spewing out, of its beginnings and endings, so that no desire arose asking to be controlled . . . Sometimes it is understandable, the doomed attempt to purify the self by adding to the disease outside . . . The nostrils, incredibly, are joined in a way that is most horrifyingly direct to the throat itself and to the entrails right through to their end.[7]

The man's oversensitive sense of smell is similar to the reaction of Soyinka's Sagoe, another character who uses the latrine as a haven to which one may retreat from an oppressive social order. The eyes and the nostrils of Armah's hero are really moral organs, however. "The man" functions as the artistic conscience of the work, although he is not exclusively so. His obsession with corruption is obliquely commented on through various parables like those of Rama Krishna, the recluse who would escape corruption but rots before he dies, and the picture of the man-child bright to school by Aboliga the Frog. Translated into political terms, the parable of the man-child preaches cultural relativism by its insistence on the universality of corruption. Corruption is in the nature of things, and the degree of corruption is relative to the time it takes to bridge the space between the beginning of growth and its end. The insanity of the man's recoil from contact appears most effectively in the scene where his wife's caesarean scar prevents him from making love to her. He is not therefore to be expected to read the more subtle lessons of inescapable decay and perpetual renewal written even in water:

> the water escaping through a gap made by the little dam and
> the far side of the ditch had a cleanness which had nothing to
> do with the thing it came from. . . . Far out, toward the mouth
> of the small stream and the sea, he could see the water already
> aging into the mud of its beginning.[8]

In spite of these comments on the *involvement* of ripeness in rotten-
ness, the man's reaction is not wholly subjective. The smell of physical
corruption which Koomson brings to the man's house on his second visit
is noticed—significantly—by a child, but not by an adult—the watchman
who "did not seem to notice the smell." Although community is not
offered as the place of salvation and well-being for the individual in *The
Beautyful Ones*, we must see the man's return to community, however
reluctantly he returns, as an acceptance of responsibility to his family.

In *Fragments,* individualism is not accepted as an alternative to a
corrupt community, even though talented individual who suffers in this
work may not look to the group for his salvation. Of the chapter titles
(which are used as comments on the action within each chapter), two—
"Gyefo" and "Osagyefo" ("Saviour" and "Saviour in war")—support
the idea tentatively offered in the novel that such individuals may look for
support only in the bond between one individual and another. But the idea
is rejected, not developed. When Juana says that "salvation is such an
empty thing when you are alone," back comes Teacher Ocran's reply that
one would not find it in the market place. However, Baako's madness is
the author's ironic comment on the chances of individualism. For in
Fragments, as in *The Beautyful Ones,* the question of value is tied to the
problem of seeing. The individual is imperfect, a fragment from the
whole. His vision is thus subjective; it is not, however, a distortion of
truth. It is a reflection of social imperfection, a mirror of that which is not
beautiful. Its reflection is justified insofar as it does not invite an adjustment of the seeing lens. But its true value is not in the accuracy of the lens
but in its diagnosis of the presence of rot and the need for a cure. This
problem gets its sharpest focus in that scene where Juana describes
Baako's isolation as "going against a general current" and receives as
reply Baako's ambiguously chosen substitute: "as a matter of fact it's
beginning to look like a cataract to me."

The cataract which caused the partial blindness of Naana, Baako's
grandmother, has the same source in the historical experience which
brought the malady of madness to people like Baako. It also suggests that
the extended family practice was never a "current" even in the past,
because the cargo mentality caused the ancestors to sell their own people
to any white slaver who came along. In spite of her physical blindness,

however, Naana's seeing is the nearest thing to completeness in the novel because she sees not the surface gleam of trinkets, but the higher Platonic beauty described in "An African Fable." She is not an isolated individual like Baako because she can relate to "Nananom"—the community of ancestors living underground. Her vision is complete and inclusive because it *contains* both the wholeness of the past and the fragments of the present:

> The larger meaning which lent sense to every small thing and every momentary happening years and years ago has shattered into a thousand and thirty useless pieces.[9]

Because Naana's values belong to a community of the past, her voice is merely the voice of the singular person left over from the past, as her name, Naana, is the singular form of Nananom.

Armah's criticism of honoured African institutions like the extended family and his frequent suggestion that the initiative for the slave trade came from Africans themselves are best seen against his argument in favour of a realistic appraisal of the African past and the future of Africa. Such realism is the topic of the conversation between Baako and his boss, Asante-Smith. Asante-Smith's objection to the allusions to slavery in Baako's film script is countered by Baako's retort that slavery has everything to do with the African past. Behind Baako's anger is the knowledge of a suffering community of slaves betrayed by their rulers.

The true test of Armah's attitude to the African past is his depiction of suffering as a communal experience, especially in *Two Thousand Seasons*. Although his first two novels deal with suffering as the experience of individuals, his heroes are individuals only because they are set against their community. Even as individuals they stand for something larger than themselves in the sense that not only does the author vest some of his themes and values in them, he also makes them the representatives of other suffering individuals in society. Moreover, the centrality of the first person narrator in the first two novels is mainly an instrument for sounding the depths of social discord, even though the nature of the seeing by either hero is done in a very personal manner. But whatever resonances of group suffering the author manages to strike by giving his characters generic names and developing their problems through his use of social institutions, suffering is most effectively conveyed in the novels through the individual experience, as when on-coming madness is seen through Baako's eyes. The irony in the author's treatment of character and experience in the novels prevents us from interpreting too simply the later argument in *Two Thousand Seasons* that the individual is nothing,

247

the group everything. What the argument does is to reinforce the horror of isolation which marks Armah's works.

It is only in *The Beautyful Ones* that we are clearly shown how close the relationship between individual suffering and a communal experience of it can be. But an author is a chameleon figure endowed with the power to assume the colour of his characters' emotions. When Armah claims and uses this privilege, he successfully focuses on the group while using the experience of the individual. He achieves this simply by leaving things unsaid and refusing to identify the actual sufferer among the group of three boys who flee from the dogs of the white man whose garden they have just raided. The outlines of the incident are clearly enough sketched to be an individual experience, although it is an experience with which many African children can identify.

> Such a lot of mangoes and such big almonds to have to leave behind, and the hole is far too small and the thorns are cruelly sharp, coming through the khaki all the painful way into the flesh. The backward glance brings terror in the shape of two dogs, and they look much larger than any angry father. . . . Can a dog also roll a child over and leave it feeling thoroughly beaten by life?[10]

The suffering here is given wider relevance because its recall by the listening man is stimulated by the speaking teacher's account of a parallel experience. Here we can at best only try to explain the method by seeing it as the experience of either three boys coalesced into one, or of one boy made to serve for three. A slightly different version of the method occurs in that scene in *Fragments* where Baako and Juana roll down the sandy beach to dry their skin. The incident is done through Juana's eyes alone and we feel the tactile sensation more fully than we do the group frenzy of the worshippers who roll down the beach in chapter two, although as far as actual sensations go, Juana's experience should be far less intense than that of the group. The group frenzy is seen—can only be seen—mainly from the outside, and it becomes less meaningful because it invites less sympathy.

In *Two Thousand Seasons,* as in the sixth chapter of *The Beautyful Ones*, Armah opts for a narrator in the plural, in contrast to the personalized narrators who dominate his first two novels in the manner of the conventional novel. The plural voice is suitable for the theme of an oppressed community which he develops in the fourth novel. But it demands that the author surrender his chameleon privilege to enter into and identify with the individual when the suffering of the group is being portrayed. Here is Armah's re-creation of a slave-branding scene:

> The askaris brought another captive forward and burned the
> mark into her flesh. When we had all been burnt the slave
> driver took the calabash and the horn from the woman. . . .
> Then walking up to each of us he dipped a piece of cloth in it
> and rubbed our raw wounds with the mixture.[11]

One cannot help noticing the hiatus in this report. The swift transition
from the third person singular, "burned . . . her flesh," to the first person
plural, "when we had all been burnt," leads us to see in the deliberate
suppression of the first person singular a reluctance to identify with the
individual, or perhaps even to acknowledge his existence.

The reason for this is made clear not only by the chosen narrative focus
but also by the credo announced at the book's close: "There is no beauty
but in relationships. Nothing cut off by itself is beautiful. . . . The group
that knows this . . . [is] itself a work of beauty." Armah is consistent in his
portrait of the migrant blacks in this novel. Individualism is not allowed.
Even Anoa, the prophetess whose utterance defined the path to the
people's salvation, is not any one individual because "she was not even
the first to bear that name."[12]

If the suffering of a community is often less intense in this work than the
suffering of individuals in the first two novels, it is nevertheless consistent
with the function of Armah's novel in showing that suffering is less
unbearable when shared. In fact, in "African Socialism: Utopian or
Scientific?", we come upon Armah's definition of community as "shared
suffering and shared hopes." This is the foundation for his attitude
towards individualism on the one hand, and socialism on the other. Placed
against this unambiguous preference for the group rather than the individual in this novel, the intensity of the focus on flawed individualism his first
two novels shows up as a call for social reform rather than a distorted
vision of society. This applies to the criticism of Nkrumah's Ghana in
both the first two novels and the essay, where the satirical emphasis falls
on the gap between word and deed. The definition of socialism in the
popular language of the latrine graffiti in *The Beautyful Ones* is both a
criticism and a reminder: "socialism chop make I chop."

The emphasis shifts from satire in *The Beautyful Ones* to patriotic
history and exhortation in *Two Thousand Seasons*. It is easy to draw a
parallel between the career of a committed writer and the emphasis in his
writing. We would not therefore learn much from pointing out that *Why
Are We So Blest?*, a novel in which Armah develops the theme of human
isolation and pessimism first sketched in "Contact,"[13] was published
when he was in the United States as a visiting lecturer. But there must be
an extra-literary significance in the East African publication of *Two
Thousand Seasons*, a work which urges the return to true socialism on the

part of all Africans, now that Armah is living in Tanzania, the land where Nyerere's practical experiment with African socialism has been launched.

This does not necessarily imply agreement with the policy which preceded the experiment, for Nyerere was as much a target of Armah's criticism in the socialism essay as Nkrumah was. Published in the Year of Ujamaa, the essay is critical of the Tanzanian programme for being "rich in sacerdotal sanctimonious piety as it is poor in political realism." But the Arusha declaration has at least one realistic feature worth mentioning here: the insistence that socialism must have a local, even rural, base. This view is extended to Nyerere's stand on Pan-Africanism, an issue on which he disagrees with Nkrumah, when he insists that African political leaders must first deal with local realities as a prelude to continental unity.[14]

The issues of socialism, Pan-Africanism and local realities are important in Armah's work. The satire in the first two novels begins from the confrontation of African socialist theories with the reality of national life. Theories are, after all, only fictions, as we infer from "African Socialism. Utopian or Scientific?":

> the socialist tradition itself [is] . . . *a mytho-poetic system.* The greatest source of power and influence available to the socialist tradition is *its acceptance and imaginative use of the archetypal dream* of total liberation, . . . the thoroughgoing negation of the repressive facts of real life.[15]

But it is as if Armah had set his sights too low when he dealt with national problems in his first two novels, for he later adjusts the focus in *Two Thousand Seasons* by developing the Pan-African theme implied in "An African Fable" along the lines of earlier Pan-African novels, from Casely-Hayford's *Ethiopia Unbound* and William Conton's *The African* to Ouologuem's *Bound to Violence*. To realize the full importance of this, his fourth novel, it is important to see it ultimately as fiction, a mytho-poetic system accepting and making use of the archtypal dream of total liberation. And like the socialist tradition which Armah analyzes in his essay, it is constructed after a Marxist mytho-poetic model: it locates an imaginary African Eden, the Way of Reciprocity, in the pre-migrations past of the Africans in the novel, and projects a socialist heaven too, in its hope for the recovery of the Way. Although Armah did not approve of the name "Kenya's Bible" given to the Kenyan document on socialism,16 *Two Thousand Seasons* is manifestly intended as "Africa's Bible" because of the explicitness of its moral exhortation and the Pan-African

manner in which it draws its characters' names from all over the continent. The very thinly disguised names and the historical framework it
adopts imply a denial that this work is primarily fiction, while its grave
relevance for the present commits us to an ethical goal that is irresistible.
But we recall that in citing the Kenyan document in support of his
criticism of African socialist theories, Armah argues that socialist intellectuals are so busy condemning religion that they do not see how they are
themselves creating a religious system.

As the author distrusts formal religion, *Two Thousand Seasons* is
offered as a kind of ethical manifesto rather than a bible for blacks.
Nevertheless, its combination of poetic form and social theory brings us
close to a magical view of art. But it is the method rather than the message
which tells us how to place the novel. The style is probably its most
important achievement. In this work Armah develops what promises to
be one of the major literary styles in Africa, finding its base in the same
tradition that encouraged Aidoo's dramatic style. The writing is not
merely oral, but oracular. Its imagery shows a preference for that which is
fundamental and unchanging. The poetic effect of the prose is sustained
without verbal inflation and dead metaphor. The essential simplicity of
the style is sustained by calling an object by its name, not its praise name.
Thus Armah avoids the convention which enables an orator to wrap his
truths and untruths in mere words. Here kings are surrounded by "flatter-
ers," not "counsellors," and the recollection of the past is a "remembrance" rather than "history." "Remembrance" suggests that memory
fails, that only what is relevant is remembered for the present and for
posterity, while "history" implies inclusiveness, accuracy and objectivity. The novel is similarly stocked with folklore elements and motifs
which, with the theme of black diaspora, give pattern and direction to the
work. Within the large tidal movement marked out by the theme of
migrations we find the tinier waves of rhythm achieved through the use of
structural parallelism, formal repetition and the repeated return to the
motif of flowing water:

> Springwater flowing to the desert, where you flow there is no
> regeneration. The desert takes. The desert knows no
> giving. . . .
> Hau, people headed after the setting sun, in that direction
> even the possibility of regeneration is dead. . . .
> Woe the headwater needing to give, giving only to floodwa-
> ter flowing desertward. Woe the link from spring to stream.
> Woe the link receiving springwater only to pass it on in a
> stream flowing to waste. . . .[17]

251

The literary model is the traditional dirge of Ghana. The function of the dirge, according to Professor Nketia, is to involve the group in the suffering of the individual, and to lessen individual grief by channelling it into collective grooves.18 The result is artistic pleasure, rather than pain, an experience of beauty which every hearer and every beholder should find in Armah's peepshow into Africa's past and present.

NOTES

1. Armah has written four novels so far: *The Beautyful Ones Are Not Yet Born* (London: Heinemann, 1969, first published in 1968); Fragments (Boston: Houghton Mifflin Co., 1970); *Why Are We So Blest?* (New York: Doubleday, 1971); *Two Thousand Seasons* (Nairobi: East African Publishing House, 1973). All quotations are from these editions.
2. *Two Thousand Seasons*, p. 285.
3. *Présence Africaine* (Paris), no. 68 (1968), pp. 192–196.
4. *The Beautyful Ones*, pp. 170, 175, 177 passim.
5. "African Socialism: Utopian or Scientific?", *Présence Africaine* (Paris), no. 64 (1967), pp. 6–30.
6. *Fragments*, p. 253.
7. *The Beautyful Ones*, pp. 28, 47–48 passim.
8. Ibid., p. 27.
9. *Fragments*, p. 280.
10. *The Beautyful Ones*, pp. 79–80.
11. *Two Thousand Seasons*, pp. 184–185.
12. The Ghanaian legend of Anoa has been re-interpreted by another Ghanaian writer, Ama Ata Aidoo in *Anowa* (London: Longman, 1970).
13. *The New African* (London), vol. IV, no. 10 (Dec. 1965), pp. 244–246, 248.
14. See interview with Nyerere in *Africa* (London & Paris), ed. Raph. Uwechue, no. 21 (May 1973), p. 13.
15. "African Socialism: Utopian or Scientific?", p. 8, italics mine.
16. "Kenya's Bible" is Kenyatta's description of Sessional Paper no. 10, 4 May 1965: *African Socialism and its Application to Planning in Kenya*, as Armah notes in his essay.
17. *Two Thousand Seasons*, p. ix.
18. J. H. Nketia, *Funeral Dirges of the Akan People* (Achimota: 1955), p. 8: " 'One mourns one's relation during the funeral of another person' . . . , says the Akan maxim . . . Grief and sorrow may be personal and private, nevertheless Akan Society expects that on the occasion of a funeral they should be expressed publicly through the singing of the dirge."

ARMAH'S *FRAGMENTS* AND THE VISION OF THE WHOLE

Edward Lobb

Ayi Kwei Armah's second novel, *Fragments,* was widely and favorably reviewed in the United States when it appeared in 1970, and has attracted similarly favorable notice elsewhere since its belated appearance in Heinemann's *African Writers Series.*[1] Gerald Moore, reviewing the novel for the *Journal of Commonwealth Literature* in 1974, said that there were "good reasons for believing that it will eventually establish itself as superior to *The Beautyful Ones Are Not Yet Born* [Armah's first novel, 1969] in quality, profundity, and originality."[2] Moore's review indicated some of the directions that subsequent criticism might take; his remarks on the use of "dislocated ritual" in the novel are particularly suggestive. *Fragments* has received some critical attention since, and Armah is generally acknowledged as one of the finest stylists among "Anglophone" African writers: but, even now, little attention has been paid to the structure of the novel or to the relation of image and themes within that structure.

The plot of the novel is slight. Baako Onipa, a Ghanaian who has just completed his university studies in the United States, returns to his own country. He has suffered a nervous breakdown during his stay in America, and returns to face his family's expectations that, as a "been-to," he will bring money, influence and prestige to the family. He finds himself alienated from his society by its open and cynical corruption, and from his family by their inability to understand that his ambitions are not primarily material ones. Doubly alone, he moves slowly towards a second breakdown; his friend and lover, Juana, a Puerto Rican psychiatrist, is away when it occurs. At the end of the novel, it seems likely that Baako and Juana will be reunited when Baako is released from hospital.

The novel bears a superficial resemblance to its predecessor, *The Beautyful Ones*. As in the earlier novel, Armah portrays Ghana as a society corrupt at every level, and embodies his sense of the moral atmosphere in vivid images of rot and sterility. Again, a single more or less good man is isolated from society by his refusal to acquiesce in its corruption; and, again, his uprightness gains him nothing and does not alter the social order. These resemblances are, however, largely matters of narrative surface. On any other level, the two books are fundamentally different.

The earlier and shorter novel has the simplicity and force of allegory. Its chief character is nameless, and encounters, in true *Everyman* fashion, type-figures of temptation and corruption before enduring a symbolic descent into Hell and a sea-rebirth which returns him to the world. The characters, scenery, and incidents of *Beautyful Ones* are in the tradition of apologue: the moralized landscape in particular reminds the reader of *The Pilgrim's Progress* rather than of "realistic" fiction. *Fragments,* on the other hand, is more obviously a novel. The elements of allegory and apologue are muted; *Beautyful Ones* is built around a few clear and appalling images, while *Fragments* is based on ambiguity and contradiction. The confrontation of the protagonist and society is particularly problematic.

In *Beautyful Ones,* the protagonist's isolation from society preserves him from the corruption of that society and constitutes a kind of proof— not least to himself—of his moral purity. After he helps his friend Koomson to escape, for example, the man feels "a vague freedom, like the untroubled loneliness he had come to like these days."[3] This sense of solitude as saving is strongly present in *Fragments* as well. When he first returns to Accra, Baako takes a room in a hotel instead of returning to his family's home: already wary of the family's expectations, he feels "an ambiguous comfort, savoring this sense of being so alone back home, connected for the moment to no one, with no one save himself knowing where he was" (pp. 92–93). Juana, whose work as a psychiatrist presents her daily with evidence of society's destructive effects, resorts to the "comforting pigeonholing reflex" and is able to push back "the threat of having to confront another human being" (p. 143). The extreme form of this desire to isolate oneself is physical flight, to which both Baako and Juana have recourse. Juana takes long drives when the hospital becomes too much for her, and Baako flees from his family twice when they try to take him to the asylum. During his second escape, Baako again experiences the joy of solitude, "the happy feeling . . . that now he could run miles and miles and sense no tiredness" (p. 236).

Even Naana, Baako's grandmother, feels the relief of being by herself. A traditional African, she has a strongly developed sense of community and the importance of communal life; but in the world of present-day Ghana her isolation (she is blind and partly deaf) appears to her as a boon: "Since so much of what remains to be seen brings fear and the sights of day are followed in the night by this silent danger which has no name, I find it a matter in which the path of my soul has been good: that my body should be closing all the holes through which the world has entered me"

(p. 279). Her first monologue, which begins the book, includes her sense that her blindess has been "sent . . . to save me from the madness that would surely have come with seeing so much that was not to be understood" (p. 14).

All of this is quite in keeping with the vision of things in *Beautyful Ones:* contact is a sort of contamination, a surrender to the corruption around the self. In *Beautyful Ones,* however, there is no real temptation to succumb; the man's isolation is practical as well as moral, since it prevents his being purged, after the *coup d'état,* by the new regime. Baako's dilemma in Fragments is that he senses the necessity of some kind of human contact even while recognizing the danger of it. This sense of human contact as something at once desirable and dangerous is shared by the other chief characters. Juana, despite her own urge to solitude, realizes that "the high flight of the individual alone, escaping the touch of life around leads only to "annihilation" (p. 271), and her last comment is the observation that "Salvation is such an empty thing when you're alone" (p. 276). Naana, in her first monologue, remembers an old ritual song: "A human being alone/ is a thing more sad than any lost animal/ and nothing destroys the soul/ like its aloneness" (p. 6).

But a satisfactory human relationship is hard to come by in a corrupt society. Baako's sister Araba, for example, is frankly manipulative in her relationship with her husband Kwesi: " '. . . the midwife says Kewsi should leave me alone for two months. If he doesn't agree to the things I'm going to ask for, I'll add another month' " (p. 127). Efua, Baako's mother, exploits her friends in order to make her grandson's outdooring ceremony profitable for the family. In fact, the only example in the novel of a life-giving relationship is the affair between Baako and Juana.

The sexual aspect of this affair is described graphically, but never very sensually; one has the impression that sex is really a metaphor for what Juana thinks of as "the human touching[,] the hunger for which continued in her in spite of everything" (p. 19). The first time Baako and Juana make love, Armah's diction itself suggest the metaphoric nature of the act. "She reached her his hand, but before she could touch it all her control went out of her body, the salt taste of the air was deep in her throat, and she was saying words she'd thought she could never use again, and there was one moment when nothing that had happened to her made any difference, and all the steadying, controlling separatenesses between things did not matter at all to her" (p. 171). The loss of control, which is equated with Juana's "separateness," is both life-giving and threatening, since Juana is now susceptible to the pain of involvement which she has carefully avoided for so long. A later sexual scene makes it clear that eroticism is not central to the relationship.

> She rubbed his nipple gently, once, and it was pure pain but
> it made him hard, and she turned slightly and took him into
> herself, lying motionless in his embrace.
> "Just stay in me, Baako," she said.
> He moved deeper, searching her for more of her warmth, his
> head filling with a fear of nameless heavy things descending
> upon him, pushing him to seek comfort in her. He pulled her
> completely to himself. She was warm against him, but in a
> moment he became aware she too was shivering. They lay
> together, neither moving. (p. 294)

What brings on Baako's second breakdown, then, is the problem of
choosing between the almost impossible alternatives of a safe but sterile
solitude on the one hand and, on the other, a potentially fruitful and loving
relationship which exposes him to the likelihood of pain if he loses
Juana—who is in fact away when he needs her most. The conflict is one
which another contemporary novelist, Angus Wilson, has expressed more
overtly in the thoughts of one of his characters: "To be alone was to
uphold one's right to the inner poetry, yet to be alone was also to be an
insufficient human being. To be two was the start of all human fulfilment;
and also of all gangs and conspiracies."[4]

The problem of human involvement refects the theme of Armah's novel
as a whole. Baako is concerned with the question of whether to remain
alone or to become part of something larger (a relationship, a society),
and *Fragments* deals essentially with the question of cosmology—
whether individual things can be made to cohere into some sort of larger
pattern. The title itself suggests that "things fall apart," and Baako has
abundant evidence that there is no coherence in the modern world. But
the novel portrays both sides of a complex issue, and suggests at least the
possibility of some kind of order.

Admittedly, the idea of any *ultimate* order appears to be mocked at
various points in *Fragments*. Baako recalls a production assistant at
Ghanavision who defines himself as a "nexologist":

> I confess it was a thrill to hear him define nexus so well,
> everything in the world connected, the air itself some connect-
> ing fluid, each man a connecting enter node set in the nexus.
> The fact of connection meaning consequence: here I wondered
> if he understood what he was implying or was sloganizing with
> doctrines swallowed, but I would not have interrupted him for
> all the world. . . . Example: a nexologist wakes up one
> morning, counts his wealth and finds he's broke, only pennies

between him and the world. . . . The practicing nexologist under such conditions does not despair, throw up his arms, lose faith in himself. On the contrary: the hopeless-looking moment is the moment not only for hope, but for the expression of faith in hope . . . he would take his last coins, find his way to a crossways, then scatter the last of his wealth in all directions. Now that wealth would be bound to return to the scatterer in one form or another, mulitiplied like grain seed. . . . He said the scattering would be answered by a wished-for return because of the nexus, because the nexus meant connections, and no such act of prayer ever took place unconnected to results that could look like magic to the blind. (pp. 228–29)

This simple-minded faith in the Emersonian unity and benevolence of the natural order reminds Baako of the cargo cults of Melanesia, and other forms of faith in the novel—Efua's adherence to a fraudulent prophet, for example—are likewise seen as mere wish-fulfillment. Throughout the book, Baako senses the separateness of things and the absence of any true nexus. As he moves towards his second breakdown, even his words fail to cohere into thought: "he opened [his notebook] and looked again at the words of the previous night. He could not not make then flow together; they remained separate words, separate letters" (pp. 238–39). The landscape itself shows a radical disorder in nature: "It was a clearing that seemed filled with broken things and with unfinished work stopped violently for some sudden reason, leaving wrenched, jagged edges that gave the eye a feeling of being grated against a thousand snapped fractions of things" (p. 254).

But it is well to remember that we see these things from Baako's point of view, one which becomes progressively more unreliable. Armah has sought, much more consciously than he did in *Beautyful Ones,* to avoid a confusion of his protagonists' point of view: when we are not experiencing Baako's sense of things, we see the world through the eyes of Juana or Naana. Naana's monologues begin and end the book, and they provide a corrective contrast to Baako's bleak vision of the world. Naana is, of course, immersed in the past, but her faith in the unity of all things cannot be passed off as naive, for she understands the fragmented state of the modern world. "The larger meaning which lent sense to every small thing and every momentary happening years and years ago has shattered into a thousand and thirty useless pieces. Things have passed which I have never seen whole, only broken and twisted against themselves. What remains of my days will be filled with more broken things" (p. 280).

257

Naana claims to have given up the effort to understand, and has, by her own account, "found rest in despair" (p. 281). Nevertheless, her monologue closes with an expression of faith in a god or God she never names. "I know of the screens in life you have left us: veils that rise in front of us, cutting into easy pieces eternity and the circle of the world, so that until we have grown tall enough to look behind the next veil we think the whole world and the whole of life is the little we are allowed to see, and this little we clutch at with such desperation" (p. 286). Her image of order, the circle, is a traditional one, and is reflected in the structure of the book. The last page of the novel returns us to the first, where Naana expresses her faith that "Each thing that goes away returns and nothing in the end is lost. The great friend throws all things apart and brings all things together again. That is the way everything goes and turns round" (p. 1). The image of the circle also is, like most of the images in the novel, an ambiguous one. Circles represent perfection and eternity, but a closing circle suggests impending doom; a ring of men closes in on the dog Juana sees killed, and a similar circle closes in on Baako to take him to the asylum (pp. 246–47). Ocran's anguished sculptures also form a circle.

It can be argued, of course, that Naana is wrong, that her faith is as naive as that of the nexologist. And, we recall, she is blind—a fact which surely says something about the quality of her perceptions. In fact, however, the other chief characters are blind as well. During her first conversation with Baako, Juana has the impression that she can see "a small but very vital blind spot which broke into the wholeness of the dome [her image of Baako], yet without which it would quite simply fall apart" (p. 148). Baako himself, when he talks about going against the current of his society, describes its force as that of a "cataract," and this delicate pun again suggest the saving nature of his partial blindness. Earlier, Juana has seen that the foreigners who survive life in Accra have deliberately become less sensitive to the life around them: "with the opening of her own mind to accept the place she had come to, Juana had found it difficult to understand the willingness with which the expatriates kept themselves imprisoned in their little blind incestuous groups. With more looking and understanding she saw it was not really blindness, but a decision quite consciously made not to see, or to see but never to let any real understanding intrude" (p. 36). Despite "the opening out of her own mind," Juana herself takes drives and walks on the beach in order to avoid facing the reality of the hospital too directly for too long. Even "Ghanavision," the state television network, is afflicted with a politic blindness: it produces only flattering portrayals of state leaders.

Blindness seems, in fact, to be preferable to any kind of clear-sighted-ness, simply because, like solitude, it spares one a good deal of pain. Lawrence Boateng, an aspiring writer, gets drunk at a literary soirée and embarasses the successful hacks who dominate official Ghanaian culture. His self-destructive behaviour is, as he says, the result of clear sight: " 'Lawrence Boateng is a drunkard, Lawrence Boateng drinks too much. I'm tired of people taking about me. I drink, yes. I see the truth when I'm drunk, and I can say what I see' " (p. 152). The sculptor Ocran conveys in a series of terra-cotta heads his anguished sense of the human condition. "They had been arranged in some kind of rough order, so that the tension captured in the heads seemed progressively to grow less and less bearable, till near the end of the whole series . . . the inward torture actually broke the outer form of the human face, and the result, when Baako looked closer, was not any new work of his master but the old, anonymous sculpture of Africa" (p. 111). Baako's breakdown is presumably the result of the same kind of vision. The economy of the novel seems to suggest that Naana is right to be thankful for her blindness.[5]

But Boateng, Ocran, and Baako are all artists, and none of them can deny his sight without denying his very being. The problem, then, is to develop a kind of sight which will encompass reality without plunging the viewer into despair. In the light of this problem, *Fragments* can be seen as an African *Kunstlerroman*—a novel about the artist's education, situation, and responsibilities—and the opposed images of the novel (isolation/ contact, fragmentation/ order, blindness/ sight) as aspects of the artists' traditional problem of reconciling apparently incompatible elements into a unified whole.[6] Baako's success in doing this is obviously far from complete, but his concern with the problem is evident. His first script for Ghanavision, for example, is an obscure symbolic drama dominated by images of a dark circle and a white square; the action reflects, on different levels, the history of Ghana and Baako's own sense of alienation from his society.[7] Baako manages, to some degree, the reconciliation of isolation and community, since his relationship with Juana overcomes his loneliness and does not implicate him in the corruption of society. At the end of the novel, however, he has apparently failed to order the fragments of his world into any significant whole—his mind itself has, in fact, fragmented. It would be wrong, however, to see the novel as essentially pessimistic. The penultimate section concludes with Juana's preparations for Baako's return, and the last section is Naana's monologue, with its assertion of faith in the circle of eternity which appears to flawed human sight in "easy pieces." It is possible that Naana's last comment on the world is also that of the novel: that we see parts of the puzzle, fragments of the whole, and live in the faith that the pattern, the completed circle, actually exists. ". . .

Still clutching the useless shreds of a world worn out, we peep behind the veil just passed and find in wonder a more fantastic world, making us fools in our own eyes to have believed that the old paltriness was all" (p. 287).

In the meantime, nothing will make the artist's lot an easy one. The particular predicaments of Boateng and Ocran are clear enough; Baako later sees the general situation of the artist embodied in a scene the meaning of which is at first elusive. As Baako and Juana watch a group of fishermen pulling in a net on the beach, a young boy tries to join the group and is knocked out of the way. Retiring from the group, he finds a double gong. The men, fatigued, slow the pace of their work. Then

> in a gap of quiet when neither the breeze nor the men's voices were high, the small boy added his voice to the beating of his gong. It was a clear voice, high as a woman's, and the song it was carrying could have been anything about the sea, like a woman's long lament for one more drowned fisherman. One irritated strong man kicked sand at the boy and shouted at him, perhaps to shut him up; he stopped his singing only briefly, recovered and continued. On the next return another big-bodied man, this one with a slow, pensive step, . . . took up the song, his voice deeper but his rhythm the same. Where the two singers paused the only refrain was the sound of the sea, till one after the other the remaining men and a few of the waiting women began also to hum endings to the song. Now the pulling took a rhythm from the general song. The men dug their feet deep into the sand and pulled from fixed positions on the rope.
>
> It was two hours at least before the bag net itself emerged from the water, but the time passed quickly, imperceptibly, and the sun mellowed to an early evening warmth. In that time the boy started separate songs, each in itself made up of long and subtly changing verses held over easy chorus hums, and the men sometimes unfixed themselves and pulled on the ropes with a slow shuffling march whose steps were all measured to the songs. (pp. 183–84)

It is a beautifully realized scene, emblematic rather than symbolic. The fluidity and shapelessness of the sea are set against the order and harmony of the boy's song, which helps the men even when they reject the singer. The various functions of art—as pastime, practical aid, form of knowledge, means of community—are all invoked without being specified or isolated. Baako is, understandably, fascinated by a scene which suggests the exalted vocation of the artist, the ignorance of society about that vocation, and the artist can expect as a result.

It is possible, of course, the hard usage that the artist's adversity can be turned to advantage. In Paris, Baako sees an inscription which reads

> TOUT HOMME CRÉE SANS LE SAVOIR
>   COMME IL RESPIRE
> MAIS L'ARTISTE SE SENT CRÉER
> SON ACTE ENGAGE TOUT SON ÉRE
> SA PEINE BIEN AIMÉE LE FORTIFIE. (p. 74)

If this is anything more than a comforting slogan, Baako's breakdown itself may be part of his education as an artist.

Throughout the novel, Armah is careful to insist upon the ambiguous nature of the reality with which the artist deals. Juana thinks, after her first meeting with Baako, that his desperation is so deep as to be "indistinguishable from hope" (p. 149), and a similar ambiguity is apparent not only in the pairs of opposed images we have already looked at but also in the multiple meanings which cluster about a single image. Water, for example, seems at first glance to have only positive associations related to the value of sexuality and "the human touching." The association is a natural one, since water and sexuality are both sources and sustainers of life; it is fitting, then, that Baako and Juana make love for the first time on the beach. Afterwards, Baako tells Juana the story of Mame Water and the musician: " 'The singer goes to the beach, playing his instrument. These days it's become a guitar. He's lonely, the singer, and he sings of that. So, well, a woman comes out of the sea, a very beautiful goddess, and they make love. She leaves him to go back to the sea, and they meet at long, fixed intervals only. It takes courage. The goddess is powerful, and the musician is filled with so much love he can't bear the separation. But then it is this separation itself which makes him sing as he has never sung before' " (p. 171).[8] The singer is strengthened, like Antaeus, by contact with an elemental force, but the water brings desolation as well as pleasure: the singer who makes love to Mame Water now knows, among other things, " 'the fear that one night he'll go to the sea and Mame Water . . . will not be coming anymore.' " (p. 172).

Elsewhere in *Fragments,* water is clearly a malign force (the lorry-driver Skido is killed in the water, for example) but it is most often associated with illusion. During one of her walks, Juana catches sight of the sea: ". . . from the hill it seemed so immediately close that for a moment Juana felt she could take one vertical step and fall straight down into it. From time to time the planted vegetation and the tall reeds parted and revealed not only the sea but a ship on it, white and solitary but looking very close. An infantile illusion, this closeness, Juana knew, thinking of forgotten days back home when she had run from her mother's restraining hold thinking she was going down to find this time a ship really touchable on the shore. Even now the urge was not entirely dead, in spite of knowledge and the passage of years" (pp. 39–40). A few pages later, Efua's "prophet" conducts an orgiastic baptism on the same stretch of beach. In these passages water suggests the infinitely fluid nature of experience, its formlessness, its susceptibility to various interpretations—suggests, in short, ambiguity itself. The relation of the singing boy and the sea is therefore analogous to that of the woman and the sea in Wallace Stevens' poem "The Idea of Order at Key West": the sharpless element is momentarily subdued and given form by the art of the singer.

Armah alludes twice in *Fragments* to the story of Ananse without relating it[9] and in part of this old Akan myth lies one aspect of the novel's largely unspoken affirmation. It is said that Ananse Kokrofu, the great spider, grew worried about the state of wisdom in the world; it was not being looked after properly, and some of it was getting lost. He decided to collect all the wisdom and store it at the top of a tree. Basil Davidson tells the rest of the story:

> In due course, the elders say, Ananse did indeed finish collecting the world's wisdom. He packed all this in a gourd and began to climb a tall palm. Halfway to the top he got into difficulties: he had tied the gourd in front of him, and it hampered his climbing. At this point his son Ntikuma, who was looking up form below, called in a shrill young voice: "Father, if you really had all the wisdom in the world up there with you, you would have tied that gourd on your back." This was to much even for Ananse, who was tired from long labour, He untied the gourd in a fit of temper and threw it down. It broke and the wisdom was scattered far and wide. After a while people who had learned their lesson came and gathered in their own gourds whatever each would find. It is this that explains why a few people have much wisdom, some have a little, but many have none at all.[10]

Here is a traditional African view of fragmentation, and one which implies, like Naana's last monologue, the order and unity we cannot see. At the end of the novel, Baako's mind and the vision of order are both fragmented, but there is a note of hope in the theme of the artist's developing perception. If Baako says, in effect, "These fragments I have shored against my ruins,"[11] the novel implies a fuller vision to which he may yet attain. The ultimate order we yearn for may exist only in the artist's mind, and the artist may be, like Baako, far from attaining his vision of the whole, but Armah seems to suggest that we must believe in the possibility of success if we are to accomplish anything at all. The artist' relation to his vision is perhaps analogous to Juana's glimpse of a beautiful bird perches on the stalk of a flower: "The impulse to touch that smooth beauty grew strong in her, and she approached the flower quietly, hoping to draw near without frightening the bird. But before she could take more than a few steps the bird flew upward, hovered almost without any motion just above the greenness, then darted swiftly sideways to settle on a reed more safely out of reach" (pp. 40–41)

Armah has shown, from the beginning of his career, a willingness to take great chances. In *Fragments,* his use of ambiguous and contradictory images runs the risk of confused or self-defeating effects, but his success in treating the theme of the artists' perception is near-complete. What I have attempted here is not, of course, a complete account of Armah's novel. *Fragments* contains, as Gerald Moore suggests, elements of the satirical *roman à clef;*[12] it also deals with alienation, of which Baako's madness is an extreme example, and—less obviously than *Beautyful Ones*—with the political ideas of Frantz Fanon. But, precisely because the apparently simple narrative suggests different interpretations, the theme of perception remains central to the novel and to our understanding of it.

NOTES

1. All references are to the first edition (Boston: Houghton Mifflin, 1970) and will be given parenthetically in the text.
2. "Armah's Second Novel," *Journal of Commonwealth Literature,* 9, no. 2 (August 1974), 69.
3. *The Beautyful Ones Are Not Yet Born* (New York: Collier, 1969), p. 176.
4. Angus Wilson, *No Laughing Matter* (Harmondsworth: Penguin, 1969), p. 293.
5. Cf. *Beautyful Ones,* p. 69; "The destructive things wee [marijuana] does is to lift the blindness and to let you see the whole of your life laid out in front of you."
6. Baako wants to write, if only for Ghanavision, but he is carefully associated with other arts as well: he plays the quitar, and we know from Ocran that he showed talent as a painter before leaving Ghana.
7. Pp. 210–13.
8. It is this myth which Baako and Juana will unconsciously act out: Baako is the musician, he and Juana do make love in the water (pp. 177–80), and Juana is absent during Baako's breakdown. Note that in the myth, as in the novel, solitude and human contact are the sources of different kinds of strength, and the artist's suffering contributes to the perfection of his art.
9. See, e.g., p. 95: ". . . the repeated figure of the protean spider Ananse, always in a

different position along the turns and radiating lines of his web." This description and parts of the myth suggest Ananse's symbolic role as a type of the artist.

10. Basil Davidson, *The African Genius: An Introduction to African Cultural and Social History* (Boston: Atlantic, Little Brown, 1970), p. 17.
11. T. S. Eliot, *The Waste Land,* 1. 431.
12. "Armah's Second Novel," 69.

KOFI AWOONOR'S *THIS EARTH, MY BROTHER* AS AN AFRICAN DIRGE

Richard K. Priebe

One of the first things we become aware of concerning the formal structure of *This Earth, My Brother* is that we are reading a prose poem which can be thought of as a novel only in the most liberal sense of the word. Yet despite the extremely thin narrative thread which runs through the book, we might try to relate what Kofi Awoonor has done to a tradition of expressionistic experimentation that can be traced from James Joyce to the present, though it is questionable how far this alone would lead us. We are hearing nothing new or necessarily helpful when we learn that the author himself has insisted on his work being thought of as a poem.[1] The final judgment will of course be left to the reader. But classification per se, whether by the artist or his critics, is a rather useless game if it fails to help us reveal perceptions into the situation the artist has given us, and there is probably little beyond the obvious that a formal analysis of this novel will yield to the critic who does not take into consideration the formal elements that come from Eweland as well as those which come from England.

Perhaps no other prose writer in Africa since Tutuola has written a work which so thoroughly defies conventional Western criticism. The cul-de-sac that Gerald Moore found in Tutuola is, more than anything, an apt description of the critic's problem where the critic is unwilling to keep in mind the traditional literature these writers are so close to. Certainly Awoonor does not write from exactly the same naive sensibility as Tutuola, for their educational backgrounds are vastly different, the former having earned his doctorate in comparative literature and the latter not having gone beyond the sixth form. Yet in discussing his poetry, Awoonor has said that he has been influenced primarily by the tradition of the Ewe song, "especially the Ewe dirge, the dirge form, the lament, and its lyrical structure with the repetition of sections, segments, lines, along with an enormous, a stark and at times almost naive quality which this poetry possessed."[2] In fact the images, motifs, and themes we find in the novel are very close to those Awoonor has employed in his poetry. He himself has written that "You must see *This Earth* and my poetry as constituting the same continuous poetic statement about man and society. My concern is not . . . to provide a picture of a particular society at a particular time, but rather to provide through a series of selected images, the idea of the continuous process of corruptibility which the human society without strength and vision can be locked in."[3] Within this context the assertion that *This Earth, My Brother* is a prose poem may have relevance if we can see how Awoonor has built it on the structure of a dirge or a lament.

This Earth, My Brother is obviously not a dirge in the traditional African sense any more than it is a conventional English novel. And even though, for the sake of analysis, we will look at the internal structure as that of a dirge modified to fit the external shell of novel, the two aspects function dialectically to forge a formal synthesis that corroborates the thematic synthesis. On the most general level the dirge is a celebration of man's conquest of death, but this dirge is also an attempt to move beyond the deadly constructions of cultural conflict. Keeping this in mind we will first look at the relationship of time an character in the novel in terms of its dramatistic basis, specifically in terms of ritual action. In order to see how this relates to the West African dirge we will then draw on J. H. Nketia's analysis of Akan funeral dirges.[4] While the Akan are a linguistic group distinct from the Ewe, they are culturally similar in many respects and in particular as regards their dirges.[5] Since we are dealing with a novel written in English the differences between the two groups can be considered minimal in our examination of the way in which Awoonor has made use of the dirge on contextual, thematic, and linguistic levels.

As there is no simple narrative pattern the pervasive tone of the lament holds the novel together and asserts its presence with more force than the actual characters. Character, in other words, is made subservient to the lyrical structure. Thus it is not so important who Amamu is, as what he represents within this framework. His position as a specific person is no more important than the characters of Lycidas and Adonais in the elegies by Milton and Shelley, for it is the expression and the transcendence of grief that becomes important for the reader. Here even more so, it is ultimately neither the death of Amamu, nor the symbolic death of a country, Ghana, which holds our imagination. These specific events serve only as reference points to focus our attention on the man and his land as individual and collective carriers of a long history of suffering. Beyond this we are left with the unstated, but implied efficacy of any such ritual move, namely individual and collective rebirth.

E. M. Foster has said that it is impossible for the novelist to abolish time from his work.[6] Perhaps this is true, yet the novelist can fracture time so completely that it ceases to be an important aspect. Rather than telling a story which proceeds in any chronological fashion, Awoonor has painted in a very cubistic manner a certain landscape from a number of different angles. We could piece sections together to give the book more chronological coherence, but that would almost totally destroy the poetic assertion which is being made. Amamu's anguish is not simply an individual's suffering, but the agony of a land, its people, and their gods, and none of this can be understood as something which is localized in time. In an essay, "The Fourth Stage," Wole Soyinka has discussed how in the African world view the element of eternity is something from which the individual does not feel estranged. The individual in Africa "is not, like European man, concerned with the purely conceptual aspects of time. . . . life, present life contains within it manifestations of ancestor, the living and the unborn."[7] Rather than making distinctions in time he makes distinctions in areas of existence. Moreover, he is painfully aware that there are great gulfs between these ares which must be bridged by ritual and sacrifice. The person most sensitive to these gifts must necessarily be a kind of priest, in short, a man such as Amamu.

Divided into fifteen chapters in which the main narrative line is developed, the book also has a poetic introduction, almost an invocation, along with eleven poetic interludes which follow the first eleven narrative chapters. Awoonor himself explains the central importance of the poetic sections:

> . . . there was a publisher's error in this. I wanted the chapters to slide on into the poetic interludes which would be indicated by the use of italics. But they decided to separate them, and this imposed a more rigid structure than I wanted. More importantly, it makes the poetry seem to be a comment on what has gone before, though it actually moves into a lot more important area than what has just been said in the story. In fact, the story plays a secondary role to the poetry rather than the other way round.[8]

Towards the end these interludes are no longer necessary as the narrative line and the poetic assertion are fully merged.

The introduction sets the tone into which all the succeeding chapters tend to modulate, and functions, moreover as a kind of poetic invocation. The protagonist has just passed through a period of loss and separation and is describing that trial which was a moment of pain for others as well as himself. Like the worshippers on the beach, he is singing "A low moan, mournful song of death and loss."[9] The immediate cause of sorrow is the separation from his woman of the sea, but beyond this are adumbrations of the decay which pervades his land, "this house whose fences were falling" (p. 6). Only at the end will we learn that he is already dead, that he is speaking here as an ancestral voice, though we are provided with a clue that makes sense only in relation to his reunification with his woman of the sea. "And I was alone. But not for long" (p. 8). This spiritual reunification further adumbrates an ultimate salvation for his land since he is better able as an ancestral force to effect the changes he had not the power to effect while living.[10]

In the opening chapter we are given a feeling of the great age of the land and the decay that pervades it. The road overseer is presented as a symbol of that decay, "a veritable picture of human lethargy translated into power at its most resigned and unconcerned pivot" (p. 10). The time is during England's colonial rule of Ghana, but as we have already stated, the specific time is not very important; it is the colonial situation in general that Awoonor is protesting against, not just British colonialism. He is establishing the recurrent dunghill image, an emblem of the land and a symbol of disorder and human corruption. Out of this comes the potential saviour, Amamu. Chapter 1a, the first poetic interlude, is a song to his birth, the pain of that birth and the hope that it offers. A heavy drum rhythm accentuates the contrasting elements that will frame his life, the necessary "death of blood" and his birth as a hunter "in the wild butterfly field in the wild field of sunflowers" (p. 20). For all the beauty that he may discover, it is necessary that he be a carrier, a sacrifice to end the cycle of suffering in his land.

The second chapter reveals Amamu as a fully grown man, an established lawyer in Accra. We move through part of a day with him seeing the corruption with which he is besieged as well as the suffering he feels is the result of witnessing the mechanical life the average man is forced to live.[11] In effect we see him taking on his role as a carrier. He assumes the anguish of the policeman who stands for years on his pedestal going through an "eternal marionette show" (p. 24) and of Richard, the barman, who knows only to serve "his new masters . . . and dream of his native land five hundred miles away" (p. 26). The interlude is then packed with invectives hurled against the "Fart-filled respectable people . . . [who] continue where the colonialists and imperialists left off" (p. 36). Yet as the dunghill imagery is intensified so is the hope for a Christ who will "let us return to the magic hour of our birth for which we mourn" (p. 37).

The rest of the book consists of images which are extensions of and variations from those presented in the first two chapters. In terms of narrative structure this makes the book sound rather facile, but as we will see, the relationships are extremely complex. Chapter three extends our perception of the situation in which Amamu grew up by showing in detail life in a colonial primary school. We are again taken forward and see the respite which Amamu has found in his relationship with his lover, Adisa. Images of suffering and joy, destruction and creation quickly and effectively alternate to form a single plaintive lyric. These alternations are paralleled by the successive moves backward and forward in time, and finally we see through a number of details such as the missing center tooth, that Adisa blends into Dede, Amamu's cousin who died when she was twelve. Together they represent his woman of the sea, Mammy Water, a metaphysical, unifying force. In a recent interview in *Transition* Awoonor has commented that

> They are aspects of Amamu's consciousness. . . . Adisa is a warm womanly woman. The essence of womanhood. The essence of Africa in a way: or one aspect of Africa. Adisa is like Africa, like the little girl who is raped and dies before she has even been initiated into the puberty rites. All that lives on is her tiny mite of woman's widom. And so we see her again as the mermaid, the woman of the sea. . . . I was trying to incorporate the imagery of that myth into another symbol of Africa. Somewhere she does exist as the final repository of wisdom. . . . she knows what I must do, what Amamu must do, what we all must do. And I must go with her in order to acquire this knowledge and survive the truncation of the soul that society imposes. Unless we follow this path to wisdom, the Dance of Death will continue, onward and onward.[12]

This female figure, then, is a link between the reality of death as loss and the ultimate transformation that death represents. Here is the very essence of the mythic consciousness. As Kenneth Burke has written, "In the sense that discursive reason is dialectical, the mythic image may be treated as figuring a motive that transcends reason. It may also make claims to be "religious," since it presumably represents man's relationships to an ultimate ground of motives not available for empirical inspection.[13] Not only in his use of this woman, but also in his extensive use of scatological imagery Awoonor is pointing towards the same "ultimate ground of motives" as Ayi Kwei Armah. The death of Amamu, an apparent suicide, seems to be a negation of everything that is good in the society. On a symbolic level we usually look for a positive transformation in the death of a villain, not a good person. As with all sacrifice, however, the symbolism becomes inverted and the victim which represents the greatest loss to the community stands out as the most efficacious offering. Add to this the fact that amongst the Ewe suicide is the greatest sin one can commit against the earth, the ultimate act of rebellion,[14] and we can clearly see Amamu's death in terms of a negation of the *present* social order. The act is progressive and futuristic in its orientation. From a historical perspective Okonkwo's death in Chinua Achebe's *Things Fall Apart* was symbolic of the necessary *specific* transformation that his people had to undergo; likewise the death of Amamu, when seen from a mythic perspective, is symbolic of the *recurrent* transformations necessary to the health of any society.

Amamu's destruction is foreshadowed in the lunatic priest, Paul Dumenyo, whose sin of the flesh turns him into a scapegoat to be stoned by young children. Both are victims of a hypocritical society that has been torn apart by culture conflict, but they are also both carriers of the collective guilt of that society, thus functioning in the same sacrificial role. Neither one is at first a willing carrier, and both pray "to let the cup pass away," though in the end they are forced to accept this in the calmness of their insanity. We will speak more about this insanity later, but for now it is enough to see how closely their seemingly disparate natures are interlocked.

In the opening lines of the chapter following the one about Paul Dumenyo we see Amamu prepared to accept his fate. "He was very calm this morning. There was a sudden quiet that surrounded him, like the peace of all times. . . ." (p. 136). The day quickly slides into evening when he goes out to a high-life bar where he experiences a love act ritual in the music of the band. But this is merely a prelude to his own final marriage to the woman of the sea. "Diminishing afternoon in the darkness of after-love a cruel mocking laughter strangles the only love left" (p. 169). He must between now and then experience the nadir of despair as initiation into complete understanding of his role. His anguish must be the anguish of his people. The sardonically twisted line from T. S. Eliot reveals both the scatological and eschatological nature of this process ("Fear death by shit trucks."), while the lines from Kierkegaard and the refrain, "Despair and Die," assert the necessary alienation. The continual references to Okigbo are to one who has already completely experienced this anguish and gone through the final *rite de passage,* death.

The flashback to the return from England of Amamu's wife and the humorous vignette of the party function as elaborations on the absurdity of the world in which Amamu must live. As a child in the cemetery recounting for the other children the circumstances around the death and burial of his cousin, Amamu had a naive understanding of a world that had order, but the dirges he remembers echo out beyond the limitations of his childlike perceptions which finally "vanished into the fast fading twilight" with his friends.

Amamu's search for his servant, Yaro, involves the assumption of yet another's anguish and the purgatorial wanderings through the slums of Nima, "the eternal dunghill," serving as a stone to put a fine edge on his awareness. Along with this new awareness comes a bitterness which is reflected in the intensive use of irony. The university is described as a "new Jerusalem in Nima's green and pleasant fields" (p. 195), and we are told of "a senseless roundabout which used to be [named] for the man they threw out, now for the abstraction for which they threw him out" (p. 186). For the third time in the novel we see how the magic of a lawyer's words can open all doors as Amamu helps Yaro see his brother who has been apprehended by the police. Earlier with the traffic officer, and another time with the customs officer, Amamu's magic had worked. But it now comes too late, for the brother has already died from the beatings he received form the police.

The final poetic interlude brings all these ironies together as a series of invectives hurled against all those people who have had a hand in ravaging the land, Africans as well as colonial administrators. The steady beat of one newspaper-like statement after another is counterpointed by understatement and intermittent personal reportage:

> We have many beautiful places in the country to which tourists, especially Americans, who will pay to see anything, can be lured with the appropriate posters and publicity material. . . .
>
> When I told them that young Africans left secondary schools speaking Latin and Greek they thought it was one of those fantastic African lies. All Africans are congenital liars. Othello was a liar (p. 208).

Though more intense here than elsewhere, there is a continuous injection of humour throughout this book. And this humour, just as the joking in an African funeral celebration, goes well beyond comic relief in a potentially tragic situation. The intensity of both the ludic and the serious elements in such close proximity to one another takes us deep into the heart of a ritual process. We are drawn into that center where everyday rigid distinctions between disorder and order, death and life are transgressed, even abrogated, and where, in effect, man can squarely face the problem of temporary/temporal existence and bridge the ontological gap inherent in this existence.[15] Framing this ritual celebration, however, is Amamu's journey, mythical in the sense that Amamu makes the heroic crossing out of society with the intention of winning the revitalizing boon held by his woman of the sea, thereby gaining communal as well as individual salvation. Literally cross-

271

ing the Volta on a ferry at Tefle, Amamu moves across that traditional area between states before making his final frenzied run to the sea.[16] But his move occurs only after the accumulated anguish of the protagonist appears to be beyond what any one man can bear, beyond any assuagement: "Our sadness itself, based upon that distant sadness which is the history of this land, defies all consolation" (p. 208). Having gone to the depths of despair, the poet turns the dirge into a poignant supplication to the woman of the sea to release the land from this perpetual anguish:

> For now believe me, the land is covered [with] blood, and more blood shall flow in it to redeem the covenant we made in that butterfly field, and under my almond. For you I renounce the salvation of madness and embrace with a singular hope, your hope . . . (p. 211).

Counterpointing the earlier refrain of "Despair and Die," we have the softer plea "return the miracle." Dramatic action and poetic assertion merge as Amamu becomes literally possessed by ancestral rhythms:

> His headache had come again this evening. Throbbing, violent, as if many drums and gongs and gongs and rattlers were playing there. There was a jerkiness, a pumping regularity in all things as he watched them. The walls seemed to shiver in different lights . . . It rested for a while in a violent glimmer. He had never seen a light like this before. The drums and the gongs and the rattlers had resumed their play in his head with a regular syncopation. They were playing a weird drum beat of this childhood . . . The drums went into a slow funeral beat of mourning. Faintly a voice emerged singing a dirge (p. 213).

Able now to see what he must do, Amamu follows the rhythms which lead him back to the sea.

As with Armah's Baako, Amamu's madness is only seen as madness by a prosaic world unable to partake of his poetic vision.[17] The true insanity is the distorted idea of reality which blinds the more prosaic world from the clear view that Amamu achieves in the moment that he is possessed by the ancestral rhythms. The pain of the initiation passes as he becomes one with that vision:

> It seemed suddenly that the centuries and the years of pain of which he was the inheritor, and the woes for which he was singled out to be carrier and the sacrifice, were being rolled

away, were being faded in that emergence. Here at last . . . was
the hour of his salvation (p. 227).

According to Soyinka, the separation of gods and men since time *ab
origine* has created a sense of anguish in both parties, though "it was the
gods. . . . who first became aware of their own incompletion. Anguish is
therefore primal transmission of the god's despair, vast, numinous, always incomprehensible."[18] Though he is concerned here with the creative
process of acting and the manner in which it enables man to be released
from destructive despair, his argument may be seen to apply to the
creative process in general and to Awoonor's work in particular. If we
follow Soyinka's criticism further, we can see how Awoonor has bridged
"the infernal gulf . . . with visionary hopes," for it is only through music,
"the sole art form which does contain tragic reality,"[19] that this bridge can
be achieved. It is, after all, through the drum that the ancestors are able to
communicate with the living.[20] After a death this anguish must be most
acute, for the living are immediately confronted with the reality of the gap
between themselves and their ancestors. At the tragic moment, namely
the moment of this intense anguish, the poet, the drummer is called upon
to serve as a mediator, thus militating against despair by means of the
communication he is able to effect in the dirge that he sings.

As we have noted, the death of the protagonist has already occurred
when the story opens. On a literal level the book is a dirge sung about his
death. Not death in the Western sense of an event, but death as an
ongoing process to be celebrated, a journey toward complete awareness.
On this level it is also a dirge for the woman of the sea whose death at an
early age first made Amamu aware of the anguish of serverance. This
moves us into an allegorical level since this woman is not merely his
cousin but a mythic figure whose fertility is in direct opposition to the
effete landscape through which Amamu moves. She personifies the
awareness that Amamu moves into and the land so desperately needs.
Thus, while the dirge is celebrating this life force, it is lamenting the land
that is without that force and dying a death quite different than the death
of Amamu: "the nation is dying on its knees, dying in its own defecation"
(p. 209).

More than just the dirge is going on here, but the dirge should be seen as
the structure within which the events of the novel occur. Likewise, during
a funeral celebration a number of things are happening while the dirge is
sung:

customary greetings and return of greetings, expression of
sympathy by word of mouth and a handshake, the serving of
drinks to visitors, the narration of the circumstances of the

> death and later events to visitors, conversation among visitors, music and dancing with accompanying comments, congratulations or even jokes and laughter . . . arguments or quarrels here and there. . . .[21]

We have seen that this is not entirely necessary to our understanding of Awoonor's expressionistic mode of presentation, and yet it does shed light on the reasons why he has pulled together such an abundance of disparate elements. The poet sings to us and we become his audience in a mimetic recreation of a funeral celebration.

Given this context we can easily find the four main themes of the dirge: references to the ancestors, references to the domicile of the ancestors and the deceased, references to the deceased, and reflections and messages.[22] The first two of these themes are immediately taken up in the opening chapter in the descriptions of Deme, Amamu's hometown, and Mr. Attipoe, Amamu's uncle. In this place of his ancestors he has received two legacies. The legacy of corruption which his uncle, the road overseer, represents is the most noticeable, but it is a legacy that Amamu is to transcend in his role as a carrier, his second legacy. During the outdooring ceremony where Amamu is to receive his name, the family priest calls forth the ancestors and a pledge is made to them that the child will be "their torchbearer and servant all his life" (p. 15). He is, in other words, to live his life as a priest.

Actually the opposition here is not as clear as it would at first appear. The greatness of Amamu's lineage is partially established with the references to his grandfather, whom he is said to resemble:

> He was a tree on which they all leaned and under whose shade they all took shelter. Nyidevu, the canoeupturning hippo, the hippos of Agave tried to upturn the canoes heaped with sand. Their necks snapped in the attempt (p. 15).

But the legacy he receives from his uncle is not entirely negative. Nketia explains that deeds of the ancestors which are seemingly uncomplimentary are often mentioned in dirges because the character trait implied in the deed is considered more important than the deed itself.[23] Thus, the intelligence and cunning of Attipoe are seen as positive attributes though this involves no overt approbation of the manner in which he used them. In addition, a man cannot be truly great unless his ancestral lineage is broad enough to encompass many different types of men.

As the novel progresses we see Amamu's role spread out beyond a relationship to his own ancestors to include all the ancestors of the land. Moreover, the legacy of corruption is not merely a localized corruption, but a corruption of the entire land. We have noted that the narrative aspect of the novel is minimal, and to the extent that the expressionistic mode is used here to shatter this temporal element, we have an increased awareness of space. We are not so aware of when things happen chronologically, as where they happen. At each place we see Amamu he is confronted by another facet of corruption, and the slums of Nima, the National Club, the colonial school, as well as Deme, are all part of this landscape.

The mention of the qualities of the deceased individual are intended to establish the significance of the loss of the individual to those who were close to him as well as the community. Our understanding of the sensitive nature of the protagonist increases in direct proportion to our expanded awareness of the landscape in which he moves. The references to his special qualities, however, are rarely as direct as they are in a dirge. His integrity, for example, is established in the second chapter where we see him in direct contrast to the various regulars of the National Club, and is effectively confirmed by his refusal to allow his vision to be compromised by the corruption which surrounds him.

It might reasonably be argued that the three themes we have so far discussed are of a general nature that we could find in any novel, but it is their specific combination with a series of reflections and messages that clearly relates the contents of this novel to the contents of a traditional dirge. The reflections are on the plight of those who are left behind and the messages are requests for aid and comfort from the dead.[24] Thus the mourner might make general comments on the death: "What were your wares that they are sold out so quickly?" or "This death has taken me by surprise."[25] In addition, he will add phrases which express more directly his own personal anguish and the loss to the community: "There is no branch above which I could grasp" or "I am in flooded waters. Who will rescue me?"[26] The reflections in *This Earth, My Brother* are similar and in fact make up a large part of the poetic sections:

> I do not know where they buried my birthcord (p. 18).

> Home is my desolation, home is my anguish, home is my drink of hyssop and tears (p. 38).

> In the gray truce of those hours we will win a temporary respite. In our penance hour, we shall pack our bags ready for a long journey homewards (p. 147).

> A nation is doing a death dance now in a banquet hall of its imaginings . . . (p. 148).

> Anger is futile, for death maybe is the only reality (p. 207).

Aside from the reflection on the dying nation these all could have come from a traditional dirge. The reflection on death as a journey, however, is particularly noteworthy: throughout the singing of the dirge, the conception of death as a journey with its implication of inevitable physical separation is not lost sight of. All the mourner's wishes for a good journey, her wish not to be left alone, her expressions of sorrow for the loss sustained and of her anxiety for the future are thought of because death makes physical separation unavoidable. This thought may culminate in yet another wish—the wish for continued fellowship when the deceased reaches his destination in the underworld.[27]

Amamu's journey into and through his society symbolizes this journey, the final *rite de passage*. The messages even more than the reflections corroborte this as they are direct addresses to those with whom he desires to be reunited:

> Mother, didn't I tell you I hated the sun, father didn't I tell you
> I hated sun, the little one was never found they must journey to
> god's house and purchase him with offerings, must buy him
> with sacrifices look after him well, mother (p. 19).

> Dear one, hold on, for I come (p. 77).
> My woman of the sea, I am leaving for the almond tree where I
> first met you. I shall be there when you rise . . . (p. 210).

Without a thorough knowledge of the Ewe language, or at least the linguistic structure of the Ewe dirge, we are very much restricted in what we can say about how *This Earth, My Brother* bears similarities to the dirge in terms of the language patterns. Nevertheless, the most distinctive prosodic features of the Ewe as well as the Akan dirge are the numerous types of repetition that occur. Each dirge is individuated by its own system of repetitions which control meaning as well as rhythm, and range from alliteration and assonance to repeated collocations and repetitions of entire sentences. We see such use in the first of Awoonor's poetic sections as well as all the subsequent interludes, and even, though to a lesser extent, in the narrative sections. The following is one of the finest examples of the way he interweaves such a complex of repetitions:

> The seventh night, deep deep night of the black black land of
> gods and deities they will come out. First the drums to-gu to-gu
> to-gu to to to-gu if they insist then I shall die the death of blood
> I shall die the death of blood. They will march through every
> lane drums echoing across no one can tell where they are now,

no one can tell. They will pause for entrance into thunderhouses the silence of crickets nocturnal wail of bullfrogs taking over from as near as Kosivi's ground water tank. If they insist and say it must be by every means, if they insist then I shall die the death of blood. The echo recedes into distant farmlands the sole witnesses of the journey the restlessness of gods if they insist if they say it must be by every every means then I shall die the death of blood (pp. 17–18).

Words, phrases and sentences are rhythmically bound together by the insistent, drum-like repetition of d's, t's and b's. The reiteration of adjectives and key phrases, as well as the parallel construction, effects an intensification of that rhythm.

It is not merely a rhythm for musical effect, but a rhythm which also carries a lot of meaning. Like Christ, the protagonist would have his cup pass from him but the drums, the voices of the ancestors, have already decided that he will "die the death of blood." His statement "if they insist" is thus counterpointed by an implicit ancestral rhythm saying "we insist, we insist." By the end of the book he has given himself entirely over to the demands which the ancestors have made upon him. When he begins to return to the sea he follows the intense rhythm of a dirge, hearing drums move into "a slow funeral beat of mourning." As there are no more worldly things distracting him the earlier insistence is no longer needed:

It was a distinct female voice singing a dirge about the day of death, of trees withered, of leaves fallen from the evergreen baobab, of a desert storm, of skulls crossing a wide impenetrable expanse of forest soaked in the desert rain. Then a voice began to talk about the searcher who finds, the searcher who finds in the wilderness the death that will kill him, the sorrow of the pallbearers, the pity he will have for them who will carry his body to the grave (p. 213).

Seeing *This Earth, My Brother* as an Ewe dirge, however transformed by the artist, establishes the coherence of the work as a whole and the vision which is the basis of that coherence. Past and present are locked in a tragic cycle which goes back to a primordial anguish of severance. Through his death, Amamu is able to serve as a mediator who can break the cycle for the future. The vision is a mythic one, but framed in a lament that might be sung to any great man in the Ewe community. Though this clarifies much that is going on in the novel it certainly makes it no less

277

complex. In fact, as Forster said about *Moby Dick,* as soon as we begin to feel the music in it the work suddenly becomes amazingly difficult.[28]

NOTES

1. Bernth Lindfors, et. al., eds., *Palaver: Interviews with Five African Writers in Texas,* Occasional Publication No. 3 (Austin, Texas: African and Afro-American Research Institute, 1972), p. 54.
2. Ibid., p. 52.
3. Personal communication, April 1973.
4. *Funeral Dirges of the Akan People* (Achimota, Ghana, 1955).
5. Confirmed by Kofi Awoonor (personal communication, April 1972).
6. *Aspects of the Novel* (Harmondsworth: Pelican, 1962), pp. 48–49.
7. In *The Moriality of Art,* ed. D. W. Jefferson (London: Routledge and Kegan Paul, 1969), p. 122.
8. Linfors, p. 61.
9. Kofi Awoonor, *This Earth, My Brother* (New York: Doubleday, 1971), p. 8. Subsequent page references to this edition given in parenthesis.
10. See Janheinz Jahn, *Muntu: An Outline of Neo-African Culture,* trans. Marjorie Grene (New York: Grove Press, 1961).
11. In the interview referred to above, Awoonor was asked whether he felt the writer should be committed to some sort of social change. His response is worth noting here:
    . . . the writer . . . by the very commitment he imposes upon himself to tell the story of our woes, sorrows and joys is a committed writer. Achebe once said, "What is the point of suffering if it is to go on forever." If suffering is not productive, it is no good. . . . The little man in the corner who goes through the grinding sorrow. . . . will perhaps one day be able to reach a little respite (Lindfors, p. 56).
12. John Goldblatt, interviewer, No. 41 (1972), p. 44.
13. *A Rhetoric of Motives* (Berkeley: Univ. of California Press, 1969), p. 203.
14. Personal communication with Kofi Awoonor, November 1972.
15. For a further elabortaion of the relation between the ludic/serious oppositionand ritual, see Roger Abrahams, "Ritual for Fun and Profit, or the Ends and Outs of Celebration," unpublished ms.
16. Cf. Awoonor's poem, "The Journey Beyond," in *Night of My Blood* (New York: Doubleday, 1971): "Kutsiami the benevolent boatman;/ when I come to the river shore/ please ferry me across. . . ." (p. 41).
17. See Lindfors, p. 60.
18. *The Morality of Art,* p. 123.
19. Ibid., p. 124.
20. See Janheinz Jahn.
21. Nketia, pp. 13–14.
22. Ibid., p. 19.
23. Ibid., p. 24.
24. Ibid., p. 44.
25. Ibid., p. 47.
26. Ibid., p. 47.
27. Ibid., p. 48.
28. *Aspects of the Novel,* p. 140.

BIBLIOGRAPHY

A BIBLIOGRAPHY OF CRITICAL STUDIES OF GHANAIAN LITERATURE

Richard K. Priebe

I have attempted to be as inclusive as possible in putting together this bibliography of critical books and essays on Ghanaian literature. Invariably, however, items do fall through the cracks. I apologize in advance for any omissions; I would also appreciate learning of any, however small or egregious, that I might include them in an updated version. (Send to Richard K. Priebe, English Department, Virginia Commonwealth University, Richmond, Virginia 23284, U.S.A.)

The organization of the bibliography generally follows that of the contents of this anthology. There is, of course, much overlap among the heading and some arbitrary placing. Thus, material on Awoonor can be found under "Poetry," "Fiction," and "Interviews;" and material on popular drama will be found under "Drama" and not under "Popular Literature." Articles with an asterick (*) are those included in this collection.

BACKGROUND AND GENERAL LITERATURE

Amegbleame, Simon. "Naissance et développement d'un corpus imprimé africain: La Littérature éwé." *L'afrique Litteraire Et Artistique* (Senegal) 39 (1976): 37–42.

Apronti, E. O. "Language and National Integration in Ghana." *Présence Africaine* 81 (1972): 162–69.

Awoonor, Kofi. *The Breast of the Earth: A Survey of the History, Culture and Literature of Africa South of the Sahara*. New York: Anchor, 1976. [Sections on Ewe and Akan oral art and on Ewe written literature.]

Colmer, Rosemary. "The Restorative Cycle: Kofi Awoonor's Theory of African Literature." *New Literature Review* 3 (1977): 23–28.

Danquah, J. B. *The Akan Doctrine of God*. London: Frank Cass, 1944.

Gérald, Albert. *African Language Literatures*. London: Longman, 1981. [Sections on the development of vernacular literature in Ghana.]

————. "Aux sources de la littérature ghánéenne." *Mélanges de Culture et de Linguistique Africaines Publiés à la Mémoire de Léo Stappers*. Ed. C. Faïk and Erika Sulzmann. Berlin: Dietrich Reimer Verlag, 1982. 259–300.

Hagan, Kwa O. "The Literary and Social Clubs of the Past: Their Role in National Awakening in Ghana." *Okyeame* 4. 2 (1969): 81–86.

Herdeck, Donald E. *African Authors: A Companion to Black African Writing Vol. I: 1300–1973*. Washington, D.C.: Black Orpheus P, 1973.

Kaplan, Irving, et al. *Area Handbook for Ghana*. Washington, D.C.: U.S. Government Printing Office, 1971.

Kayper-Mensah, A.W. and Horst Wolff, eds. *Ghanaian Writing: Ghana as seen by her own Writers as well as German Authors*. Tübingen: Horst Erdmann, 1972.

Kotei, S. I. A. "Themes for Children's Literature in Ghana." *African Book Publishing Record* 4 (1978): 233–39.

McFarland, Daniel Miles. *Historical Dictionary of Ghana*. African Historical Dictionaries 39. Metuchen, New Jersey: The Scarecrow P, 1985.

Okai, Atukwei. "Vision, Image, and Symbol in Ghanaian Literature." *Pacific Quarterly* (Moana) 6.3–4 (1981): 51–61.

Opoku, Kofi A. "The Destiny of Man in Akan Traditional Religious Thought." *Conch* 7.1–2 (1975): 15–25.

Rattray, R. S. *Ashanti*. Oxford: Clarendon, 1927.

Sangster, Ellen G. "Student Creative Writing in Ghana." *Okyeame* 4.2 (1969): 87–92.

Senanu, K. E. "Creative Writing in Ghana." *RE: Arts and Letters* 6.2 (1972): 1–14.

Stewart, Danièle. "Ghanaian Writing in Prose: A Critical Survey." *Présence Africaine* 91 (1974): 73–105.

Ward, William E. F. *A History of Ghana*. 4th ed. London: George Allen and Unwin, 1967.

Zell, Hans M., Carol Bundy and Virginia Coulon. *A New Reader's Guide to African Literature*. 2nd. ed. New York: Africana, 1983.

BIBLIOGRAPHY

Jahn, Janheinz and Claus Peter Dressler. *Bibliography of Creative African Writing*. Millwood, New York: Kraus-Thompson, 1973.

Lindfors, Bernth. *Black African Literature in English: A Guide to Information Sources*. American Literature, English Literature and World Literatures in English Information Guide Series 23. Detroit: Gale Research, 1979.

Modern Language Association Bibliography. New York: Modern Language Association. [An annual.]

Patten, Margaret D. *Ghanaian Imaginative Writing in English, 1950—1969*. Legon: U of Ghana, Dept. of Library Studies, 1971.

Priebe, Richard K. "A Bibliography of Popular Writing in Ghana." *Research In African Literatures* 9.3 (1978): 425–32.

INTERVIEWS AND BIOGRAPHICAL STATEMENTS

Assensah, A.B. "Interviews: Dr. Kofi Awoonor." *Afroscope* 8.10 (1978): 25, 27, 29.

Awoonor, Kofi. "Coming from My Own Tradition." *Compass* (Kutztown, Pa.) 5/6 (1974): 3–6. [Autobiographical statement.]

Goldblatt, John. "Kofi Awoonor: An Interview." *Transition* 41 (1972): 42–44.

"Kofi Awoonor on Poetry and Prison." *West Africa* 17 (April 1978): 750-51.

Lautré, Maxine. "Efua Sutherland." *African Writers Talking.* Ed. Dennis Duerden and Cosmo Pieterse. New York: Africana, 1972. 183-95. [Interview.]

Lindfors, Bernth. "Interview with Joe de Graft." *World Literature Written in English* 18 (1979): 314-31.

Lindfors, Bernth, et al. "Interview with Kofi Awoonor." *Palaver.* Occasional Publication of the African and Afro-American Research Institute, 3. Austin: African and Afro-American Research Institute, U of Texas, 1972. 46-64.

McDowell, Robert. "J. W. Abruquah Talks About Ghana." *World Literature Written in English.* 20 (1971): 27-36.

McGregor, Maxine. "Ama Ata Aidoo." *African Writers Talking.* Ed. Dennis Duerden and Cosmo Pieterse. New York: Africana, 1972. 19-27. [Interview.]

Morell, Karen L. "Kofi Awoonor." *In Person: Achebe, Awoonor and Soyinka.* Ed. Karen L. Morell. Seattle, Washington: Institute for Comparative and Foreign Area Studies, U of Washington, 1975. 133-160. [Lecture, interview.]

Munro, Ian H. and Wayne Kamin. "Kofi Awoonor: Interview," *Kunapipi* 1.2 (1979): 76-83.

Serumaga, Robert and Dennis Duerden. "Kofi Awoonor." *African Writers Talking.* Ed. Dennis Duerden and Cosmo Pieterse. New York: Africana, 1972. 29-50. [Interview.]

Wästberg, Per. *The Writer in Modern Africa.* New York: Africana, 1969. [Remarks by George Awoonor-Williams (Kofi Awoonor) on African Literature and growing up in Africa.]

ORAL ART

Abarry, Abu Shardow. "Rhetoric and Poetics of Oral African Literature: A Study of the Ga of Ghana." *Dissertation Abstracts International* 38 (1978): 5119A.

Adali-Mortty, Geormbeeyi. "Ewe Poetry." *Introduction to African Literature.* 2nd ed. Ed. Ulli Beier. London: Longman, 1979, 3-11.

Addo, Peter E. *Ghana Folk Tales: Ananse Stories from Africa.* New York: Exposition, 1968.

Agalic, James. "Story-Telling Among the Bulsa of Northern Ghana." *Zeitschrift für Ethnol.* (Braunschweig) 103.2 (1978): 261-78.

Amegbleame, S. A. "Le Conte et l' imprimé dans une société africaine: L'Exemple ewe." *Présence Francophone: Revue Littéraire* 16 (1978): 163-74.

Ameyaw, K. and E. Y. Aduamah. "Collections of Oral Traditions from the Volta Basin." *Research Bulletin* 1.2 (1965): 20-22.

Anyidoho, Kofi. "Henoga Domegbe and His Songs of Sorrow." *Greenfield Review* 8.1-2 (1980): 55-58.

Appiah, Michael Anthony. *"Okyeame:* An Integrative Model of Communication Behavior." *Dissertation Abstracts International* 4 (1979): 1745A [On proverbs.]

Apronti, E. O. "On the Structural Unity of the Akan Dirge." *Research Review* 8.2 (1972): 32-40.

Awoonor, Kofi. *Fire in the Valley: Ewe Folktales.* New York: Nok, 1973.

———. *Guardians of the Sacred Word: Ewe Poetry.* New York: Nok, 1974.

———. "Some Notes on the Poetry of the Ewe." *Alcheringa* 3 (1971): 13-15.

*Boadi, Lawrence A. "The Language of the Proverb in Akan." *African Folklore.* Ed. Richard Dorson. Garden City: Anchor Bks, 1972, 183-91.

Brookman-Amissah, J. "Some Observations on the Proverbs of the Akan-speaking People of Ghana." *Afrika und Übersee* 55 (1971–72): 262–67.

Bruner, Charlotte H. "Make Sure of All Things, Hold Fast to What is Fine." *Africa Report* 18.5 (1973): 24–25. [On oral art in Ghana.]

Christensen, James B. "The Role of Proverbs in Fante Culture." *Africa* 28 (1958): 232–43.

Dakubu, M. E. Kropp. "Akaja: A Ga Song Type in Twi." *Research Review* 8.2 (1972): 44–61.

Daaku, Kwame Y. "History in the Oral Traditions of the Akan." *Journal of The Folklore Institute* (Indiana U) 8 (1971): 114–26.

Dseagu, S. A. "Proverbs and Folktales of Ghana: Their Forms and Uses." *Conch* 7. 1–2 (1975): 80–92.

Egblewogbe, J. Y. *Games and Songs as Education Media among the Ewes of Ghana*. Tema: Ghana, 1974.

Fikry-Atallah, Mona. "Ghana: Tales Collected from the Wala of Wa." *African Folklore*. Ed. Richard Dorson. Garden City: Anchor Bks, 1972. 395–440.

Finnegan, Ruth. *Oral Literature in Africa*. Oxford: Clarendon P, 1970.

Goody, Jack. *The Myth of the Bagre*. Oxford: Clarendon P, 1972.

Henige, David P. "The Problem of Feedback in Oral Tradition: Four Examples from the Fante Coastlands." *Journal of African History* 14 (1973): 223–35.

McDermott, Gerald. *Anansi the Spider*. New York: Holt, Rinehart and Winston, 1971.

Nketia, Kwabena. "Akan Poetry." *Introduction to African Literature*. 2nd. Ed. Ulli Beier. London: Longman, 1979. 23–33.

Nketia, J. H. *The Folk Songs of Ghana*. Accra: Ghana UP, 1974.

——. *Funeral Dirges of the Akan People*. Achimota, Ghana, 1955.

——. "The Poetry of Akan Drums." *Black Orpheus*. 2.2 (1968): 27–35.

Oduyoye, Amba. "The Asante Woman: Socialization Through Proverbs (Part I)." *African Notes: Journal of the Institute of African Studies* 8.1 (1979): 5–11.

Pelton, Robert D. "Ananse: Spinner of Ashanti Doubleness." *The Trickster In West Africa: A Study of Mythic Irony and Sacred Delight*. Berkeley: U of California P, 1980. 25–70.

Rapp, Eugen Ludwig. "Eräzhlung der Guang von Boso in Ghana (Guang-Studien IV)." *Wort Und Religion. Kalima Na Dini. Studien Zur Afrikanistik*. Ed., Hans-Jürgen Greschat und Herrmann Jungraithmayr. Stuttgart: Evangelischer Missionsverlag, 1969. 94–106.

Rattray, R. S. *Akan-Ashanti Folktales*. Oxford: Clarendon P, 1930.

——. *Ashanti Proverbs*. Oxford: Clarendon P, 1916.

Sprigge, R. G. S. "Eweland's Adangbe: An Enquiry into an Oral Tradition." *Transactions of the Historical Society of Ghana* (Legon) 10 (1969): 87–128.

Sutherland, E. *Anansegoro (Story Telling Drama in Ghana)*. Accra: Afram (Afram African Studies Library), 1975.

Turkson, A. A.R. *Ghanaian Wit in Song*. Ghana Today 6. Accra-Tema: Ghana Info. Service, n.d.

Warren, Dennis M., and Owusu Brempong. "Attacking Deviations from the Norm: Poetic Insults In Bono (Ghana)." *Maledicta* 1 (1977): 141–66.

Yankah, Kwesi. "From Loose Abuse to Poetic Couplets: The Case of the Fante Tone Riddle." *Maledicta* 7 (1983): 167–77.

——. "To Praise or Not to Praise the King: The Akan *Apae* in the Context of Referential Poetry." *Research in African Literatures* 14.3 (1983): 381–400.

——. "Voicing and Drumming The Poetry of Praise.: The Case for Aural

Literature." *Interdisciplinary Dimensions of African Literature.* Annual Selected Papers of the African Literature Association 8. Washington, D.C.: Three Continents P, 1985. 139–53.

――――. "The Akan Highlife Song: A Medium of Cultural Reflection or Deflection?" Forthcoming in *Research in African Literatures.*

EARLY WRITERS (PRE-1920)

Afesi, John D. "J. E. Casely Hayford: From Gold Coast Cultural Nationalism to Pan-African Political Nationalism." *Mazungumzo* (East Landing, Michigan) 1.2 (1971): 49–54.

Brentjes, Burchard. "Anton Wilhelm Amo in Halle, Wittenberg and Jena." *Universitas* (Legon) 6.1 (1977): 39–55.

――――. "250 Jahre Anton Wilhelm Amo." *Asien-Afrika-Latein-Amerika* 5 (1977): 785–88.

Dathorne, O. R. "The Beginnings of the West African Novel." *Nigeria Magazine* 93 (1967): 168–70. [On R.E. Obeng and E. Casely-Hayford.]

Eluwa, G. I. C. "Casely Hayford and African Emancipation." *Pan-African Journal* 7 (1974): 111–18.

Fikes, Robert, Jr. "Confirming Intellectual Capacity: Black Scholars in Europe During the Renaissance and the Enlightenment." *Présence Africaine* 114 (1980): 120–31. [On Anthony William Amo.]

Hussain, Arif. "Iqbal and Casely Hayford: A Phase in Afro-Asian Philosophy." *Ibadan* 29 (1971): 45–52.

Nwala, T. Uzodima. "Anthony William Amo of Ghana on the Mind-Body Problem." *Présence Africaine* 108 (1978): 158–65.

Ofosu-Appiah, L. H. *Joseph Ephraim Casely Hayford: The Man of Vision and Faith.* J. B. Danquah Memorial Lectures 8. Legon: U Bookshop, 1975.

Piłaszewicz, Stanisław. " 'The Arrival of the Christians': A Hausa Poem on the Colonial Conquest of West Africa by al-Hadji' Umaru." *Africana Bulletin* (Warsaw) 22 (1975): 55–129.

――――. " 'The Song of Poverty and of Wealth': A Hausa Poem on Social Problems by al-Hadji' Umaru." *Africana Bulletin* 21 (1974): 67–115.

Sölken, Heinz. "Zur Biographie des Imam 'Umaru von Kete-Kratyi." *Africana Marburgensia* 3.2 (1970): 24–30.

Ugonna, Nnabuenyi. "Casely Hayford: The Fictive Dimension of African Personality." *Ufahamu* 7.2 (1977): 159–71.

POPULAR LITERATURE

Collins, E. J. "Ghanaian Highlife." *African Arts* 9.4 (1976): 30–34, 101.

Coplan, David. "Go to My Town, Cape Coast: The Social History of Ghanaian Highlife." *Eight Urban Musical Cultures: Tradition and Change.* Ed. Bruno Nettl. Urbana: U of Illinois P, 1978.

Geest, Sjaak van der. "The Image of Death in Akan Highlife Songs of Ghana." *Research in African Literatures* 11 (1980): 145–74.

Geest, Sjaak van der, and Nimrod K. Asante-Darko. "The Political Meaning of Highlife Songs in Ghana." *African Studies Review* 25.1 (1982): 27–35.

Grant, Stephen H. "Publisher for the Many." *Africa Report* 17.1 (1972): 26–27. [On Asare Konadu.]

*Ikiddeh, Ime. "The Character of Popular Fiction in Ghana." *Perspectives on African Literature*. Ed. Christopher Heywood. New York: Africana, 1971. 106–16.

Mensah, Atta A. "The Popular Song and Ghanaian Writer." Okyeame 4.1 (1968): 110–19.

Priebe, Richard K. "Popular Writing in Ghana: A Sociology and Rhetoric." *Research in African Literatures* 9.3 (1978): 395–432.

POETRY

Amegbleame, Simon Agbeko. "La Poésie Ewe: Structures formelles et contenu." *Revue de Littérature and d'Esthétique Négro-Africaines* 3 (1981): 89–101. [Rpt. from *Asemka* 5 (1979): 63–77].

*Anyidoho, Kofi. "Atukwei Okai and His Poetic Territory." *New West African Literature*. Ed. Kolawole Ogungbesan. London: Heinemann, 1979. 45–59.

*————. "Kofi Awoonor and the Ewe Tradition of Songs of Abuse *(Halo)*." *Toward Defining the African Aesthetic*. Ed. Lemuel A. Johnson, et al. Washington, D.C.: Three Continents P, 1982. 17–29.

Apronti, Jawa. "Ghanaian Poetry in the 1970's." *New West African Literature*. Ed. Kolawole Ogungbesan. London: Heinemann, 1979. 31–44.

————. "John Atukwei Okai: The Growth of a Poet." *Universitas* (Legon, Ghana) 2.1 (1972): 117–29.

Awoonor, Kofi. "The Imagery of Fire: A Critical Assessment of the Poetry of Joe de Graft." *Okike* 19 (1981): 70–79.

*————. "The Poem, the Poet, the Human Condition: Some Aspects of Recent West African Poetry." *Asemka* (Cape Coast, Ghana) 5 (1979): 1–20. [Rpt. here as "Three Young Ghanaian Poets."]

Colmer, Rosemary. "Kofi Awoonor: Critical Prescriptions and Creative Practice." *ACLALS Bulletin* (Mysore, India) 5.1 (1978): 22–31.

*Early, L.R. "Kofi Awoonor's Poetry." *Ariel: A Review of International English Literature*. 6.1 (1975): 51–67.

Egudu, Romanus N. *Four Modern West African Poets*. New York: Nok, 1977. [On Kofi Awoonor.]

Goodwin, K. L. "Kofi Awoonor." *Understanding African Poetry* London: Heinemann, 1982. 93–106.

Hodghin, T. "The Islamic Literary Tradition in Ghana." *Islam in Tropical Africa*. Ed. I. M. Lewis. London: Oxford UP, 1966. 442–60.

Kayper-Mensah, A. W. "Kwesi Brew and His Poetry." *Legacy* (Legon) 3.1 (1976): 27–32.

Knipp, Thomas R. "Myth, History and the Poetry of Kofi Awoonor." *African Literature Today* 11 (1980): 39–61.

Kubayanda, J. Bekunuru. "Polyrhythmics and African Print Poetics: Guillén, Césaire, and Atukwei Okai." *Interdisciplinary Dimensions of African Literature*. Annual selected Papers of the African Literature Association 8. Washington, D.C.: Three Continents P, 1985. 155–69.

Moore, Gerald. "Kofi Awoonor: The Neglected Gods." *Twelve African Writers*. Bloomington: Indiana UP, 1980. 237–60.

Okwu, Edward Chukwuemeka. "The Artist-Figure in Modern West African Poetry: An Approach to the Poetry of Awoonor, Okigbo, and Soyinka." *Dissertation Abstracts International* 39 (1979): 5505A.

Orraca-Tetteh, Kwei. "Atukwei Okai Revisited." *Legacy* (Legon) 1.3 (1973): 27–34.

*Thumboo, Edwin. "Kwesi Brew: The Poetry of Statement and Situation." *African Literature Today* 4 (1970): 19–36.

Sander, Reinhard. "Joe de Graft's 'Two Views from a Window.' " *Greenfield Review* 2.3 (1972): 23–30.

Uré, J. " 'Funeral' by Jawa Apronti." *Actes du heitième congrès international de linguistique africaine, Abidjan 24–28 mars 1969.* 2 vols. Abidjan: U of Abidjan, and the West African Linguistic Society, 1971. 589–97.

DRAMA

Acquaye, Saka. "Modern Folk Opera in Ghana." *African Arts* 4.2 (1971): 60–65, 80.

*Adelugba, Dapo. "Language and Drama: Ama Ata Aidoo." *African Literature Today* 8 (1976): 72–84.

Agovi, J. K. "The Ghana Dance Ensemble and the Contemporary Ghanaian Theatre." *Legon Observer* 12.9 (1980): 213–15.

*Angmor, Charles. "Drama in Ghana." *Theatre in Africa.* Ed. Oyin Ogunba and Abiola Irele. Ibadan: Ibadan UP, 1976.

Asante, S. K. B. "The Politics of Confrontation: The Case of Kobina Sekyi and the Colonial System in Ghana." *Universitas* (Legon) 6.2 (1977): 15–38.

Bame, K. N. "Comic Play in Ghana." *African Arts* 1.4 (1968): 30–34, 101.

———. "Comic Plays in Ghana: An Indigenous Art Form for Rural Social Change." *Rural Africana* 27 (1975): 25–41.

———. "Des origines et du development du 'concert party' au Ghana." *Revue d' Histoire du Théâtre* 27 (1975): 10–20.

———. "The Influence of Contemporary Ghanaian Traditional Drama on the Attitudes and Behavior of Play-Goers." *Research Review* (Ghana) 9.2 (1978) 26–32.

———. "The Popular Theatre in Ghana." *Research Review* (Legon) 3.2 (1967): 34–39.

Bamikunle, Aderemi. "The Two Plays of Aidoo—A Commentary." *Work in Progress: 1.* Zaria, Nigeria: English Dept., Ahmadu Bello U, 1972. 170–83.

Banham, Martin. "Efua Sutherland, Joe de Graft, Ama Ata Aidoo, and Notes on Other Playwrights." *African Theatre Today.* Bath: Pitman, 1976. 50–56.

*Collins, E. J. "Comic Opera in Ghana." *African Arts* 9.2 (1976): 50–57.

de Graft, J. C. "Roots in African Drama and Theatre." *African Literature Today* 8 (1976): 1–25. [Deals with Ghanaian drama.]

Gibbs, James M. "Mohammed ben Abdallah and the Legon Road Theatre." *African Arts* 5.4 (1972): 33–34.

Graham-White, A. "J.B. Danquah, Evolué Playwright." *Journal of the New African Literature and the Arts* 2 (1966): 49–52.

Hachten, Harva. "The Lost Fisherman." *Topic* 76 (1973): 24–25. [On an opera by Saka Acquaye.]

Hill-Lubin, Mildred A. "The Relationship of African-Americans and Africans: A

Recurring Theme in the Works of Ata Aidoo." *Présence Africaine* 124 (1982): 190-201.

Kennedy, Scott. *In Search of African Theatre.* New York: Scribners, 1973. [Personal impressions of drama and theater in Ghana.]

Kennedy, J. Scott. "Le bilinguisme: Une possibilité pour le développement du théâtre au Ghana." *La culture africaine: Le Symposium d'Alger (21 juillet-ler août 1969).* Alger: S.N.E.D., 1969. 388–94.

———. "The National Theatre in Ghana." *East Africa Journal* (Nairobi) 6.7 (1969): 38–45.

Kilson, Marion. "Women and African Literature." *Journal of African Studies* 4 (1977): 161–66. [Deals with Ama Ata Aidoo.]

Langley, J. Ayo. "Introduction to *The Blinkards* by Kobina Sekyi." London: Heinemann, 1974. 1–17.

Morisseau-Leroy, Félix. "Le rôle du théâtre africain dans le développement." *La culture africaine: Le Symposium d'Alger (21 juillet-ler août 1969).* Alger: S.N.E.D., 1969. 271–74.

Nagenda, John. "Generation in Conflict." *Protest and Conflict in African Literature.* Ed. Cosmo Pieterse and Donald Munro. New York: Africana, 1969. 101–08. [On Ama Ata Aidoo and J. C. deGraft.]

Okafor, Chinyere. "Parallelism Versus Influence in African Literature: The Case of Efua Sutherland's *Edufa.*" *Kiabàrà* 3.1 (1980): 113–131.

Ricard, Alain. "Le Théâtre entre l'oral et l'écrit au Ghana et au Nigeria." *Französich Heute* 2 (1982): 147–56.

Ridden, Geoffrey M. "Language and Social Status in Ama Ata Aidoo." *Style* 8 (1974): 452–61.

Sutherland, Efua T. *Bob Johnson.* Accra: Anowuo Educational Publications, 1970.

Talbert, Linda Lee. "*Alcestis* and *Edufa:* The Transitional Individual." *World Literature Written in English* 22.2 (1983): 183–90. [On Efua Sutherland.]

Yerenkyi, Asiedu. "Kobina Sekyi: The Founding Father of Ghanaian Theatre." *Legacy* (Legon) 3.2 (1977). 39–47.

FICTION

Adeyemi, N. A. "The Major Artistic Achievements of Armah in *The Beautyful Ones Are Not Yet Born.*" *Shuttle* (Lagos) 8 (1980): 46–48.

Aidoo, Ama Ata. "No Saviours." *African Writers on African Writing.* Ed. G. D. Killam. Evanston: Northwestern UP, 1973. 14–18. [On Armah's *The Beautyful Ones Are Not Yet Born.*]

Amegbleame, Simon Agbeko. "La Fiction narrative dans la production littérature ewe: La Nouvelle et le roman." *Africa* (London) 50 (1980): 24–36.

Amuta, Chidi. "Ayi Kwei Armah, History and 'The Way': The Importance of *Two Thousand Seasons.*" *Komparatistische Hefte* 3 (1981): 79–86.

———. "Ayi Kwei Armah and the Mythopoesis of Mental Decolonization." *Ufahamu* 10.3 (1981): 44–56.

———. "Potraits of the Contemporary African Artist in Armah's Novels." *World Literature Written in English* 21.3 (1982): 467–76.

Amuzu, Koku. "The Theme of Corruption in *A Man of the People* and *The Beautyful Ones Are Not Yet Born.*" *Legacy* (Legon) 3.2 (1977): 18–23.

Booth, James. *"Why Are We So Blest?* and the Limits of Metaphor." *Journal of Commonwealth Literature* 15.1 (1980): 50–64.

Britwum, Atta. "Hero-Worshipping in the African Novel: The Case of Ayi Kwei Armah and Others." *Asemka* 3 (1975): 1–18.

*Brown, Lloyd W. "Ama Ata Aidoo: The Art of the Short Story and Sexual Roles in Africa." *World Literature Written in English* 13 (1974): 172–83.

Bruner, Charlotte. "Child Africa as Depicted by Bessie Head and Ama Ata Aidoo." *Studies in the Humanities* 7.2 (1979): 5–11.

Burness, Donald B. "Womanhood in the Short Stories of Ama Ata Aidoo." *Studies in Black Literature* 4.2 (1973): 21–24.

Chakava, Henry. "Ayi Kwei Armah and a Commonwealth of Souls." *Standpoints on African Literature: A Critical Anthology*. Nairobi: East Africa Literature Bureau, 1973. 197–208.

Chapman, Karen C. "Introduction to Ama Ata Aidoo's *Dilemma of a Ghost*." *Sturdy Black Bridges: Visions of Black Women in Literature*. Ed. Roseann P. Bell, et al. Garden City, N.Y.: Doubleday (Anchor), 1979. 25–38.

Collins, Harold R. "The Ironic Imagery of Armah's *The Beautyful Ones Are Not Yet Born:* The Putrescent Vision." *World Literature Written in English* 20 (1971): 37–50.

Colmer, Rosemary. "The Human and the Divine: *Fragments* and *Why Are We So Blest?*" *Kunapipi* 2.2 (1980): 77–90.

Coustel, J. C. "Un Enfant noir à la recherche de son identité." *Annales de l'Université de Toulouse: Le Mirail* 13.1 (1977): 47–54. [On Francis Selormey.].

Duclos, Jocelyn-Robert. " 'The Butterfly and the Pile of Manure': A Study of Kofi Awoonor's Novel, *This Earth, My Brother*." *Canadian Journal of African Studies* 9 (1975): 511–21.

Egharevba, Chris. "Relation of Style and Meaning in Kofi Awoonor's *This Earth, My Brother.* . . ." *Kuka* (Zaria) (1978–79): 55–62.

Evans, Jenny. "Women of 'The Way': *Two Thousand Seasons,* Female Images and Black Identity." *ACLALS Bulletin* (Mysore, India) 6.1 (1982): 17–26.

Folarin, Margaret. "An Additional Comment on Ayi Kwei Armah's *The Beautyful Ones Are Not Yet Born*." *African Literature Today* 5 (1971): 116–29.

Fraser, Robert. "The American Background in *Why Are We So Blest?*" *African Literature Today* 9 (1978): 39–46.

———. *The Novels of Ayi Kwei Armah: A Study in Polemical Fiction*. London: Heinemann, 1980.

Goldie, Terry. "A Connection of Images: The Structure of Symbols in *The Beautyful Ones Are Not Yet Born*." *Kunapipi* 1.1 (1979): 94–107.

*Griffiths, Gareth. "Structure and Image in Kwei Armah's *The Beautyful Ones Are Not Yet Born*." *Studies in Black Literature* 2.2 (1971): 1–9.

Ikyegh, J. I. "K. Awoonor's *This Earth, My Brother:* An Interpretation." *Mirror* (Zaria) 1 (1975–76): 45–48.

*Izevbaye, D.S. "Ayi Kwei Armah and the 'I' of the Beholder." *A Celebration of Black and African Writing*. Ed. Bruce King and Kolawole Ogungbesan. Zaria, Nigeria: Ahmadu Bello UP, 1975. 232–44.

Johnson, Joyce. "The Promethean 'Factor' in Ayi Kwei Armah's *Fragments* and *Why Are We So Blest?*" *World Literature Written in English* 21.3 (1982): 488–98.

Kibera, Leonard. "Pessimism and the African Novelist: Ayi Kwei Armah's *The*

Beautyful Ones Are Not Yet Born." The Journal of Commonwealth Literature 14.1 (1979): 64–72.

Lindfors, Bernth. "Armah's Histories." *African Literature Today* 11 (1980): 85–86.

*Lobb, Edward. "Armah's *Fragments* and the Vision of the Whole." *Ariel: A Review of International English Literature* 10.1 (1979): 25–38.

———. "Personal and Political Fate in Armah's *Why Are We So Blest?*" *World Literature Written in English* 19 (1980): 5–19.

Lurie, Joe. "*Fragments* Between the Loved Ones and the Community." *Ba Shiru* 5.1 (1973): 31–41.

Massa, Daniel. "The Postcolonial Dream." *World Literature Written in English* 20.1 (1981): 135–49. [On Armah's Fragments.]

McCaffrey, Kathleen. "Images of the Mother in the Stories of Ama Ata Aidoo." *Africa Woman* 23 (1979): 40–41.

*McDowell, Robert E. "Four Ghanaian Novels." *Journal of the New African Literature and the Arts* 4 (1967): 22–27. [On Abruquah, Selormey and Konadu. Rpt. here as "Three Ghanaian Novels."]

Nicholson, Mary. "The Organization of Symbols in Ayi Kwei Armah's *The Beautyful Ones Are Not Yet Born.*" *Asemka* 1.2 (1974): 7–15.

Nnolim, Charles E. "Dialectic as Form: Pejorism in the Novels of Armah." *African Literature Today* 10 (1979): 207–23.

Obiechina, E.N. "Post-Independence Disillusionment in Three African Novels." *Nsukka Studies in African Literature* 1.1 (1978): 54–78. [Deals with *The Beautyful Ones Are Not Yet Born.*]

Ogungbesan, Kolawole. "Symbol and Meaning in *The Beautyful Ones Are Not Yet Born.*" *African Literature Today* 7 (1975): 93–110.

Ojo-Ade, Femi. "Madness in the African Novel: Awoonor's *This Earth, My Brother. . . .*" *African Literature Today* 10 (1979): 134–52.

Okpewho, Isidore. "Myth and Modern Fiction: Armah's *Two Thousand Seasons.*" *African Literature Today* 13 (1983): 1–23.

Palmer, Eustace. "Ayi Kwei Armah: *The Beautyful Ones Are Not Yet Born.*" *An Introduction to the African Novel.* London: Heinemann, 1972. 129–42.

———. "Ayi Kwei Armah: *Two Thousand Seasons.*" *The Growth of the African Novel.* London: Heinemann, 1979. 220–39.

Petersen, Kirsten Holst. "Loss and Frustration: An Analysis of Armah's *Fragments.*" *Kunapipi* 1.1 (1979): 53–65.

Piłaszewicz, Stanisław. "Stories from Northern Ghana: A Hausa Text from the IASAR/22 Manuscript." *Rocznik Orientalistyczny* (Warszawa) 34.2 (1971): 73–110.

Priebe, Richard K. "Demonic Imagery and the Apocalyptic Vision in the Novels of Ayi Kwei Armah." *Yale French Studies* 53 (1976): 102–36.

———. "The Ghanaian Novel After Independence." *European-Language Writing in Sub-Saharan Africa.* Ed. Albert S. Gérard. Forthcoming, 1987.

*———. "Kofi Awoonor's *This Earth, My Brother* as an African Dirge." *The Benin Review* 1 (1975): 95–106.

Rassner, Ron. "*Fragments:* The Cargo Mentality." *Ba Shiru* 5.2 (1974): 55-64.

Saint-Andre-Utudjian, E. "Un Pionnier littérature de la Côte de l'Or: Le Romancier R. E. Obeng." *Annales de l'université du Bénin, Togo: Série Lettres* 4.1 (1977): 75–90.

Solomon, Jean. "A Commentary on Ayi Kwei Armah's *The Beautyful Ones Are Not Yet Born." English in Africa* 1.2 (1974): 25–31.

Staudt, Kathleen. "The Characterization of Women in Soyinka and Armah." *Ba Shiru* 8.2 (1977): 63–69.

Steele, Shelby. "Existentialism in the Novels of Ayi Kwei Armah." *Obsidian* 3.1 (1977): 5–13.

Stewart, Danièle. "L'être et le monde dans les premiers romans d'Ayi Kwei Armah." *Présence Africaine* 85 (1973): 192-208.

Walker, William Alexander, Jr. "Major Ghanaian Fiction in English: A Study of the Novels of Ayi Kwei Armah and Kofi Awoonor." *Dissertation Abstracts International* 36 (1975): 2816A.

Yankson, Kofi. "*This Earth, My Brother* . . .: A Study in Despair." *U of Cape Coast English Dept. Working Papers* 4 (1972): 67–71.

———. "*Fragments:* 'The Eagle that Refused to Soar.' " *Asemka* 1.1 (1974): 53–59.

INDEX

CONTRIBUTORS

CONTRIBUTORS*

Dapo Adelubga is a Senior Lecturer in Theatre Arts at Ibadan University.

Charles Angmor teaches in the Department of English at the Advanced Training College, Winneba, Ghana.

Kofi Anyidoho is a Lecturer in the English Department at the University of Ghana, Legon.

Kofi Awoonor is Ghana's Ambassador to Brazil and is on leave from the University of Cape Coast where he is Professor of English.

Laurence Boadi teaches in the Department of Linguistics at the University of Ghana, Legon.

Lloyd W. Brown is a Professor of Comparative Literature at the University of Southern California.

E. J. Collins teaches in the Philosophy Department at the University of Ghana, Legon.

D. S. Izevbaye is a Senior Lecturer in English at the University of Ibadan.

Robert McDowell is a Professor of English at the University of Texas, Arlington.

Richard Priebe is an Associate Professor of English at Virginia Commonwealth University.

Edwin Thumboo is the Head of the Department of English Language and Literature, National University of Singapore.

Kwesi Yankah is a Lecturer in the Linguistics Department, University of Ghana, Legon.

Jonas Yeboa-Dankwa is a Research Fellow in the Language Centre at the University of Ghana, Legon.

---

*As I was unable to obtain information on the current positions of all the contributors, I must apologize for any errors or omissions. I would appreciate updated information so that I might make corrections in any subsequent edition.